Sport and Society

Series Editors
Benjamin G. Rader
Randy Roberts

A list of books in the series appears at the end of the volume.

Leftist Theories of Sport

Leftist
Theories
of
Sport

A CRITIQUE AND
RECONSTRUCTION

WILLIAM J. MORGAN

University of Illinois Press
Urbana and Chicago

This book is printed on acid-free paper.

Library of Congress Cataloging-in-Publication Data
Morgan, William John, 1948–
    Leftist theories of sport : a critique and reconstruction /
William J. Morgan.
        p.   cm. — (Sport and society)
    Includes bibliographical references and index.
    ISBN 0-252-02068-5 (alk. paper). — ISBN 0-252-06361-9 (pbk.
alk. paper)
    1. Sports—Philosophy. 2. Sports—Sociological aspects.
I. Title. II. Series.
GV706.M6   1994
796'.01—dc20   93-24135
                                                         CIP

In loving memory of my mother, Helen Morgan (1909–93), and my uncle, Robert Timlin (1912–92)

Contents

Preface

The overriding purpose of this study is to reconstruct a formidable critical theory of sport. I aim to do so by putting critical theory on a surer argumentative footing, shoring up some of the weak conceptual buttresses that have undercut its critical and practical interests. I believe that a new critical theory would help make sport a more humane, compelling, and substantive undertaking than it presently is.

My conviction that I can fashion a better and stronger critical theory of sport by going conceptual, by making it accountable to arguments that are more persuasive than those it has so far received, is perhaps a testimony to my own inveterate rationalism. For that, I offer no apology. I believe that presenting the most powerful arguments we can muster to support the abiding convictions we hold—and that we want others to hold—is the only alternative we have to coercion, political demagoguery, and countless forms of rhetorical sleight of hand. It is, in short, all we can offer each other in an intellectual and social community that doesn't demean our beliefs in the course of making them known to others. The arguments I bring to bear on my critical study of sport do not measure their strength by whether they "set up reverberations in the brain" such that "if the person refuses to accept the conclusion, he dies," as Nozick jests (*Philosophical Explanations* [Cambridge, Mass.: Harvard University Press, 1981], pp. 4–5). Instead, their effectiveness lies in their impact on the ways in which critical theory has been formulated to date, and in their ability to advance that theory's critical causes.

The main intent of my book is to fashion a conceptually reinforced critical theory of sport. Its subplot, however, is the rapprochement of the philosophy and the social theory of sport. I wrote this book in part to convince my colleagues in the philosophy of sport that a more direct acquaintance with the work of social theorists of sport is worthwhile; likewise I would like to convince my colleagues in the sociology of sport that a closer attention to the argumentative detail of philosophical accounts of sport could fortify and enrich their own accounts. Each of these subdisciplines, along with the history of sport, has for too long been virtually ignorant of the contributions that the other has made to the study of sport, and the field of sport studies is the poorer for it.

The intended audience for my book is broad. It includes scholars of sport studies whose orientation might be toward the history, philosophy, or sociology of sport. However, the book was also written for aficionados of sport, for students of the game whose quest for understanding its allure and mysteries is not satisfied by the local sports page or other standard sporting forums. Finally, it was written for political and critical theorists as well as for students of political and critical theory, who might be intrigued by the rich cultural and political possibilities of our pastimes and their effect on the larger public and the body politic. Though I have singled out the political Left here, by which I mean both the Marxist Left and the liberal Left, I believe my book might be instructive for the more conservative political and cultural critics.

The writing of this book has been largely a solitary project, but I have been generously encouraged and helped along the way by scholarly organizations and many able scholars in sport studies. I wish to acknowledge and thank the Council for International Exchange of Scholars for awarding me a Fulbright Scholar Award for a semester of study and writing at Marburg Universität in the spring of 1988, in what was then called the Federal Republic of Germany. This award provided me with much-needed time, not to mention cultural stimulation, to get a good start on my book. It also afforded me an invaluable opportunity to discuss my ideas with some of the most prominent critical theorists of sport in the Federal Republic. In this regard I want to thank especially Gunter Gebauer, Freie Universität; Bero Rigauer, Oldenberg Universität; and Peter Becker, Marburg Universität, for their congeniality and for their willingness to engage in critical dialogue. I also wish to express my special gratitude to Allen Guttmann for his evenhanded and sympathetic criticisms of my work. I would be remiss if I failed to recognize the various symposia sponsored by the Philosophic Society for the Study of Sport and by the North American Society for the Sociology of Sport, which gave me an opportunity to try out some of my ideas in a critically conducive environment. The graduate students who participated in my seminars helped shape, through their spirited questions, some of the ideas in this book.

I also wish to acknowledge a delightful association with the University of Illinois Press, in particular, with the director and editor, Richard L. Wentworth; the associate editor, Richard Martin; and the editors of its Sport and Society series, Ben Rader of the University of Nebraska and Randy Roberts of Purdue University. I owe a special note of gratitude in this regard to my copyeditor, Carol Bolton Betts, for her expert and thorough editing of my text.

I want to recognize and thank most of all my wife, Susan, and my children, Jennifer and Melanie, for their forbearance and patience. Without them I could not have written this book.

Introduction

The signs of the degradation of sport are all around us. The mania for winning, the widespread cheating, the economic and political trivialization of sport, the thirst for crude sensationalism and eccentric spectacle, the manipulation by the mass media, the cult of athletic stars and celebrity, and the mindless bureaucratization are just some of the more ominous signs. These signs are too pervasive to deny, too steeped in our social milieu to pass off as anything other than social pathology, and too entrenched in our present social configurations to require anything short of a wholesale revamping of our major social institutions.

This picture of sport can hardly be ignored—not, that is, if a more humane and civil form of sport is to be salvaged. Indeed, I am convinced that the critical rehabilitation of sport is crucial to the critical rehabilitation of society itself. The aim of my present study is to fashion a critical social theory of sport whose practical intent is to rid sport of its current social ills. This theoretical and practical interest in emancipation distinguishes the critical theory I am about to advance from traditional, or so-called pure, theory's understanding of itself as a "disinterested" enterprise,[1] whereby it forswears any *substantive* interest in the historical and social affairs of human life. Furthermore, it is this linkage of theory and practice that defines my materialist reading of the emancipation project: that the corruption of contemporary sport can only be overcome by a transformation of its existing material conditions.

I am well aware that the practical interest in emancipation that informs my study must confront what Wendell Berry correctly identifies as the "great obstacle" to social change in general: "the conception that we cannot change because we are dependent on what is wrong."[2] Applied to sport, that conception gives rise to the claim that sport cannot thrive and prosper without the pernicious institutions that currently support it and the aggressive and shameless media that promote it. If that argument has a familiar ring, it is because it is the fashionable way that we rationalize "bad things" in our society today. In its substance it is no different than the claim that the maintenance of our standard of living requires environmental policies that rob and pillage nature, and economic and political policies that rob and pillage those less well off than we. That these are not really tenable arguments at all, but bald-face excuses, and that they are excuses that borrow, as Berry astutely observes, from the self-deluding rationalizations of the addict, amply explains why we should not take them seriously. There is nothing in them that should deter us from doing what should be done to make sport and human life more charming and happy affairs than they are now.

In spite of my avowed practical aim, however, the present study follows an unmistakably theoretical path. Indeed, compared to what one typically finds in this critical genre of social theory, the treatment that follows may strike the reader as markedly abstract. That quality is a product of the historical situation in which we find ourselves. In other words, there are good historical reasons why the critical theory I propound assumes an abstract approach to the study of sport.

It is important to be clear about what is at issue here. One will search in vain in the following pages for any specific program of action to unshackle sport from its social chains. This is neither especially noteworthy nor controversial; it merely testifies to the limitation of any critical theory regarding manifestly practical matters. Theory in itself is incapable of legitimating a particular political program. As Foucault nicely puts it, "critique doesn't have to be the premise of a deduction that concludes: This then is what needs to be done."[3] While theory can inform the work of enlightenment, it cannot prescribe the risky decisions of strategic action at the political level. These can only be justified by the participants themselves, who in their practical discourse with one another decide what strategies to follow and what risks to take with what expectations.[4]

The abstract temperament of the present work cannot be attributed to its failure to recommend a detailed blueprint of how sport might be rid of its current abuses. Instead, this abstract quality emerges because this study refrains from identifying any specific group that might take up and practically carry out its theoretical directives. In failing to target a specific addressee for its theory, it violates a sacred canon of critical theory, which insists that theory must maintain an internal connection to an extratheoretical, political movement to execute its various insights. That demand, I argue, can no longer be honored. Furthermore, it can no longer be honored because there does not seem to be a social class, a social formation, or what Marcuse at times called a "catalyst" group that can be singled out as the bearer of correct knowledge, or as representative of a general interest that has not been violated and that could serve as an agent of real change. I am claiming, in short, that there is not a particular social group to which we might appeal to ground critical theory, to anchor critical insights and claims that are above ideological suspicion.

This is a large and controversial claim that will be defended in the course of my investigation. For now, however, it must be qualified. To hold the view that there is no social class to which theory might turn to carry out its critical mandate does not require that we regard subordinate classes as simply dupes of the system, nor that we view them as entirely unaware of their objective historical situation. Neither does it demand that we give up on all such social groups in perpetuity, or that we abandon microanalyses of how social groups and formations come into existence, operate, and change, what Corrigan aptly calls "thick descriptions" that make clear the "textures of social relations."[5] Nor, finally, does it require despair at the prospect of reconstructing the status quo, a kind of pessimism that reeks of intellectual arrogance and a scornful, dismissive insensitivity to the course of the real world and to the thoughts and actions of real people locked in all too real struggles.

The foregoing admission of the absence of an addressee for theory does require, however, a sober recognition of our present situation. This situation suggests, I argue, that we are not living in a period ripe for radical change. Part and parcel of that judgment, of course, is the mounting historical evidence regarding the conservative and often reformist manner of the working class and other less privileged social groups in advanced capitalist society. That conservatism is apparent not only in the overt political practices of these groups, but especially in the cultural fare characteristic of class-life in the modern age, not the least of which includes so-called popular culture and, perhaps most conspicuously, sport itself. To recognize and come to terms with such historical developments is part of the never-ending confrontation that must be waged between theory and history, a confrontation that theory must not skirt if it is to be adequate to its times.

To put the point somewhat differently, I am claiming that we must counter the notion that action for the sake of action, commitment and political engagement for their own sake—a notion common in many critical circles today—is superior to and somehow an alternative to theory. I contend that present conditions require a fundamental re-thinking of our current plight, a return to theoretical concerns, especially as these apply to popular pursuits like sport. To ignore this theoretical imperative—to continue to insist, for example, on the "creative strength" of the working class in spite of the evidence to the contrary—is not only a theoretical evasion but also a practical one that only makes social groups like the working class weaker than they need be.[6]

Perhaps the most troubling aspect of the ill-founded attempt to make one social group or another a cause célèbre of the revolution is that it risks the political instrumentalization of critical theory itself. The uncritical tailoring of theory to social groups that lack revolutionary zeal and/or substance succeeds only in mimicking the dominant positivist standpoint of social theory and research, in particular its preoccupation with useful knowledge that seeks to resolve everyday problems of life—where the resolution of such problems means the solidification of the status quo. What begins, therefore, as a critical effort to make theory responsive to the strategic and tactical demands of a particular social group ends as simply another specialized science that allows the consideration of various practical techniques to mobilize groups into effective political units to take precedence over a consideration of the substantive ends that inform such groups. This emasculation of the critical project by turning it into a useful science is emblematic of a larger tendency in our culture that substitutes technical canons of utility and reason for enlightened action or, in Habermasian terms, falsely presumes "that the practical mastery of history can be reduced to technical control of objectified processes."[7]

The inability to target a specific addressee for theory does not cancel or otherwise deflect the practical aspirations of the critical theory I am about to propound. On the contrary, it indicates the theoretical route critical theory must first traverse today in order to bear practical fruit. That route leads, I argue, to philosophical reflection, to an abstract type of thinking geared to uncovering distinctive features of social life-forms and to the traces of reason found within them. This turn to philosophical theory, I hasten to emphasize, is not a detour in the grand dialectic of Enlightenment; it is a necessary move to sustain the critical enterprise itself and ultimately to effect the realization of reason in history.

The suggestion that philosophical reflection is the next step and, by implication, the best hope for a critically inspired social theory of sport is not likely to sit well with theorists who work in this area. In fact, the critical pretensions of the sort of abstract thinking I champion here run against the grain of current intellectual fashion, a fashion that, after Nietzsche, feeds on all manner of relativist thought that parades itself quite fashionably as historicist thought. It is no exaggeration to say that, for critical theorists, the very mention of philosophy in this context is anathema. This is true of the theorists that work out of both the Marxist Left and the liberal Left traditions. The Marxist Left despises and shuns the abstract temperament of philosophical reason because it is thought to be at odds with history, with the historical conditions that give rise to and ultimately shape social practices like sport. Those theorists maintain, therefore, that philosophical and historical treatments of sport do not and cannot mix, that the former is given to idealistic and romantic portrayals of the ennobling qualities of sport that slight the historical facts of the case and lead inexorably to the reification and depoliticization of sport.[8] The liberal Left believes that because of the dense manner and disputed character of abstract philosophical thought, it does not lend itself to the sort of public agreement and consensus that is vital to the sustenance of democratic societies. In this view, taking a light-minded approach to deep philosophical questions—staying, so to speak, on the surface philosophically—is a requirement of democracy itself.[9]

I do not take either of these charges lightly, and, accordingly, I will attempt to fend them off whenever they spring up in the ensuing analysis. For now, they require me to make good on another central tenet of critical theory: its reflexive status. Critical theory distinguishes itself from traditional theory not only in its aim to enlighten, but also in its self-referential character; its attempts to explain social reality include an attempt to give account of itself, its own origin and application, as an integral feature of that social reality.[10] This feature of critical theory impels me in the present context to show why the preservation of the critical role of theory at this historical juncture makes it necessary to resort to the kind of philosophical reflection I sketch above.

The original, orthodox position regarding the relation of philosophy to social theory in Marxist thought sought to liquidate philosophy's idealistic conception of itself as pure thought and place in its stead a socially instantiated form of reason committed to the construction of a rational society. According to this version, the realization of reason in society would signal the end of philosophy. All of this is forecast in Marx's famous eleventh thesis on Feuerbach: "The philosophers have only *interpreted* the world, in various ways; the point, however, is to change it."[11] But if the development anticipated by theory does not occur, if the social forces that were intended to bring reason into the world have been effectively muted, then theory must collect and reorient itself in ways that bring to light human capacities and objective developments that lie dormant in the present social situation. A fundamental part of that theoretical reorientation, I have argued, involves a return to philosophical concerns and modes of analysis. Thus, the old charge that philosophy has merely interpreted the world has lost its critical luster; when resurrected in the present, that charge unwittingly serves as a pretext "to choke, as vain, whatever critical thoughts . . . practical change would require."[12]

My advocacy of philosophical reflection as a pivotal element of critical theory is, therefore, a historical one. It is the tenor of the times that recommends—even demands—such advocacy. Of course, philosophy itself has not escaped the historical fate of the contemporary age. The purity of thought has been sullied as well. There is no longer the option of returning to an unvarnished notion of philosophy, of a pristine, unadulterated form of reason that gives an absolute guarantee to our knowledge claims. The belief that there are "nontrivial knowledge claims that are immune from criticism," what Bernstein calls "absolutism,"[13] has been demolished. So the claims and pretensions of "first philosophy" (*Ursprungsphilosophie*) to provide nonfallibilistic backups for theoretical discourse must be relinquished. Giving those up requires philosophy to turn from pure reason to the reason embedded in social practices, from a pure, transcendental ego to a socially formed subject (individual or group) that is nothing more nor less than the sum of its social practices and institutions. This shift is anticipated in Rorty's trenchant reminders that "there is nothing deep down inside us except what we have put there ourselves," that "socialization, and . . . historical circumstance, goes all the way down—there is nothing 'beneath' socialization or prior to history which is definatory of the human," that there are no "natural starting points that are distinct from cultural traditions."[14]

However, what must not be given up is the critical standpoint of philosophical reflection, its tendency to think beyond and say more than what present social circumstance recognizes or allows. What must be resisted, in short, is the reduction of philosophical logic to the particular logic of science, or to the therapeutic function of uncovering linguistic puzzlements, or to the general view—apparent in both positivism and many currents of Marxist thinking—that philosophy cannot of its own accord offer a positive account of the world.

These views speak with virtual unanimity on the point that reflection, and the truth it captures, is an inescapably local matter, and that theoretical forays beyond this limit only give rise to "objectivist" illusions. Horkheimer has long since detected in this line of thought an effort not to "explain the social function [and content] of philosophy, but rather to perform one oneself, namely, to discourage thought from its practical tendency of pointing to the future."[15]

If my endorsement of Bernstein's and Rorty's misgivings about "first philosophy" seems to run counter to my insistence that philosophy not abandon its critical perspective, its interrogation of prevailing conceptions of truth and justification, that is only because those misgivings are thought to rule out, or at the very least call into question, philosophy's critical impulse. That claim, I contend, is a mistaken one. Once we rid ourselves of the false "metaphysical comfort" provided by the philosophical tradition's production of "abstract doubles" of our real self and world, we must come to terms with social practices themselves. Once we do, it quickly becomes apparent that certain social practices, a short list of which would surely include sport, possess a social logic that is not reducible to, or directly translatable into, the local vocabularies and idioms of prevailing cultural institutions and fixtures. That is to say, while the reason embedded in these practices is immanent to them (not found outside of these specific practices), it cannot be read back into the particular cultural constellations in which they find themselves at any given moment. What we find when we go deep down inside these practices is not something natural or inviolate, but neither is it something culturally specific to, say, capitalism. This is why the standards of rationality accepted by a culture cannot exhaustively define the rationality of all the social practices that fall within its boundaries, and why those standards cannot be put to use as an algorithm to judge and evaluate such social practices.[16]

The turn from pure reason to social practices, therefore, does not undercut the critical standpoint of philosophy but safeguards it. The only way to give such practices their due is to say something definitive about their immanent logic, which requires a philosophical consideration of what might cautiously be called their "deep" structures. Such an analysis is not concerned with the attributes of transcendental consciousness as such (whatever they might be), nor with the conventions that underlie present social arrangements, but with the logical structures of social forms of life and the historical traditions that inform and sustain them, and that are binding on all social subjects. Lest anyone think that I am speaking strictly in theoretical terms here,

I hasten to add that the turn to philosophical reflection is what historical circumstances themselves demand of a social theory interested in practical change. It is an important way to discern human capacities and objective developments that would otherwise be imperceptible in the present social situation. To conjoin Foucault's jargon with mine, the philosophical recourse to the immanent logic of social practices is a particularly powerful way of showing that the current ways in which we treat, value, organize, and institutionalize such practices are not natural, indispensable, or self-evident. The "breach of self-evidence" that Foucault tries to effect by historical means to show that things "weren't as necessary as all that" is what I argue can best be effected, given existing historical conditions, by philosophical means.[17] At any rate, this is the sense I give to Horkheimer's epigram that "the whole historical dynamic has placed philosophy in the center of social actuality, and social actuality in the center of philosophy."[18]

The kind of philosophical depth I wish to bring to bear on my critical study of sport is not that of an abstruse metaphysics, not the sort of "abstraction by essentialization" practiced, for example, by Heidegger in his arcane meditations on the Being of beings; nor is it a formal epistemology, not the sort of transcendental deduction carried out, for example, by Kant in his critical tribunal of "pure reason." Indeed, I, like Rorty, entertain no secret wish to be "buffaloed by German depth" or derailed by what he calls "French subtlety."[19] Rather, the philosophical depth I seek and attempt to put into practice in my ensuing analysis tries to achieve a deeper, richer, and more complex understanding of sport itself. Specifically, the contrast between the philosophical depth I aspire to and the philosophical abstinence and/or superficiality the Left espouses is roughly analogous to the distinction Charles Taylor draws between "strong evaluation" and "simple weighing."[20] Simple weighing is the type of reflection an individual pursues when he or she is considering the "desirability of different consummations" of de facto desires. Strong evaluation, by contrast, is the type of reflection pursued by an individual seeking to achieve a better understanding of the sort of being who holds these desires in the first place. While the first reflection encourages individuals to stay on the surface of their existing desires, the second requires them to penetrate to the center of their very being in order to understand just who they are. If we turn from Taylor's focus on individual reflection and evaluation to social reflection and evaluation, the contrast becomes clear. In that case, simple weighing reduces to considering what our existing institutions allow us to say and do, to what we can get away with saying and doing within those institutions' boundaries;[21] strong evaluation reduces to considering how one can get past such institutions in order to understand and appreciate better the social practices they envelop—to learn how to penetrate our present institutional setups and their face-value justifications to determine what they distort and/or exclude from our reflective grasp of such social practices. It is my central argument that the configuration of social and historical forces arrayed against us have made philosophical depth the path of choice to pursue strong evaluation. It is, of course, a corollary of that thesis that the philosophical indifference of the Left truncates its critical scope to simple weighing, which in part explains its view that there is nothing *in* a social practice like sport that is not accounted for by its institutionalization; thus, it has no effective way to get beyond the institutional entanglements of sport it must in order to justify its own status as a critical theory.

The embrace of philosophical depth and critical social analysis that I endorse here, however, takes a different form than it did in the old critique of political economy. The task posed for philosophy in that critique was the conceptual one of transforming bourgeois concepts into their opposites: calling, for example, free exchange by its right name—social injustice. The task historically posed for philosophy today is not one of decoding the truth potential of language but of redeeming the truth potential of cultural practices. The new practical light in which the discursive orientation of philosophy thus appears is that of rational redemption, reclaiming the rational potential of social forms like sport that have been covered over in prevailing social reality. With one important qualification, Adorno's following remarks capture well the substance of this new philosophical task: "The only philosophy that can be responsibly practiced in the face of despair is the attempt to contemplate all things as they would appear from the standpoint of redemption. . . . Perspectives must be fashioned that displace and estrange the world, that reveal its lacerations and cracks as indigent and distorted as they will appear in the messianic light. To gain such perspectives without caprice or violence . . . this and this alone is the last task of thought."[22]

What must be qualified in Adorno's otherwise sage pronouncement is its pessimistic pathos. The new redemptive task of philosophy is not one rooted in despair, nor does it insinuate Adorno's rather hopeless and pathetic *Flaschenpost* (message in a bottle) address to an imaginary witness. Rather, it grows, as argued above, directly out of changed historical conditions, which themselves stake out, as always, the terrain in which the practical critique of the existing order can work itself out. Those conditions open up a critical space for a philo-sophically informed practical critique that speaks to certain central features of sport, which, though not rooted in or directed to the pat-terned responses or systems of belief of any particular social group, fall within the orbit of experience of all social agents. It is to this or-bit of experience, captured philosophically, and to the social agents it binds together, and not some hypostatized "imaginary witness," that the present critical theory of sport is directed.

Methodology

A social theory that purports to give a reputable and binding account of social reality must address the methodological question of how it gains access to that reality in a sufficiently critical way.[23] I have cho-sen to address that question sooner rather than later for essentially two reasons: first, its explication affords me the opportunity to lay out the structure of the entire study, giving some sense of its over-riding aims and abiding concerns, and second, it allows me to fix the right mode of presentation for the substantive questions I will tackle in the remainder of this study.

The method I employ in this book, and which I apply in various ways and at various levels, is that of immanent critique.[24] Immanent critique, however, is not a method in any conventional sense of the term. It does not, for instance, abide by any fixed formula for treat-ing social reality. It has, as such, no clearly defined beginning or end-ing points. But neither is it a wholly arbitrary procedure. It derives its legitimacy from its object of study, from the terms of social expe-rience itself and our various conceptions of that experience. Indeed, the distinguishing feature of immanent critique is that it makes no pretense of separating itself from its object, instead taking its point of departure directly from its subject matter and seeking to make com-mon cause with it. Our various experiences and conceptions of the social world are, therefore, to be examined and scrutinized by way of principles and standards that are intrinsic to them, that are, in other words, not imposed on them from the outside.

That immanent critique is, as Michael Rosen so felicitously puts it, "not so much a method as a commitment to take one's . . . method from the exigencies of the particular critical situation"[25] means that its visage changes in accord with historical shifts in particular criti-cal situations. These shifts account for the curious development im-manent critique has undergone as a method leading from Hegel through Marx to critical theorists like Adorno. It also accounts, of course, for the changing visage of critical theory itself. In any case, my own use of immanent critique takes its point of departure from Marx and the critical tradition, that is, from conflicts of practical reason that repose within social forms of life as opposed to theoretical conflicts of reason that repose within detached intellectual constructions. By taking apart internally these contradictions between the conceptions of social experience provided by prevailing society and the effective experience of the social actors that operate within them, we can expose the gap between what a society appears to be and what it actually is. Further, it is this gap between the institutions and the effective practices of a society that supplies immanent critique with the critical vantage point it needs to launch a radical critique of modern society. My interest in the contradictions and gaps that fracture the apparent unity of the social constellations of advanced capitalist society center, of course, on their effect on the development of sport as a form of life. I propose to analyze them by way of an immanent analysis of sport that proceeds along two fronts corresponding to the two major divisions of my critical study of sport.

My first employment of immanent critique, and the first part of my study, will be directed toward the theoretical arena in which the practical conflicts that have characterized the social evolution of sport have been conceptually mapped out and debated. In this regard, I will canvas and criticize what I regard to be two of the leading currents of critical sport theory, the New Left and hegemony theory. Accordingly, Chapter 1 will take up the New Left (Neo-Marxist) critique of sport, and Chapter 2, the hegemonic critique of sport. I will argue that the respective manner in which these theories treat sport fail to do justice to its complex social composition. My criticisms, however, will in each case be qualified and determinate ones, and so they will be devoted in part to redeeming select features of their conceptions that can later be reworked—in a subsequent chapter—into a more comprehensive and powerful theory of sport. Chapter 3, which ends Part 1, strikes an ideologically critical note. It will try to accomplish two goals. First, it will offer a diagnosis of what ails contemporary sport, using Alaisdair MacIntyre's pivotal distinction between social practices and institutions; and second, it will argue that the Left's critique of sport misconstrues the source and character of that pathology thereby accentuating, rather than ameliorating, its corrosive effects.

My next use of immanent critique, in Part 2, will be devoted to the development of a new critical theory of sport. Chapter 4 will lay the groundwork for that theory by retracing the path that the Left itself followed in its unsuccessful bid to come up with standards of criticism capable of understanding and undoing the social and ideological bind in which practices like sport presently find themselves. After considering the different ways in which the Left tried to divine such standards, I will settle on a particular—I should add unconventional, by leftist measures at any rate—immanent critique of sport. This critique takes its point of departure from sport conceived as a social practice, and from a critically extended, socialized version of the liberal device of separation, a device that recognizes that certain practices and the goods they trade in fare better in certain social contexts than others and that tries to situate them in those favored social contexts so that they might flourish. In Chapter 5, I will put that liberal-socialist device of separation to work and reconstruct a new critical theory of sport, a new social map of sport whose boundaries are drawn in two principal ways: first, by reference to the internal logic of sport itself, and second, by reference to our critically backed shared conceptions of the social goods we regard to be intrinsic to its practice. The first reference, I will argue, requires an immanent analysis of what I call, after Walzer, the "characteristic normative structures" of sport; the second requires an immanent analysis of its practice-community, of what I call, after Lyotard, the *litige* of its deliberative proceedings.

I will close my critical study of sport with a final justificatory effort that takes the larger, rather than the internal, measure of sport in order to answer some questions about the immanent justification I provide it in Chapter 5. Here I will show how sport connects with other social undertakings, and how it might be justified in this larger scheme of things. Once again I will invoke a liberal notion, this time the ideal of pluralism, clothe it in democratic-socialist garb, and put it to work in a critical capacity. Specifically, I will argue that a well-ordered society is a pluralistic one, and that one salient mark of a vibrant pluralistic society is that it affords room for practices like sport that make the pursuit of excellence their central aim.

NOTES

1. See Max Horkheimer's classic essay, "Traditional and Critical Theory," *Critical Theory* (New York: Herder and Herder, 1972). Although my conception of critical theory, and its distinction from traditional theory, derives its major inspiration from this essay by Horkheimer and largely conforms to the program of "critical theory" set out by other writers associated in one way or another with the so-called Frankfurt school (most notably, Adorno, Marcuse, and Habermas), it is not synonymous with that school. By critical the-

ory I mean the attempt to understand rationally and explain the manifold forms of domination in society in order to enable human agents to come to grips with those forms of domination and practically overcome them. In this sense, critical theory has obvious affinities with many strands of Marxist and feminist theory as well as liberal theory and other practically disposed social theories. For a similar account of critical theory and a catalogue of the sorts of theories it captures, see Brian Fay, *Critical Social Science* (Ithaca: Cornell University Press, 1987), pp. 5–6.

2. Wendell Berry, "The Futility of Global Thinking," *Harper's*, Sept. 1989, p. 19.

3. Michel Foucault, "Questions of Method," in *After Philosophy: End or Transformation?* ed. Kenneth Baynes et al. (Cambridge, Mass.: MIT Press, 1987), p. 114.

4. See Jürgen Habermas, *Theory and Practice* (Boston: Beacon Press, 1973), pp. 33–34. It bears mentioning in this regard that Habermas criticized Lukács's attempt to derive theoretical claims from the political and organizational concerns of the Party for this very same reason.

5. Philip Corrigan, "The Politics of Feeling Good," in *Popular Cultures and Political Practices*, ed. Richard B. Gruneau (Toronto: Garamond Press, 1988), p. 46.

6. See Horkheimer, "Traditional and Critical Theory," p. 214.

7. Jürgen Habermas, *Knowledge and Human Interests* (Boston: Beacon Press, 1971), p. 316.

8. Gruneau argues along these lines. See his *Class, Sports, and Social Development* (Amherst: University of Massachusetts Press, 1983), pp. 34, 139.

9. On this point see Richard Rorty's essay "The Priority of Democracy to Philosophy," in *The Virginia Statute of Religious Freedom*, ed. Merill Peterson and Robert Vaughn (Cambridge: Cambridge University Press, 1988), pp. 261–63; and John Rawls's essay "Justice as Fairness: Political Not Metaphysical," *Philosophy and Public Affairs* 14 (Summer 1985): 230–31.

10. Traditional theory, in accord with its objectivistic tenor, strictly separates itself from its object of study and so conceals the social interests that tie it to its object. See Horkheimer, "Traditional and Critical Theory," p. 229.

11. Karl Marx, "Theses on Feuerbach," in *Marx and Engels: Basic Writings on Politics and Philosophy*, ed. Lewis Feuer (New York: Anchor Books, 1959), p. 245.

12. Theodor Adorno, *Negative Dialectics* (New York: Continuum, 1973), p. 3. This is also the sense of Foucault's contention that "the necessity of reform mustn't be allowed to become a form of blackmail serving to limit, reduce, or halt the exercise of criticism." "Questions of Method," p. 114.

13. Richard Bernstein, *Beyond Objectivism and Relativism* (Philadelphia: University of Pennsylvania Press, 1985), p. 12.

14. Richard Rorty, "Pragmatism and Philosophy," in *After Philosophy*, ed. Baynes et al., p. 60; idem, *Contingency, Irony, and Solidarity* (Cambridge: Cambridge University Press, 1989), p. xii; idem, "Pragmatism and Philosophy," p. 54.

15. Max Horkheimer, "The Social Function of Philosophy," *Critical Theory* (New York: Herder and Herder, 1972), p. 263. Horkheimer's specific target in this regard was the sociology of knowledge.

16. I owe this point to Hilary Putnam. See his essay "Why Reason Can't Be Naturalized," in *After Philosophy*, ed. Baynes et al., p. 228. In this same essay, Putnam makes the further trenchant point that theorists who overlook the immanence of reason get caught up in philosophical fantasies of "absolutism," whereas theorists who overlook the irreducible character of reason become ensnared by cultural and historical relativism—one of the most pernicious forms of which is a cultural "imperialism" that holds that truth is defined by the norms of *my* culture. See pp. 228 and 232 of the same essay.

17. Foucault's historical decomposition of the matter-of-fact way in which cultures talk and think about madness, normality, illness, crime, and punishment stops short of any effort to subvert such cultural talk or practice. His restraint in such matters stems clearly and consistently from his belief that one can speak of reason only in the instrumental and relative sense in which it is inscribed in this or that system of practice and in this or that culture. Since there is no other way to measure reason save in relation to the activity it comes to occupy, all that Foucault can plausibly hope to achieve by his genealogical probing is to make us think twice about what we say or do regarding prisons and mental institutions. Of course, that gives us no foothold either to criticize such institutions, or any onus or guide to replace them with something better. Viewed from Putnam's schema of rationality, Foucault's reticence to undertake or recommend a program of social reform is a product of his championing the immanence of reason at the expense of its irreducibility, which, as Putnam further argues, eliminates the normative altogether. Foucault, "Questions of Method," pp. 107–8, 112; Putnam, "Why Reason Can't Be Naturalized," pp. 240–41.

18. Horkheimer, "The Social Function of Philosophy," p. 268.

19. Richard Rorty, "Pragmatism without a Method," in his *Objectivity, Relativism, and Truth* (Cambridge: Cambridge University Press, 1991), p. 76.

20. As cited in Michael Sandel's *Liberalism and the Limits of Justice* (Cambridge: Cambridge University Press, 1982), pp. 160–61.

21. Rorty uses language like this in his essay "Epistemological Behaviorism and the De-transcendentalization of Analytic Philosophy," in *Hermeneutics and Praxis*, ed. Robert Hollinger (Notre Dame, Ind.: University of Notre Dame Press, 1985), p. 98.

22. Theodor Adorno, *Minima Moralia* (London: Verso, 1985), p. 247. The quotation as I give it, however, is actually an amended translation that appears in Helmut Dubiel's *Theory and Politics: Studies in the Development of Critical Theory* (Cambridge, Mass.: MIT Press, 1985), p. 97.

23. Analogously, any social theory that purports to give an account of what the social world is actually like can scarcely avoid the metatheoretical question of just what constitutes a good explanation of the social world. See Fay, *Critical Social Science*, p. 3.

24. For an excellent discussion of the character of immanent critique and

its historical evolution as a method of critical inquiry, see the following sources: Michael Rosen, *Hegel's Dialectic and Its Criticism* (Cambridge: Cambridge University Press, 1982); Charles Taylor, "The Opening Arguments of the Phenomenology," in *Hegel: A Collection of Original Essays,* ed. Alaisdair MacIntyre (New York: Doubleday, 1972); Alan Montefiore and Charles Taylor, "From an Analytical Perspective," introductory essay to Garbis Kortian's *Metacritique: The Philosophical Argument of Jürgen Habermas* (Cambridge: Cambridge University Press, 1980).

    25. Rosen, *Hegel's Dialectic and Its Criticism,* p. 39.

1 THE CRITIQUE

ONE

The New Left Theory of Sport

The New Left critique of sport was launched in the late 1960s and early 1970s. Among its proponents were theorists of German, French, Canadian, and American lineage. As intellectual circles go, this was, and is, a rather large one.[1] My analysis, however, will concentrate on a select, though representative, number of its authors and texts. Primary among them are Bero Rigauer's *Sport and Work,* Jean-Marie Brohm's *Sport a Prison of Measured Time,* Rob Beamish's various overlapping essays on sport, Richard Lipsky's *How We Play the Game,* and Paul Hoch's *Rip Off the Big Game.*[2] I will also consider, to a lesser extent, the more discrete analyses (mainly essay literature) by critics such as Ike Balbus and John McMurtry.[3] Throughout, I will use the term "Neo-Marxist" interchangeably with the term "New Left."

Critical Goals and Tasks

The New Left theory of sport is quite literally defined by its practical, emancipatory intent. Indeed, in its view the legitimacy of any social theory rises or falls on its practical import. The whole point of theory after all, to paraphrase Marx's well-worn epigram, is not simply to comprehend the world of sport but to change it. Hence, any effort at comprehension must be inextricably and palpably tied to the practice of sport.

The kind of comprehension peculiar to a theory with emancipatory intent is one, according to this view, that engages our critical reflection of sport. That is, it is one that unmasks and demystifies our perceptions, beliefs, values, and views of the sport realm. It seeks to jar our critical sensibilities about sport, to press beyond their stubborn and stultifying familiarity. This requires not the "denigration" but the penetration of sport by calling it and its larger connection to society into question.[4] Only in such a way, it is argued, is the pervasive corruption of modern sport wrought by bourgeois society likely to be overcome and real emancipation achieved.

That a social theory with practical intent has little truck with standard academic theories and methods of inquiry is hardly surprising. It eschews the traditional division of academic labor one finds in sport studies (applying, for example, the disciplines of philosophy, history, sociology, or anthropology to sport), a splintering that privileges discrete treatments at the expense of "totalizing critiques." It further distances itself from idealistic studies that ignore the material, historical roots of sport. For example, the kind of abstract definitions of sport one typically finds in philosophical texts are branded as "almost entirely worthless" and are replaced by contextual (socially and historically delimited) definitions.[5] Finally, as a critically oriented sociology it marks itself off from empirical sociology, a form of social inquiry that fails to take into consideration its own problematic relation to society and that of the social actors it studies through largely quantitative means. If the aim of an emancipatory social theory is to penetrate the social facade of sport, then it cannot rest content with "empirically obtained results about sports [which are themselves] socially predetermined and [which, therefore,] cannot provide reliable information about sports."[6]

An integral part of the New Left's efforts to nurture a critical regard for sport was to correct the Left's own failure to do so. It is no secret that the Left has had a long and deep-seated antipathy for sport despite the working class's evident enjoyment of and widespread involvement in sport.[7] Sport was customarily passed off by the Left intelligentsia as an inane, utterly frivolous enterprise, one that functioned exclusively, it was maintained, as a prop of the status quo. Valentinov, a close friend of Lenin who shared his carefully veiled interest in sport, commented that "to Lenin's other companions the subject [of sport] made no more sense than embroidery or knitting,"[8] a remark that reveals the Left's general regard for sport.

The situation has changed little in the present era. Although the roots of the French and German radical critiques of sport were tied respectively to the disturbances in French society of May-June 1968 and the student revolts in Germany in the sixties, neither of these social movements had much, if anything, to do with sport. As Brohm argued, while most institutions of French society were bitterly attacked by the students, sport "remained an analytical blind-spot, an untroubled oasis in the desert of challenge to the established order."[9] In fact, Brohm argued, not only did sport survive these social uprisings unscathed, it served as a protective shield for other embattled social institutions, thereby stabilizing an otherwise tenuous situation. Things were much the same in the student uprisings that racked West German society.

Hence, the impetus for the New Left's critical interest in sport had less to do with these movements themselves than it did with their failure to take up sport in the first place. However, in one important respect there is a certain irony in the New Left's indictment of its radical predecessors. Though it is certainly true, as noted above, that the Left virtually ignored, if not disdained, sport, it is also true that their disinterest in and opposition to sport were by no means complete. In fact, despite formidable social obstacles, which were only compounded by the intransigence of Marxist doctrine, a workers' sport movement was inaugurated at the turn of the twentieth century. It was formed as a "humanistic alternative" to the excesses of bourgeois sport. Although it never achieved the prominence of bourgeois sport before its demise in the cold-war period of the forties, it was not an insignificant social movement: in the late twenties, for example, it claimed well over two million members, and its variously sponsored Workers' Olympics attracted throngs of competitors and spectators.[10] Moreover, during the interwar period this politically active and self-conscious working-class movement was privy to "socialist manifestos," such as Fritz Wildung's *Arbeitersport* and Helmut Wagner's *Sport und Arbeitersport,* which championed socialist values through sport and which made many of the same criticisms that, as we will soon see, the New Left were to press against bourgeois sport.[11]

The New Left's indictment of its leftist counterparts, then, is not completely compelling. Nonetheless, it can scarcely be denied that its taking on the established institutions of modern sport represents a long overdue and important correction of a deeply entrenched, recalcitrant Marxist orthodoxy.[12]

Principal Claims and Arguments

The major claims and arguments advanced by the New Left are part and parcel of its materialist approach to the study of sport. That approach places labor at the forefront of any investigation of sport and culture.[13] The prominence accorded labor in this regard is derived from the primary role it allegedly plays in the self-genesis of human-kind and social history, to include, of course, sport.[14] Here the radical critics are simply following the lead of Marx, who claimed that "labor, *life-activity, productive life* itself, . . . is the life of the species . . . life-engendering life," and that "the history of *industry* and the established *objective* existence of industry are the *open book of man's essential powers.*"[15]

If, as the radical critics insist above, the analysis of sport must be based on an analysis of labor (work), then the question arises as to what sort of relation holds between work and sport. This question must not be broached, they admonish, in an abstract manner. The important connection to be explored here is not between labor and sport per se (labor and sport considered apart from their social context), but between the socially determinate forms of labor and sport one finds in a particular historical context.[16] In the present context, that means the relation between the commodity form of capitalist production and sport. Therefore, the question that must be asked here is, To what extent has this dominant mode of production compromised sport? The response supplied by New Left critics suggests two, rather different answers, and thus two, rather different accounts of the labor-sport linkage.

The first rendering of the work-sport relation is characteristic of the analyses of Brohm and Rigauer and of most of the work of Beamish; it takes its point of departure from a consideration of the correspondences apparent between work and sport in a capitalist social setting. This consideration gives rise to the claim that sport and work are analogous to and resemble each other in many important respects. The resemblances, these analyses argue, hold even at the structural level, in which a certain inner structural similarity (*innere Strukturähnlichkeit*) and conformity (*strukturell konforme*) is clearly manifest between sport and work. What is perhaps even more important, in the view of Brohm, Rigauer, and Beamish, is the patterned nature of these resemblances, which conform to a rather rigidly interpreted Marxist base-superstructure explanatory model.

Sport is treated in this vein as little more than an "auxiliary structure of capitalism," literally a "subsystem" of bourgeois society, which receives its principal, if not sole, determination from the dominant mode of production.[17] In particular, it is said to originate from work, to derive its particular forms and functions from work, and in turn to "facilitate techniques of movement which can be applied to the productive process."[18] As Young, speculating on the primitive origins of baseball, put it, "baseball is little else but the skilled use of the bludgeon."[19] So the specific character and complexion of sport, it is claimed, can be directly read from the specific character and complexion of the social labor that undergirds it.

The second version of the work-sport relation is peculiar to certain selected writings of Beamish and is based less on a consideration of observed correspondences than it is on a conceptual identification of work with sport.[20] Sport, Beamish claims, does not so much resemble work as it instantiates it, as it counts itself as a determinate instance of work. Beamish seems to throw caution to the wind here regarding his own previous strictures against abstract treatments of work and sport, speaking rather apocryphally of certain universal features of labor that are shared by sport.[21] His argument rests on a fairly sweeping conception of labor as a creative form of externalization (*Entgegenständlichung*), a conception that he regards as a faithful rendition of Marx's own understanding of labor. As he avers, "For Marx, labor, as a generic practice, is the way humans externalize their unique capacities and actualize human potential."[22] Such a conception of labor, Beamish maintains, can easily capture the sort of actualization of potential that goes on in sport, not to mention, he adds, practices "ranging from a game of Class Struggle or Anti-monopoly, through ballet, rhythmics and box lacrosse, to building a Lego house or a garden."[23] The conclusion thus easily follows that sport itself is merely a particular instance of social labor; or to put it more directly, "the Rules of the Game of life [production] in capitalist society are . . . built right into [the] rules [of sport].[24]

Notwithstanding the real differences between the correspondence and the identity versions of the work-sport relation, the actual assessment they provide of this relation—that "sport labor is no different than social labor"[25]—is largely the same. That is, although the correspondence approach, unlike the identitarian one, does not maintain an a priori sameness between sport and labor, the sheer number and deep-seated nature of the resemblances it turns up commands the conclusion that sport is not an alternative to work but a replica of it.[26] On either account then, sport is depicted as a mere double of work, duplicating its techniques and laws of production, its forms of organization, and its innermost mores and values.[27] Viewed in this light, it seems of little consequence whether this entwinement of work and sport is one of (found) analogous or (presumed) identical structures.

What is of direct consequence, however, is the process of production that is said to give rise to sport.[28] It is the logic of this social process, it is argued, that causes certain kinds of sporting practices to come into existence that both reflect this logic and sustain it as a dominant force. McMurtry gives perhaps the most forceful and clear account of this reciprocal causal relation: "the major spectator sports of a society are paradigms of it . . . [that do not] merely *mirror* the social order in which they occur, but more importantly, *cause this order to be maintained intact* by evangelizing in popular form its essential structure of action."[29] This is why Brohm and his colleagues so stoutly insist that "it is impossible to separate sporting activity . . . from its capitalist, . . . material base."[30]

The causal effect of production on sport works itself out, they argue, as a process of incorporation. In the correspondence version, incorporation marks the encroachment of the technical logic and ethos of production on the logic and ethos of sport; whereas in the identitarian version it marks the reinforcement and affirmation of the underlying technical character of sport itself. With respect to the former, Rigauer argues that the techniques and norms of work "impose" themselves on leisure activities like sport.[31] The idea here is that economic and technical structures of capitalist production actually burrow themselves into sport, turning it into just another commodity and technical activity. This process of insertion or incorporation is described as a kind of mimesis in which sport is said to variously "imitate" and "internalize" worklike behaviors as dictated by the imperatives of production.[32] Moreover, though the economic and technical infiltration of sport is centered on top-level, elite sport, it is not confined to it. Rather, insofar as elite sport is the driving force behind the whole social system of sport, the technical assimilation extends to mass, leisure-oriented sport as well.[33] As Brohm bluntly puts it, "there are not several kinds of sport but only one: bourgeois sport."[34]

What sport is claimed to "internalize" from the productive apparatus of capitalist society in this manner is just about everything imaginable that can be linked in one way or another to that apparatus. A short list would include the following stock items of industrial capitalism: the "performance principle" (also known as the "achievement principle"), competition, quantification, division of labor, techniques of training, normative standards of individual conduct, and in general the methodical manner and rationalized style of bourgeois life.[35] Indeed, in this view there is little if anything about the social composition of sport that cannot be accounted for in this rigid contextual fashion.

The Question of Agency and Emancipation

That one might exercise in an actual and effective manner one's distinctly human agency in sport, or find in sport any emancipatory opportunity, seems, in this account, a foregone and entirely negative conclusion. On the contrary, the whole thrust of the New Left's argument to this point suggests just the opposite: that neither the expression of individual or collective will in sport nor the use of sport as an emancipatory agent is achievable by our present social principles.

To begin with the latter claim, the critics contend that there is nothing about the social makeup of sport that suggests it possesses any emancipatory potential. So by sheer dint of argument the emancipatory claim has to be rejected in favor of its stark opposite: that sport is a repressive force. Scarcely any other conclusion is possible: if in fact the alienating features of capitalist work are, as argued, inscribed in sport, if alienated work and sport are of the same piece, then sport is condemned to actuate and extend that social alienation. Moreover, if the interpenetration of work and sport, as further argued, saturates sport at every level, if the practice of sport is everywhere the same,[36] then there is no place to turn in the world of sport, no current practice or institution of sport to single out, that might soften this critical indictment of sport. Indeed, the only tenable claim that can be offered here is the invidious one that "sports belong to the realm of unfreedom, no matter where they are organized."[37]

Implicit in the denial of any emancipatory capacity to sport is the denial of any genuine expression of agency within its compass. If the very logic and innermost structures of sport are bound up with the dominant mode of production, then it follows that sport is an "agent of socialization through which the actor is forced to conform to the forms and contents of society's framework of relationships."[38] The deeper, structural shortcomings of sport that disqualify it as a liberating agent explain, therefore, why sport can't be used as a dramatic, critical vehicle to express the interests of the underclass. Sport is locked into its bourgeois social context, and so cannot *be put to different uses independently of the social production relations in which it grew up and within which it is reproduced.*"[39] While critics like Beamish readily concede that some cultural forms (namely, television, photography, painting, sculpture, and writing) possess critical elements that enable them to demystify and even overturn the social forces of domination, sport, Beamish argues, contains no such critical elements and so is practically condemned to carry out the repressive decrees handed down by society. Unlike the former cultural forms whose subversive effects are embedded in "the very nature of their concrete use-value," all that one can find in the concrete use-value of sport are the sedimentations of an alienated social order. Hence the conclusion that actors in sport are "bearers of other social relations and ideas" rather than active, reflective agents, and the sober prognosis that "sport is a *positivist system* and as such always plays an integrating and never an oppositional role."[40]

The dim prognosis regarding the transformative potential of sport only worsens with the critics' further contention that sport actively promotes intraclass factions and interclass collaboration. Sport not only fails the subordinate classes as an instrument of class expression and struggle, they argue, but it actually impedes such expression by disrupting class solidarity in ways that directly play into the hands of the dominant class. The blame can once again be assigned to the structures of alienated labor that reside within sport, which "*inculcate* [an] *attachment to the established order.*"[41] This explains why sport is able so effectively to co-opt the masses.

The interest in and promotion of sport is, therefore, considered synonymous with the interest in and promotion of bourgeois society. The telltale slogans that sport is an "opiate of the people" and a way of "regimenting youth" gain their currency here.[42] In addition to these familiar refrains, the mythic and symbolic undercurrents of sport that attract many people to its variegated world also come under criticism in this context. Lipsky argues, for example, that the sense of identity and community which people seek in sport deflect them from the true source of their *angst*-filled seeking, faulty political and social structures, in favor of the delusions and fantasies offered by hero worship and sport fandom. Since this turning to sport and the mass adulation accompanying it are at bottom nothing more than false remedies for a real social problem, sport "can be cathartic," he asserts, "but never therapeutic."[43] With this, the critical indictment of sport comes full circle.

Ideology Critique

The notion of ideology in leftist circles is an unambiguous one; it denotes a "false consciousness of existing social realities."[44] The notion of ideology critique, therefore, is also unambiguous. It means a critical excavation of the roots of our false perceptions and conceptions of the social world, an excavation that does not rest content until the particular social interests served by these false beliefs and values are uncovered. In a capitalist society, of course, the social group directly implicated in the distortion of social reality is the bourgeois class itself.

The argument has been forcefully made that sport is intimately bound up with the material, productive base of capitalist society. If that is so—if sport is indeed structurally homologous or identical to work—then an errant conception of modern sport would be one that denies such resemblance or identity; it would argue for a fundamental structural dissimilarity between work and sport. The error is incurred, in this argument, in the attempt to sever this irrevocable connection. It remains for the critic to specify the various forms this errant conception of sport takes and to inquire into the reasons and interests that lie behind its fallacious formulation.

According to Rigauer and his cohorts, the principal way that work is detached from sport is by linking it to "purposeless" play. In particular, sport is presented as a paradigmatic instance of play that carries over its founding values into the realm of competitive activity. Play is defined in turn as a purposeless, autotelic activity, which nicely sets up the contrast to work defined as activity pursued in the interests of self-preservation or survival.[45] With a few deft conceptual manipulations, the sought-after opposition between work and sport is accomplished.

However, the sport-play connection is pitched in different ways by bourgeois ideologues. One, perhaps the chief, way it is pitched is in the manner noted above. It is simply claimed that sport and play are integrally related, and that this connection disqualifies any regard for sport as work. A slightly more sophisticated version holds that while sport and work may occasionally run together, it is essentially a matter of how one engages in sport that determines whether it is experienced "as a pleasurable satisfaction or as the fulfillment of a duty."[46] Yet another version of this relation drives what Brohm calls the "confiscated theory" of sport, which maintains that sport is basically a neutral, if not inherently healthy, practice that is "confiscated" by outside social forces in ways that deform its true character.[47] What makes sport a healthy enterprise on this account is precisely its deep connection to play that protects it, it is alleged, from the ravages of a crooked capitalist modernity.

What is mistaken about such views of sport has already been noted: they ignore or otherwise cover up the complicity of sport in the productive affairs of capitalist society. One question remains, however: What does the dominant class hope to achieve by its false portrayal of sport as play? The answers are manifold, but they tend to coalesce around two points, both of which, of course, have as their avowed aim the maintenance of the status quo.

The first point cited by the critics is that by passing sport off as just another form of play, its internalization of the norms and techniques of work can be effectively disguised thereby making it an ideal medium for the transmission of distinctly bourgeois virtues and ideals of life. If the critics are to be believed, sport has proved itself to be an important cog in the bourgeois ideological machine. An impressive array of bourgeois-like actions and beliefs have come to occupy a niche in sport and have seemingly thrived in that ambience. Some of the more prominent of these include: the teaching and valuation of achievement-oriented action, the inculcation of respect for authority and blind obedience, the glorification of discipline, sacrifice and the cult of duty for its own sake, the celebration of anti-intellectualism, the sublimation of sexual pleasure, the mortification of the body that trades on the masochistic theme "pain is pleasure," and the continuance of the belief in linear, unlimited progress.[48] In short, all the accouterments of bourgeois-class practices and ideals are claimed to find ready acceptance and reinforcement in modern sport.

The second point has less to do with ideological content per se—with the message—than it does with the medium in which this content is conveyed and filtered through sport. A consideration of this medium reveals how easily and smoothly it can pass through sport unnoticed, and how powerful an ideological weapon sport really is. The critics focus here again on the presentation of sport as an autonomous enterprise (which is itself, of course, a mainstay of the sport-as-play thesis), a presentation that, they argue, effectively transforms the social actions assimilated by sport into natural ones. If the assortment of elements and values that comprise sport are in fact separable from the material base of society and its various derivatives, and if these elements and values are historically continuous and persistent ones (the timeless thesis), then it clearly follows that they are not social (in the sense of conventional) but natural properties. Their separability in this case is taken as proof of their natural (asocial) status. So, for example, on this account the competitive motif of sport is treated not as a strand of bourgeois social life woven into the fabric of sport, but as a condition of human nature itself, as something we are inclined to do not because we live in a capitalist society but because we are the human beings we are. As such, an attack on the expression of this competitive urge in sport is construed as an assault on our human nature, on those things we do by virtue of being human.

This same aura of "naturalness" that attaches itself so easily to (autonomous) sport also inspires a certain sense of innocence and naiveté that is no less, ideologically speaking, ominous. The notion that sport is a thing *sui generis*, a bracketed world beholden only to itself, conjures up, as Lipsky argues, a symbolic world of sport rife with mythic images of pleasure and fantasy, images that beckon our indulgence and incite our longing for those things that elude us in everyday life.[49]

The mythologization of sport goes hand in hand here with its depoliticization, whose hidden but very real political effect is compounded. On the one hand, politics is ostensibly separated from sport, but, on the other hand, the residual political content concealed within its inner recesses is conveyed in a festive atmosphere virtually absent of critical reflection, debate, or dissension. It is sport's ability to fashion such a "social canopy" of beliefs and values, a social canopy whose political impact is often more powerful than that of standard political ideologies, that makes it, Lipsky argues, such a formidable ideological tool.[50] This is no doubt why he insists that one of the central tasks facing a political theory of sport today is to bring to light the subtle relation between political socialization and sport as a symbolic refuge.[51]

The Critical Resolution of Alienated Sport

Although the specific measures recommended by the New Left to rectify the problematic status of sport are not always uniform, and in some cases not as clear as they might be, there is one point upon which they are all in accord: that "sports cannot be 'better' than their social context and circumstances."[52] To be sure, this cautionary note is itself open to various interpretations. One weaker interpretation of it suggests that sport cannot be changed without some correlative change in society, or that at the very least, change in the former must be linked in some demonstrable way to change in the latter. There is, however, another, much stronger interpretation that can be made here, and it is this stronger one that the critics have in mind. On this account, the resolution of alienated sport requires nothing less than the radical transformation of the larger society, a complete overhaul of its material base and productive relations. As Hoch avers, "to reform the mirror [sport] while leaving the society untouched would change nothing at all. We will have humane, creative sports when we have built a humane and creative society—and not until then."[53]

The militancy of the New Left on this point is not surprising since this idea follows from the main argument it has pressed all along: that the logic and ethos of capitalist production is directly inscribed in the logic and ethos of sport. Moreover, what is true of sport in this instance is true of the entire ensemble of cultural endeavors. All have been infected by the pervasive influence of social production. There are no privileged places or experiences left within the social totality; it is a seamless whole that admits of no exceptions. Society as a whole is therefore unfree, and sport is merely one demonstrable example of this. This is why, as Brohm boldly asserts, "the task is to denounce bourgeois sport as such, and not to try to reform it."[54]

Once we get past the "denouncing," "smashing" part, however, things get slightly muddled regarding the specifics of the New Left's program of emancipation. The chief issue that arises is what if anything is to replace bourgeois sport in a future, truly humane society. On this score, as I intimate above, the New Left does not speak with one voice. Nonetheless, Rigauer and Brohm provide the two most definitive options to come out of the Neo-Marxist camp. Of the two proposals for emancipation, Rigauer's is arguably the more detailed. For starters, he lays out four conditions for the development of a new "self-conception" of sport:

1. the dissolution of all worklike structures of behavior in sport, to include the fetish on achievement and the repressive features associated with the rationalization of production
2. the dissolution of all manner of conformist thought, and the democratization of choice in sport
3. the politicization of sport so that individual athletes are able to express "their genuine political interests"
4. the demystification of sport based on a critical awareness of the connections between sport and society[55]

The collective realization of these conditions, Rigauer argues, would allow sport to dedicate itself to "social and educational tasks" and would make "the satisfaction of individual needs the central purpose of doing sports."[56] Of course, it scarcely needs mentioning that such a realization would require that every trace of alienated labor be purged from the structures of sport, which would be possible only if the present alienating mode of production were replaced *in toto* by a nonalienating one.

As to what kind of sport we will have in the future, or what specific role it will play in a socialist society, Rigauer has little to say. There is some hint on his part that it will feature noncompetitive physical activities.[57] Perhaps the most tantalizing clue he leaves us in this regard is his call for "the unity [*Einheit*] of sports and work under social conditions of autonomy and self-determination."[58] It thus appears that a rather tight, intimate relation will obtain between sport and work in a humane society, but what sort of relation he envisages this to be (for example, a strictly instrumental or functional relationship), and whether or not he has something in mind, such as Marcuse's integration of play (the realm of freedom) within work (the realm of necessity), is exceedingly hard to say.[59]

Unfortunately, Brohm's emancipatory sketch is not particularly detailed either, but it does break some new ground. It is clear enough from his analysis that he thinks that sport is little more than an embellished shadow of capitalist society. Thus, he argues that sport, along with bourgeois society, will simply *"disappear in a universal communist society."*[60] But Brohm says next to nothing about a replacement for sport as such. What he does say has to be deciphered from his other critical comments, in particular, from the sallies he directed against the students' handling of sport during the riots of the late sixties. In such instances, he speaks in Foucaultian terms of giving a new status to the body, and of nurturing new forms of bodily development "in which the body would find its rightful aesthetic, playful, erotic and intellectual place."[61] The concern for the body as framed by play, in which the body is treated "not as a vehicle of performance, but as [a] vessel of pleasure and fulfillment,"[62] is Brohm's idea of a non-alienated form of leisure, one he finds perfectly compatible with a socialist conception of society. Although his remarks here are more provocative than definitive, they do pose an interesting alternative to standard leftist fare on this matter.

Critique of the New Left Theory of Sport

Not surprisingly, the New Left indictment of sport has attracted its fair share of critics. Some of the critics have made significant dents in the Neo-Marxist case against sport, especially in their attack on the empirical strain of the New Left argument. Despite the Left's explicit disavowal of empirically oriented research, a considerable part of its critique consists of straightforward empirical claims, many of which have effectively been disposed of by critics like Guttmann.[63]

However, the critics have not been as successful, in my estimation, in dealing with the conceptual nucleus of the New Left's critique of sport, that is, with the conceptual approach, claims, and arguments that undergird its coupling of sport and work. On this subject, the critics' arguments have been less forceful and crisp than they might have been, and at times downright disingenuous.[64] Indeed, I maintain that the conceptual edifice upon which the New Left indictment of sport rests has hardly been grazed by its critical detractors.

I intend, therefore, to make this conceptual edifice the point of departure of my own critique of the New Left. I will focus my criticism, accordingly, on its central resort to labor as the *explanans* of sport, in particular, on its pivotal claim that sport can best be understood and treated as a form of social labor. I will argue that this approach is itself conceptually problematic and fails in its effort to provide a plausible explanation of sport. In this regard, a major part of my argument will attempt to show that sport is not directly implicated in the productive logic of labor. I will not, however, claim that the New Left approach to sport via labor is an altogether bankrupt one, but will argue that it has limited utility and import as an explanation of certain of its social features and tendencies.

As previously noted, the first level at which the argument of labor as *explanans* of sport is pursued is, for the Left at any rate, an extraordinarily abstract one. I am referring here to Beamish's argument that sport is a virtual conceptual clone of work, that it is a direct instantiation of labor. Though the abstract way in which this claim is framed might induce "fear and trembling" among those Marxist theorists who are uncomfortable with discussing anything other than the concrete present, specifically the concrete present of social labor, that does not especially give me pause. Rather, it is because the theoretical identification of work with sport is a poor, unfruitful abstraction that I wish to criticize it.

Ironically, when it comes to the pitfalls of dealing with labor and sport as theoretical concepts, it is Beamish who issues the appropriate caveat against reducing everything in the social landscape to labor. Doing this, he rightly observes, inflates the concept of labor to such a degree "that it no longer possesses any discriminating powers."[65]

But Beamish ignores his own warning when he later argues for the integration of sport and labor. His argument in this latter regard appeals to the bedrock of the labor process itself, to the sense in which human beings creatively express themselves by objectifying and externalizing their human faculties and powers via labor. Beamish correctly contends that such a conception of labor can easily accommodate, in the sense of include and explain, sport and its particular brand of rational activity, since it too can be plausibly viewed as simply another way human beings "externalize their unique capacities and actualize [their] human potential."[66] But he fails to point out that his notion of labor can also accommodate, again without noticeable conceptual duress, nearly every kind of activity in which a human being might engage. As Marx himself argued, the self externalizes itself in "religion, family, state, law, morality, science, art, etc."[67] By adding sport to the list Beamish only succeeds in confirming his earlier suspicion that at a sufficiently abstract point almost anything can be collapsed under the concept of labor. The price paid for doing so here is the same one he duly noted above: labor loses any power to discriminate among the welter of human affairs. If labor refers to everything, then it refers to nothing in particular. If it refers to nothing in particular, then the claim that sport is labor, or art, or religion has little, if any, import. There can be a concept of labor, or a concept of anything for that matter, if and only if it has some determinate landmarks, be they vague or mutable ones, by which it can be picked out. Beamish's whole manner of argument then, as he himself foresaw and forewarned, is self-defeating.

Beamish's conceptual equation of sport with labor is thus to be rejected as an infertile abstraction since it fails to provide the theoretical explanation of sport that it purports to provide. Indeed, at the nebulous abstract level at which it operates, it can no more explain the practice of sport than it can that of music.

However, the matter does not rest here. Beamish's rendering of labor also undermines what has to rank as the major explanatory abstraction employed in Marxist theory: Marx's important claim that the level of development of the productive forces of a society is the key to explaining that society's general course of development and complexion. No matter how loosely or strictly one reads this claim, it presupposes that the material productive forces of society can be separated somehow from its productive relations and superstructure. Beamish's account of labor, I maintain, does not allow for any such meaningful separation. Rather, tethering labor to externalization in its most abstract sense makes labor a synonym for every other human enterprise in the social totality. More precisely, labor becomes the social totality because its conceptual net now captures the very activities that collectively make up the superstructure. The result of this theoretical emasculation of labor is the predictable one that Marx's explanatory scheme is emptied of its explanatory power. This scheme is reduced either to a trivialism—that the material base of a society explains it now means that economic, political, religious, and various other cultural fare (remembering that these are all now included in the mode of production as forms of labor) explain society— or to an absurdity: that labor explains labor. That Marx escapes such conceptual ignominies is a modest tribute to the conceptual soundness of his own social theory.

To reiterate, Beamish went awry not by indulging in a theoretical consideration of labor and sport, but in pushing his abstractions too far. Although his efforts got him the linkage between labor and sport he sought, they did so without the desired explanatory force they were meant to have. But if suitably constrained, I argue, an abstract treatment of labor and sport need not lead us into this conceptual cul de sac. Neither, to be sure, does it lead to the explanatory regression from sport to labor Beamish was intent on establishing. Rather, a careful theoretical analysis of labor and sport turns up important differences between them that undercut any such regression.

With regard to a consideration of the general features of labor, one need look no further than Marx. One finds in his writings a definite, quite cogent account of labor per se, or as he put it, a study of "the labor-process" independent of "the form it assumes under given social conditions."[68] Such an abstract study of labor reveals, according to Marx, that labor is a "special productive activity" carried out with the definite aim of securing human survival. It is from its focus on human sustenance that it derives both its instrumental temperament and logic—its purposive nature—and its characteristic "damned seriousness."[69] Hence, for Marx what defines an activity as a materially productive one, as a labor activity, is its production of useful things, and what defines a thing as a useful thing, as a thing with use-value, is its satisfaction of quite specific, concrete human needs.[70] It is in this sense that Marx regards labor as the necessary condition of the existence of the human race and as the foundation of the material exchange between human beings and nature.[71]

An abstract study of sport, stripped of its immediate social elements, reveals a rather different kind of human activity.[72] The logic that governs sport and defines its general temperament is anything but a productive one. True enough, like labor and other technical activities, sport is centered about a specific aim and selects from among a determinate number of options the means likely to satisfy that aim. But the manner in which it goes about this whole task has an inherent unproductivity, as required by the rules, that has no analogue in labor; that is, in sport the permissible means to attain the goal are always narrower in scope than the possible means to attain it. This follows from the special restrictions introduced by game rules, which always proscribe the most expedient and direct way of achieving the goal in favor of some less expedient, indirect way. Thus, for example, it is useful but proscribed to hand-carry the ball to the hole in golf.

Contrary to labor then, sport is at bottom an unproductive activity that cleaves to a gratuitous, as opposed to an instrumental, brand of rationality. Though it is true that one may engage in a game for a variety of reasons, including productive ones (as in professional sports, which individuals take up ostensibly to earn a living), one must be careful to distinguish sport and its peculiar logic from the various social purposes for which it might be used. Otherwise, the use of the game as an instrument is likely to be confused with the game itself, and it is the latter, no matter what the purpose it is used for, that requires that we abide by the rules and its arbitrary limitations. Thus, although people who play games for instrumental reasons (professionals) have a different regard for those games than people who play them for intrinsic reasons (amateurs), they have the same regard for the rules of those games: namely, that the rules must be accepted because they make the activity of the game possible. This is why Suits argues that one "can have no reason for accepting the rules which is not also a reason for playing the game."[73]

So it is apparently the case, contra Beamish, that labor and sport are quite different activities, and that a treatment of the general features of each clearly establishes this to be the case. In due course, I will show the importance of such abstract considerations for the social criticism of sport. However, presently my intent is merely to forestall the view that a conceptual analysis of labor and sport is in itself wrong-headed and, accordingly, to be avoided because unfruitful. On the contrary, it is only wrong-headed abstractions that are to be avoided because unfruitful. Unfortunately, the New Left is doctrinally inclined to the former view and so is disposed to condemn all conceptual undertakings, save its own more or less covert ones, as inherently bankrupt. Thus, Lenk's legitimate criticism of Rigauer's failure to delimit adequately his abstract concept of labor at certain important points wrings a prompt concession from Rigauer as well as the promise that in the future he will confine his analysis to social labor.[74] This almost complete abhorrence of conceptual analysis, and the focus on the so-called concrete social and historical forms of labor and sport, typifies the New Left's second approach to the study of sport.

This second approach, as noted above, dispenses for the most part with a general regard for labor and sport, and insists that sport can best be explained by comparing it to the dominant capitalist form of social production. Such a comparison, or check for likenesses and resemblances, reveals an important structural correspondence between labor and sport upon which it is asserted that both a substantial identity and a strong causal link obtains between them. That sport resembles labor is interpreted to mean not just that they are more alike than different, but that labor, as the more primary of the two, is the causal force behind sport, of whatever particular social shapes and forms it assumes. Consequently, changes in the social texture of labor are alleged, on this account, to have a profound effect on the social character of sport.

It is plain to see that the kind of resemblance appealed to here is not a terribly sophisticated one. It has neither the hint of complexity of Adorno's notion of the "dialectical image," with all its complicated mediations, nor the ingenuity of Benjamin's constellation of, for instance, the ragpickers, bohemians, and new poetic methods of Paris in the Second Empire.[75] What we get in their stead is a rather crude linkage of sport to labor in which the social dynamics of sport are simply subsumed under those of labor.

It is equally clear that the causal account that is spun out of these discovered resemblances is not an especially powerful one either. That Y resembles X does not entail that X causes Y. The converse is also not compelling. That is, a lack of resemblance between X and Y doesn't warrant the conclusion that no causal relation obtains between them. In short, resemblance in itself seems to have little, if anything, to do with the attribution of causal power to some agent, thing, or event. Thus, the criticism leveled by Eichberg and Hopf, and after them by Hoberman,[76] that such accounts illicitly move from analogy to causality appears to be well founded. Also well founded, it seems, is these critics' suspicion that the search for analogies merely masks the "real" problem of explaining sport, since by effectively reducing sport to labor it preempts, by fiat rather than argument, alternative accounts of sport.

There is, however, another way of pitching this argument that makes the explanatory regression from sport to social labor a more plausible one. In this instance, the resemblance between sport and labor is not in itself construed to be the substance of the causal relation between them, but it is treated as good evidence for supposing that such a causal relation exists. Although one may reasonably inquire as to how much resemblance counts as sufficient evidence to establish such a causal claim,[77] this manner of drawing inferences and making generalizations from available data cannot so easily be convicted of "leaping from analogy to causality."

But what sort of explanatory scheme do we have here? The answer, I argue, is a refurbished version of the base-superstructure argument recast in the form of a functional explanation. It is precisely the sort of argument McMurtry had made when, as quoted earlier, he contended that "the major spectator sports of a society are paradigms of it . . . pure-type versions . . . [that do] not merely *mirror* the social order in which they occur, but, more importantly, *cause this order to be maintained intact* by evangelizing in popular form its essential structure of action."[78] There are two parts to this argument that I want to unpack to show how it is able to meet successfully the objections raised above, and to establish its particular, but limited, promise as an explanation of sport.

The first part of McMurtry's argument involves a straightforward recounting of the base-superstructure argument in which sport is said to mirror the social order and its determinate material base. This view retains the standard leftist identitarian thesis that sport and labor are more or less the same sort of enterprises. That it is able to combine this identificatory claim without impugning its base-superstructure explanatory model is something of a coup, for there are two horns of a dilemma that must be grappled with in this regard. On the one hand, if one maintains that sport and labor are structurally identical to one another, then it seems as if one has disarmed any way of distinguishing between the base and the superstructure, and so, any way of employing the model on which this distinction is based as an explanatory device. This, it will be remembered, was the fate that befell Beamish, who by passing sport off as a clone of work wreaked havoc on Marx's materialistically grounded theory of history. On the other hand, the very resort to a base-superstructure style of argument, as Gruneau has argued,[79] appears simply to parrot, in left-wing guise, the separation of culture from its material base so characteristic of idealistically oriented cultural analyses.

The dilemma, however, is only an apparent one, and can be resolved by clearing up a systematic ambiguity in the above use of the term "base." As G. A. Cohen has persuasively argued,[80] if X is alleged to be the "basis" or "foundation" of Y, then it follows that Y rests in some sense on X. Now, what Y rests on may or may not be a part of Y. The foundation, for example, upon which a house rests is arguably a part of the house. But the plinth upon which a statue rests is not part of the statue. Thus, we can distinguish, after Cohen, between two senses of the term "basis":

X is basis^1 of Y = X is that part of Y on which (the rest of) Y rests.

X is basis^2 of Y = X is external to Y and is that on which (the whole of) Y rests.

I contend that McMurtry's argument can be profitably read as a variation of basis^1, above. Let L stand for labor and S for sport, and we get the following claim:

L is basis^1 of S = L is that part of S on which (the rest of) S rests.

This way of putting the argument allows McMurtry to maintain a strong identity between sport and labor without collapsing all distinctions between them; sport, like work, is a technical activity but is distinguishable as an idealized version of the latter, and without succumbing to the idealist trick that sport is somehow autonomous from labor. Marx, I believe, had something like this in mind when he argued that "religion, family, state, law, morality, science, art, etc. are only particular modes of production, and fall under its general law."[81] In other words, while superstructural activities like sport are not synonymous with their material base, they share a kindred productive logic that is derived from labor.

The second part of McMurtry's argument establishes it as a functional explanation, or more correctly, as an argument that purports to be a functional one. To illustrate this point, however, it may be helpful to start with some general examples of such arguments drawn from Marx.[82] In his writings, Marx often made the following sorts of claims: the relations of production *correspond* to the productive forces; the legal, political, and intellectual superstructure *is conditioned by* the mode of production; consciousness *is determined by* social being. Notice that in each of these instances Marx distinguishes between two elements, the second of which is said to be explanatory in some fashion of the first. What Marx is after here, to take his first assertion as our example, seems to be this: to say that the relations of production *correspond* to the productive forces is to claim that the relations of production have the particular character that they do because they stabilize or otherwise promote the development of the productive forces. Marx is not simply attributing in this case an effect to the productive relations, that they do in fact promote the productive forces, but, more important, is proposing an explanation of the rise and very existence of the productive relations on the basis of that effect. This is a prototypical functional explanation in which it is alleged that the effects of a phenomenon contribute to an explanation of it.

If I am right, a species of the New Left argument, as apparent in McMurtry's above thesis, can be treated as a causal argument of the functional type. If so, it is important to recognize that the explanation of sport it purports to give is not the same as a "benefit" explanation.[83] For the latter, an explanation of X entails only a calculation of the useful effects/functions of X. This, I take it, is precisely the sort of explanation of sport Adorno entertained in his *Introduction to the Sociology of Music,* in which he likened the social function of music to that of sport and argued that both restore to the body particular functions that were expropriated from it by the machine.[84] Since Adorno's analysis of sport does not go beyond a reckoning of its useful effects, and makes no pretense to explain why it is able to carry out the social functions that it does, his is a benefit rather than a functional explanation.

What differentiates Adorno's account from McMurtry's, then, is that the latter stakes an additional, stronger claim on sport's alleged ability to influence society: namely, that sport has the particular character that it does because of the positive effects it has on society at large. Indeed, for McMurtry the very point of sport is that it acts to reinforce the social order to which it belongs. Its capacity to reinforce that social order hinges once again on its structural equivalence to society, that, in other words, the logic of sport is not different from that of social life but merely exemplifies it. This homology between the "social game" and the "sportive game" is apparent, he argues, in each of their particulars: in their territorial-acquisitive style of action, in their aim to achieve a monopoly over their opponents, and in their accumulation of assets and points.[85] Hence, in a pattern of argument that bears all the marks of a functional explanation, McMurtry explains sport by citing its effects on society, argues that sport has the particular character that it does because of those effects, and reasons that sport is able to exercise such effects only because society is structured in the way that it is.

If we can construe the New Left argument through the eyes of McMurtry in this fashion, then the causal account it offers does not fall prey, as I intimated earlier, to the howler that resemblance equals causality. That is, it does not mistake the drawing of an analogy with the making of a causal claim. However, the ability to avoid an elementary mistake of this kind, does not in itself, of course, make for good theory. And so it may be appropriately asked if the above revised account is indeed a compelling theory of sport. Though it clearly is a better theory than its predecessor, there are good reasons, I contend, for holding that it does not adequately explain sport.

There is first of all the problem of how a Marxist theory worth its salt can simply dispense with an analysis of the productive relations of a society, and spend virtually the whole of its time and energy engaged in a study of its productive forces. Despite some rhetoric to the contrary that proudly touts the importance of matters of social class and the like, this is exactly what the New Left does in its treatment of sport. Thus, while largely supportive of the Left's strategy to study sport via the concept of labor, Gruneau criticizes it for not taking up the cudgels of class analysis.[86] To frame the argument in Habermas's terms, "the self-constitution of the species takes place not only in the context of men's instrumental action upon nature but simultaneously in the dimension of power relations that regulate men's interaction among themselves."[87] Either way the argument is put, the New Left stands accused of ignoring the integral part social interaction plays in the production and reproduction of human life.

There is a further problem here that goes to the very core of the

kind of functional explanation I have attributed to critics like Mc-
Murtry. In order to see this, I have to retrace my steps a bit. Let us
suppose for the sake of argument that a capitalistic society much like
our own requires, for whatever reasons, sport in order to prosper fully
and thrive. Additionally, let us suppose that sport admirably fulfills
this social need, so that the society that it allegedly serves is able to
flourish in a way that would otherwise not be possible. The question
now arises of whether by showing that there is a need for sport, and
that sport satisfies that need, we have in fact explained sport. The answer, I contend, is a resounding not at all. That a society needs sport
doesn't in itself explain its having the one that it does unless—and
this requires an additional move—it can also be shown that there are
not other, quite unrelated, reasons why it happens to have the sport
it needs.[88] This, however, has not been shown, and, I contend, cannot
be shown, because there is another, more compelling reason that explains sport without appealing to its social utility—though it is able
to account for that utility.

Although I will discuss that reason shortly, my more immediate
concern is to show that McMurtry has not provided a functional explanation of sport at all, but a benefit explanation masquerading as a
functional one. That it appears to be a genuine functional explanation is owed, I argue further, to a bit of conceptual chicanery that underlies not only McMurtry's argument but this whole second line of
Neo-Marxist inquiry: their main thesis that sport is simply the sum
of its capitalist circumstances. To discover what is problematic about
this conceptual artifice—and I underscore that it is indeed a conceptual ploy that is the beguiling force here—I must resort to our previously discussed nature-convention distinction, whose importance for
critical social theory can now be shown.

It has been sufficiently established that this second brand of Marxist
analysis holds no brief for abstract conceptions of sport and labor, and
regards such conceptions as little more than vacuous intellectual exercises.[89] But what often goes unnoticed is that in fixing its analytic
gaze on the sport-social labor connection, this analysis too avails itself of a definitional apparatus, which, though concretely rather than
abstractly oriented, is no less a conceptual scheme. The standard definitions, it turns out, include the following:

> top-level sports . . . [are] a complex of social behavior which is
> directed toward the best possible individual and team athletic
> achievements. Top-level sports may include both amateurs and
> professionals.

sport is a complex system of institutionalized social practices, governed by the principles of maximum output, training, competition, and selection.

sport is an institutionalized system of competition, delimited, codified and conventionally governed physical practices which have the avowed aim of selecting the best competitor—the champion—or recording the best performance—the record—on the basis of comparing performances.[90]

Brohm, for one, calls this type of definition construction a *"dialectical materialist definition of the phenomenon of sport as a whole."*[91]

Defined in this way, the parallels between sport and society (labor) are unmistakable, perhaps unassailable. This rendering, that there is sport and that it is needed, commands the conclusion that there is sport because it is needed. It can scarcely be any other way, since other possible explanations have been conceptually legislated out of existence: there is only the sport that we see in the functionally sensitive division of labor of present society.

But the argument only works within this conceptual framework. Hence, everything turns on the cogency of the Left's socially delimited conceptions of sport. Yet, nary a word, let alone a critical word, is furnished by the critics on behalf of such conceptions. Indeed, one searches in vain for any kind of critical defense, unless the diatribe against abstract definitions of sport counts as one. That this definitional strategy might be a short-sighted one thus appears lost on all of its practitioners except perhaps Beamish.

In his brief fling with abstractions, Beamish made an important observation that I believe gets to the root of the problem. Citing Marx's own work, Beamish astutely noted that "it is by contrasting human labor as a generic practice which actualizes human potential with alienated labor that constitutes a central core to Marx's total *oeuvre* and focuses attention upon the actualization of humanist conceptions in practical reality [rather] than merely expressing them in abstract, philosophical discourse."[92] I believe Beamish has got it right. By critically elaborating on his point as it applies both to labor and sport, I intend to show that the New Left's definitional scheme cannot carry the explanatory load it was designed to carry.

To begin with labor and, therefore, as Beamish suggests, with Marx's treatment of labor, we have already noted that Marx had an abstract theory of labor, and that he depicted it as the material basis of the human agent's interchange with nature. What needs to be brought into sharper relief now is that in addition to this theory of labor per se, Marx had a particular social theory of labor; that is, Marx distinguished between the "material" properties of labor and its "social" properties. While labor's material properties establish the ontological significance of labor as the driving force of human life itself, its social properties determine the particular historical significance of labor within a discrete social system. Thus, machinery, for instance, "is no more an economic category than the bullough that drags the plough," but under the productive relations of capitalism it assumes a definite social form as a "social production relation, an economic category."[93] Marx, therefore, gives two different readings of labor depending on whether he views it from a material or a social standpoint.

The point in drawing attention to this distinction in Marx's thought is not to privilege the material over the social side of labor nor to privilege the social over the material side. Neither is it to deny the quite real social features of labor nor, conversely, to deny its equally real material ones. Rather, the point is that however one conceives labor, it has both material and social properties (though it may be conceded that some activities might be wholly social ones and others wholly material ones). The key is to understand the relation between these disparate sets of properties. The point Marx seems to have in mind is that whenever labor takes on a specific social form, it always drags along a certain part of it that is at bottom nonsocial (material), that is neither exhausted nor completely subsumed by its social context. Just as a human being is more than the set of social descriptions that define it as a bourgeois citizen, so labor is more than the social descriptions that define it as wage labor. Moreover, the basic material properties of labor cannot be deduced or strictly inferred from its social ones. To paraphrase Cohen's more exact formulation, labor or wage labor is not wage labor in virtue of what is necessary and sufficient to make it labor.[94]

Just as it is important to grasp the relation of the material to the social properties of labor, it is also important to grasp the relation of the material to the social standpoint of labor that grounds these two sets of properties. Clearly, the task of deciphering the necessary and sufficient conditions of labor falls to philosophy, while that of deciphering the social form of wage labor falls to political economy. A philosophical analysis of labor per se has no direct interest in a description of the social properties of labor any more than political economy has a direct interest in its necessary and sufficient conditions, yet the distinction and relation between them are not idle intellectual matters. Indeed, everything hangs—and this is the gist of Beamish's point—on the critical relation between them. The specification of the universal features of labor provides Marx with a normative standard by which to judge deformations in the various social forms labor assumes, be it the slave labor of antiquity, the serf labor of feudalism, or the wage labor of capitalism. Without such a standard, critical determinations of the liberating or constraining character of a particular kind of labor would have to defer to a simple social description of the diverse types of labor that have been produced in different historical periods. What is more, the heritage of philosophy as a critique of ideology, as well as the very distinction between theory and ideology, would collapse, and along with it the critical power to unmask the ideological disposition on the part of most, if not all, societies to pass off their determinate modes of production as the only possible and conceivable modes of production.[95] In short, the kinds of criticisms Marx made of bourgeois political economists like Adam Smith, who among other things argued that the repressive features of wage labor were endemic to labor itself, would lose their critical force.

A similar case, I contend, can be made for sport. It has already been established that sport possesses its own peculiar kind of rational action, and that at its very core, quite aside from any consideration of social context, it is a gratuitous, unproductive enterprise. It is also the case, of course, that sport has a social context, and that the social properties that emanate from this context conjoin with the material properties of sport in various configurations. Thus, for example, in a capitalist setting, sport takes on the social characteristics of a commodity and is thereby subject to all the constraints associated with other types of wage labor. Nonetheless, at bottom, sport is no more a commodity than machinery is a commodity.

Like labor, sport can be viewed from either an abstract material standpoint or a concrete social one. Depending on the viewpoint one adopts, sport can appear either as a distinctive kind of activity or as simply one commodity among other commodities. But again the point is not to privilege one viewpoint over the other nor to deny that sport is a special activity or a commodity, but to recognize that it is both. This means that the material properties that define sport as a gratuitous endeavor cannot be deduced or directly inferred from its social ones, and, conversely, that its social properties cannot be deduced or directly inferred from its material ones. Sport or commodity sport is not, therefore, commodity sport by virtue of what is necessary and sufficient to make it sport.

Again, the crucial issue in all of this is what sort of relation is to hold between the material and social viewpoints we take on sport. If, following Beamish's lead, we use the previous example of labor as our model, then we can expect that philosophy will occupy itself with an investigation of the necessary and sufficient conditions of sport, and that a critically informed political economy will concern itself with the entanglements of sport in the dominant mode of production. The results of the former inquiry, in turn, will be used as the normative base for our critical judgments about the emancipatory or repressive features of sport in its specific social station. The philosophical consideration of sport, in other words, will discharge its time-honored function as a critique of ideology.

Curiously enough, however, while Beamish does submit sport to a thoroughgoing social analysis from the perspective of a critique of political economy, he repudiates any attempt to anchor such a critique in a philosophical consideration of the basic character of sport. Not even his stillborn abstract effort to pass off sport as a kind of "externalization" contains the faintest hint of this. On the contrary, he is every bit as adamant as his cohorts in insisting that sport is synonymous with its capitalist setting, that there is nothing to sport save its social form, that "sport is totally tied to social labor."[96] When he uses the oxymoron "sport labor" it is always in this socially constricted sense.

Hence, Beamish's important reminder of how Marx made use of philosophically gleaned insights about the nature of labor in his critique of social labor stops short precisely at the point we left our discussion of McMurtry and this whole second line of Marxist inquiry into sport: that sport is exclusively a bourgeois instrument and so is to be explained functionally in terms of its support of the dominant mode of production. Notwithstanding Beamish's refusal to carry through the above model of analysis to sport, we are in a position to do so; we have achieved a better vantage point with which to see what is wrongheaded about this whole line of Neo-Marxist thought.

I stated earlier that in the Left's truncated account of sport, the fact that a social need exists and that sport fulfills that need is sufficient proof that sport exists because it fulfills that need. I conjectured, however, that the latter conclusion follows only if there is not another relevant reason to explain the existence of sport, and that the Left's definitional rendering of sport simply preempts the possibility of such an alternative explanation. This can now be demonstrated by appealing to the nature-convention distinction mentioned above. There is at least one other good and compelling reason that explains the complexion and attraction of modern sport that is rooted in the logic of sport itself. I am referring here to the gratuitous manner of sport, to the way in which it contrives challenging situations by introducing unnecessary obstacles to the achievement of an end. This feature of sport most clearly distinguishes sport from the rest of ordinary life—in ordinary life, after all, an unnecessary obstacle is no obstacle at all. This feature also explains, in a fundamental way, why sport draws so on our attention. It is not because we don't get enough opportunities in everyday life to do and see the kind of things that go on in sport that it commands our attention, but that we don't get a chance to do or see such things in everyday life at all.[97] In other words, sport is so interesting to us largely because it is utterly unlike the rest of ordinary life.

This explanation provides all the evidence we need to discredit the claim that sport owes its existence exclusively to social necessity. Further, if sport can be explained in terms of its internal material logic, then the entire causal account that backs up the Left's functional explanations of sport collapses as well. No matter how one pitches its base-superstructure causal argument, labor (L) can no longer be plausibly cast as the causal agent of sport (S). L cannot be said to be the causal basis[1] of S, since L is not that part of S on which (the rest of) S rests. Nor can it be said that L is the causal basis[2] of S, since although L is external to S, it is not that on which (the whole of) S rests. On this revised reading, the autonomous standing of sport is of sufficient strength to crush the identitarian strain that runs through both of these causal accounts.

In claiming, however, that sport cannot be adequately explained in terms of its social effects, nor causally grounded in social labor, I am not claiming that those social effects are of no consequence or that they have no explanatory power at all. Rather, my intent was to show that whatever import or explanatory power they have is itself parasitic on the logic of sport. It is because sport is a special undertaking that it has the power to captivate us, and it is because it captivates us that it proves useful to society in so many ways.[98] Understood in this way, a consideration of the functional effects of sport genuinely explains why certain features of sport are singled out for attention and others ignored, and why sport takes on the various social hues that it does. But since these accounts can only catalogue the useful effects of sport, its ostensible benefits, they cannot claim that these effects are explanatory of sport in some more fundamental and penetrating way.

What we have in the case of the social-effects argument then, as I argued above, is a benefit explanation. In fact, it is the same kind of explanation that McMurtry explicitly proposes at the end of his essay when, commenting on those features of sport he finds most distinctive of it—its demands for extraordinary physical courage and instant "system-analysis" ability—he reasons that "these 'higher' norms of spectator football . . . [are what] enable it to be so effective as a glorified model of our social order: endowing thereby this social order . . . [with] the false *Schein*, of heroic mindedness."[99] One can say no more or less about the social utility of sport, though what is left unsaid about sport itself here, and how it figures in all of this, is considerable.

Still, the explanatory power that can be mustered for the New Left argument in this regard cannot make up for the New Left's mistakes, nor can it contain the further damage to its position incurred by those mistakes. If its explanations and causal claims founder because they take no account of the nature of sport, then its resort to labor as the normative foundation of its critique of sport can hardly avoid a similar fate. Indeed, as should be clear by now, virtually all of the central claims the New Left presses against sport suffer from the same logical affliction: the insistence on treating a complex phenomenon like sport as a simple social one.[100] As a result, sport is treated rather like one would treat the institution of banking and its assorted activities of writing checks, making withdrawals and deposits, and investing money. Like sport, all of these activities are bourgeois practices through and through, and each, in its own inimitable but socially defined way, acts to further the goals and aims of capitalist society. In a word, one and all function as instruments of capital.

By bending this familiar line of thought in a slightly different way, the New Left is able to ground its critique of sport in labor. It argues simply that since sport and company are merely social constructions, they are hardly capable of criticizing the social order to which they owe their own existence. That prosecutorial task is reserved only for the activity and stratum of human experience that are not coextensive with its social definition, in short, for the complex praxis of labor. The Left turns then quite "naturally" to labor to polish off its critique of modern society and sport.

Once again, however, the claim that sport is a product of its social setting while labor is not, and that sport is, therefore, unsuited to any critical task it may be called on to perform, cannot be sustained if the assumptions that underlie it are contested. To reiterate, sport is no more synonymous with its commodity form than labor is with wage labor. Once this distinction is grasped, the whole idea of basing a critique of sport on labor can be seen as an unintelligible one.

It has already been argued that sport is a gratuitous human venture, that in a game it is perfectly rational, even essential, for the players to put unnecessary obstacles in their path so as to make their pursuit of their goal an interesting and challenging one. Viewed from the standpoint of labor, one would be hard pressed not to conclude that sport is a queer, if not a patently absurd, undertaking. In fact, it is this gratuitous side of sport that accounts, no doubt, for much of the vitriol the Left has consistently spewed against sport in the past. It is the basic "uselessness" and futility of sport that continue to make it "odious," as Lasch writes,[101] to many modern-day enlighteners—from the Left and the Right—for enlighteners and reformers tend to be dyed-in-the-wool instrumentalists, at least when it comes to moral and political matters. What meager interest the Left has shown in sport has to do with its limited success in putting sport to use to advance its own social and political agendas—though it must be noted that the Right has been more inclined and quicker to seize on the political and cultural "capital" of sport. The irony in all of this, of course, is that whatever social and political currency sport has in this regard is inextricably bound up with, in one way or another, its basic superfluity.

However, it is not sport itself that turns out to be an odd thing, but rather the attempt to understand it from the perspective of labor. Such an attempt would have weight only if sport really were no different than going to work, or shopping, or cutting a business deal. But sport is at bottom nothing like any of these everyday activities; it is governed by an entirely different rational order. To deny this— to regard sport, as the Left so tenaciously does, as a mere instrument of capitalism—is to lapse into a strange and incoherent account of sport, into what Suits aptly calls a "radically instrumentalist" account of sport.

It has already been conceded that sport may well be used as a device to attain a variety of other ends and purposes. But these other purposes were known, and were known by the players, to be separate from the game as such. The view that Suits calls "radical instrumentalism" is the view that denies that games can be separated from the purposes to which they are put. I contend that this is precisely the view that the Left has been trying to foist on us all along. It is perfectly consistent with its central argument that sport is literally constituted by the social purposes it subserves, an argument that closes off any significant way of separating sport from its social surroundings. But if this were so, a sport like football, to borrow McMurtry's example, could not be more unsuited to its appointed social task. The very worst way to achieve a practical objective, as Suits tells us, would be to make it the goal of a game; one would be obliged quite arbitrarily to rule out the easiest, most expedient way to achieve it in favor of some other indirect, more difficult way.

Finally, if we agree that sport is a complex activity, if, that is, it is more than a product of the dominant capitalist mode of production, then the New Left's program for the emancipation of sport must be considered suspect as well.[102] Its treatment of sport as a bourgeois concoction merely creates a seamless whole, a social totality without fissures, where there is none. The New Left's call for "the destruction of sport" attempts to consummate at a practical level what has already been achieved at a theoretical level: the conflation of sport with social labor. Indeed, because the Left's demand that sport be dismantled is based on such a conflation, it must be taken, despite Rigauer's contentions to the contrary,[103] in the most literal sense—that is, both the material properties (now misconstrued as capitalist ones) and the social properties of sport are targeted for elimination, evidently leaving nothing in their wake.[104]

This criticism extends to the particulars of its revolutionary packages. Thus, Rigauer's proposal to mold somehow labor and sport into a unified whole, assuming there is anything left of sport to mold, must also be rejected for reasons previously adduced. The underlying premise of Rigauer's recommendation is that the incorporation of worklike structures into sport is not in itself problematic, only the incorporation of the wrong ones. However, if we take Rigauer at his word here, his proposal is unintelligible. As we have noted, the instrumental rationality of labor cannot simply be combined with the gratuitous rationality of sport, not, that is, without considerable theoretical and practical cost.

However, Brohm's turning to play is no less problematic, not the least of which because it constitutes a reflex response to the mistaken view that sport is merely another form of alienated labor. The impression is quickly driven home that the relation between sport and play is very much like that between work and play: namely, that they are opposites, and that as such they cannot be linked in any meaningful way. But this is not the case. To be sure, the blind assertion that sport is by definition a form of play, regardless of its social circumstance, is sheer ideological hocus-pocus. It doesn't follow from this, however, that sport and play are opposites, only that they do not logically entail one another. In other words, that one is doing sport doesn't entail that one is playing, and that one is playing doesn't entail that one is doing sport. Nonetheless, it may very well be the case that if one is engaged in sport one is also playing (literally playing that sport), and vice versa, since the logic of play and the manner in which it maintains a certain distance from the ordinary world is not incompatible with the logic and manner of sport. It is not the sport-play relation that is to be rejected as disingenuous, then, but rather Brohm's attempt to pass it off as merely another variant of the work-play relation.

The Left's turning to play as a resolution to the problem of alienated sport has additionally been criticized, by theorists of such diverse stripes as Guttmann and Gruneau,[105] as a reactionary and Romantic rejection of modernism itself, of the technological complexion and bent of modern society, and by extension modern sport. Hoberman further claims to have detected in the Left's enchantment with play an element of the Volkish critique of modernism and sport, which sought to replace the asphalt ambience of modern, technological sport with the natural ambience of premodern sport, the cement stadium and the cinder track with the unadorned, untrammeled meadow.[106]

These claims are not without merit, and in their particulars they are even persuasive. But whatever real or imagined antimodernist elements may have infiltrated the Left's turning to play as a way of resolving the problem of alienated sport, it is not at all clear, nor has a case been made, that play is itself either exclusively a vestige of the premodern era or an arch enemy of modernism. Indeed, if Marx's argument that the "realm of freedom" is the proper telos of the "realm of necessity" has any credence,[107] then it seems that play is at least as good a candidate as any other human endeavor that populates the realm of freedom to bring about the actual realization of the project of enlightened modernity: the attainment of a rational society predicated on the freedom, justice, and happiness of its members.

The validity of this claim, of course, is not germane to the present discussion. What is germane, however, and what leads to my rather different criticism of the Left's advocacy of play, has to do with the amorphous and open-ended way in which the Left portrays play as an alternative to alienated praxis. That is, it is not its turning to play itself that I find troublesome, but rather its depiction of play as the erotic space of bodily expression, and its conception of the "ludic" body as a pure vessel of pleasure. Such portrayals, I maintain, prompt the identification of play with the irrational itself, in which the invitation to play becomes the invitation to plunge into the abyss, to sample in an unadulterated way the delightful fruits of the irrational, to reject the claims of reason—whatever their lineage—and to wallow in the radical "otherness" of reason. Moreover, they countenance an undifferentiated pleasure seeking that is equally at home with what Jaspers called the urge toward "eccentric possibilities" characteristic of bourgeois individualism and its penchant for crude forms of sensationalism, as it is with the Fascist preoccupation with the pleasures of the flesh rooted in exhibitionistic displays of the body.[108] The Left's turning to play, therefore, is suspect because it represents, in my estimation, a crass and false *Aufhebung* of alienated labor.

Critical Appropriation of the New Left Theory of Sport

Obviously, there is much about the New Left critique of modern sport that I flatly reject. Perhaps most important in this regard is my criticism of its attempt to account for sport as a general or specific derivative of labor. Such an approach, I maintain, is fraught with conceptual problems and at bottom untenable.

In keeping with my notion of immanent critique, however, I am convinced that there are also important lessons to be learned from the New Left criticism of sport, and that these lessons deserve to be a part of any critically oriented theory of modern sport. Perhaps most notable among these are Beamish's important recognition of the need to establish a normative foundation for the critique of sport; the various social "benefit" explanations of sport authored by several Neo-Marxist writers; and the forms of ideology-critique these writers developed as spinoffs of these same "benefit" explanations.

Beyond these lessons, it is often the case that a particular theory will occasionally run up against the limits of its own theoretical position, at times even transgressing those limits. When it does, that theory is often able to garner new and important insights, but the costs are always high; the paramount cost, of course, is to its own theoretical status as a tenable, viable theory, and the minimal cost is the emergence of some rather striking inconsistencies that must be dealt with or explained away in some fashion. Nonetheless, these transgressions are more often than not instructive ones, and so ones that warrant our critical attention.

Just such a theoretical transgression has occurred in the New Left critical literature on sport, and an important lesson can be derived from it. I have in mind here two specific instances in which Rigauer makes claims regarding the basic character of sport action that quite explicitly violate his own treatment of sport. While the claims—really, disclaimers—are not completely conceded on his part, they are nonetheless striking. Rigauer says:

> In contrast to the world of work, the individual person still brings together these individual sequences during the "moment of truth" in the contest itself. During the athletic action the rational analysis disappears. Nonetheless, the division-of-labor dif-

ferentiation of the teaching and training process remains socio-logically relevant because the teaching and training process takes up more time than the contest does.

In the contest itself, the pattern of socialized behavior is applied in complex plays and can even be improvised. In contrast to the narrowly determined, analytical demands of work, the playing field offers the possibility for independent solutions to problems. Nonetheless, the break-it-into-parts method of tactical team training remains the basis for learning game behavior. In train-ing, team sports copy the forms of the division of labor even if the analytical scheme can be set aside during the contest itself so that new solutions to specific playing situations can be found.[109]

What is significant about Rigauer's claims is that they challenge the whole thrust and force of his argument in *Sport und Arbeit*. They insinuate that sport is at its core quite unlike labor and, consequent-ly, that it is recalcitrant to any simple reduction to labor. Unfortunate-ly, Rigauer chooses not to deal with these obvious discrepancies in his account, but rather lamely seeks to explain them away. We are, therefore, reassured that in spite of the different tenor and complex-ion of sportive action in the contest itself, where rationalization pro-cesses can be set aside and where even opportunities arise for impro-visation, the atomistic, division of labor procedures of training remain the basis of learning sport, and that training is more important, so-ciologically speaking, than the sportive action itself because it is of longer duration. That one learns to perform certain feats in sport by training for it says nothing at all about the character of sport itself; that training is of greater social relevance because it takes up more time than the contest itself is absurd on its face—not to mention that it apes the achievement-oriented society Rigauer so disdains, a soci-ety that habitually misconstrues quantitative matters for qualitative ones. Indeed, the reverse is actually the case; training derives its in-telligibility and its basic sense and orientation from its subordinate relation to sport, not vice versa. Indeed, whatever social relevance training may have is always parasitic on the game itself.[110]

Hence, these concessions cannot be explained away in this fash-ion because they are incompatible with the theoretical framework on which Rigauer bases his critique of sport. In order to do them jus-tice, therefore, to give them their full due as insights into the nature of sportive action, it is the theoretical framework itself that must be shed. In my view, this is the important lesson to be learned from

Rigauer's transgressions. Before this lesson can be effectively incorporated into a reworked critical theory of sport, we need to consider the other major branch of leftist sport theory, one that takes its inspiration from Gramsci's hegemonic turn.

NOTES

1. The pivotal works of the inaugural phase of the Neo-Marxist (this term will be used interchangeably with the term New Left) movement were written by German and French theorists and included Gerhard Vinnai, *Fußallsport als Ideologie* (Frankfurt: Europäische Verlagsanstadt, 1970); Ulrike Prokop, *Soziologie der Olympischen Spiele* (München, 1971); Jac-Olaf Böhme et al., *Sport im Spätkapitalism* (Frankfurt: Limpert, 1971); Ginette Berthaud et al., *Sport, culture et repression* (Paris: François Maspero, 1972); Jean-Marie Brohm, *Critiques du sport* (Paris: Christian Bourgeois, 1976). The New Left movement in Germany, with which I am more familiar, still continues to thrive, but for all intents and purposes it has split into two rival, though largely friendly, camps. On the one side, a more orthodox and dogmatic Marxism prevails; it endorses the top-level sport of Eastern bloc countries but is quite critical of the achievement-oriented sport of Western countries. The major leader of this faction is the Polish sociologist Andrzej Wohl, whose principal works have been translated into German; see in particular his book *Soziologie des Sports* (Pahl-Rugenstein, 1979). The other important leaders and representative works of this group include Sven Güldenpfennig, *Sensumotorisches Lernen und Sport als Reproduktion der Arbeitskraft* (Cologne, 1974), and Peter Weinberg, *Handlungstheorie und Sportwissenschaft* (Cologne, 1978). The second camp has been heavily influenced by the work of Habermas; it argues that a complex activity such as sport cannot be adequately understood by an appeal to any one theory. Hence, members of this camp emphasize a multitheoretical approach to sport (one that even sanctions critically directed empirical research) in which the accent is no longer placed on labor as such, but on the broader notion of "behavior." The major figures and works of this faction include Bero Rigauer, *Warenstrukturelle Bedingungen leistungssportlichen Handelns* (Andreas Achenbach Lollar, 1979); idem, *Sportsoziologie: Grundlagen, Methoden, Analysen* (Hamburg: Rowohlt, 1982); Klaus Cachey, *Sportspiel und Sozialisation* (Schorndorf, 1978); Elk Franke, *Theorie und Bedeutung sportlicher Handlugen* (Schorndorf, 1978); Kerstin Kirsch, *Zeitgenössiche Sportphilosophie als Kritische Sporttheorie der Neuen Linken* (Frankfurt am Main: Peter Lang, 1986); Karen Rittner, *Sport und Arbeitsteilung* (Bad Homberg, 1976). The interest of the latter group of New Left theorists in a multitheoretical approach to sport suggests some possible lines of rapprochement with the similarly inclined work of Anglo-Saxon sport theorists such as Chris Rojek. See his important book *Capitalism and Leisure Theory* (London: Tavistock, 1985). There is one final qualification. Not all critically oriented theorists, of course, can be grouped neatly into one or the other of these camps. Gunter Gebauer's work is a notable example in this

regard. Gebauer's writings reveal an interest in both critical theory and grand theory. Thus, he has not given up on the notion of a unitary, comprehensive theory of sport. See his latest book, *Körper-Und Einbildungskraft: Inszenierungen Des Helden Im Sport* (Berlin: Dietrich Reiner, 1988).

2. Bero Rigauer, *Sport and Work*, trans. Allen Guttmann (New York: Columbia University Press, 1981); Jean-Marie Brohm, *Sport: A Prison of Measured Time*, trans. Ian Fraser (London: Ink Links, 1978); Rob Beamish, "Central Issues in the Materialist Study of Sport as a Cultural Practice," in *Sociology of Sport: Diverse Perspectives*, ed. Susan Greendorfer and Andrew Yiannakis (New York: Leisure Press, 1981); idem, "Materialism and the Comprehension of Gender-Related Issues in Sport," in *Sport and the Sociological Imagination*, ed. Nancy Theberge and Peter Donnelly (Forth Worth, Tex.: Texas Christian University Press, 1984), pp. 60–81; idem, "Sport and the Logic of Capitalism," in *Sport, Culture, and the Modern State*, ed. Hart Cantelon and Richard Gruneau (Toronto: University of Toronto Press, 1982), pp. 142–97; idem, "The Materialist Approach to Sport Study," *Quest* 1 (1981): 55–71; idem, "Understanding Labor as a Concept for the Study of Sport," *Sociology of Sport Journal* 2 (1985): 357–64; Richard Lipsky, *How We Play the Game: Why Sports Dominate American Life* (Boston: Beacon Press, 1981); Paul Hoch, *Rip Off the Big Game* (New York: Doubleday, 1972).

3. Ike Balbus, "Politics as Sports," in *Sport Sociology: Contemporary Themes*, ed. Andrew Yiannakis et al. (Dubuque, Iowa: Kendall Hunt, 1979), pp. 75–80; John McMurtry, "The Illusions of a Football Fan: A Reply to Michalos," *Journal of the Philosophy of Sport* 4 (1977): 11–14.

4. Rigauer, *Sport and Work*, p. 111.

5. Hoch, *Rip Off the Big Game*, p. 14. For a sampling of such contextual definitions see Brohm, *Sport: A Prison of Measured Time*, pp. 68–69.

6. Rigauer, *Sport and Work*, pp. 2–3.

7. See Robert Wheeler, "Organized Sport and Organized Labour: The Workers' Sports Movement," *Journal of Contemporary History* 13 (1978): 191–210; David Steinberg, "The Workers' Sport Internationals, 1920–28," *Journal of Contemporary History* 13 (1978): 233–51; John Hoberman, *Sport and Political Ideology* (Austin, Tex.: University of Texas Press, 1984), pp. 109–14.

8. Hoberman, *Sport and Political Ideology*, p. 188.

9. Brohm, *Sport: A Prison of Measured Time*, p. 140.

10. Wheeler, "Organized Sport and Organized Labour," pp. 196–97; Steinberg, "The Workers' Sport Internationals, 1920–28," p. 233; James Riordan, "The Workers' Olympics," in *Five Ring Circus: Money, Power and Politics at the Olympic Games*, ed. Alan Tomlinson and Gary Whannel (London: Pluto Press, 1984), p. 98.

11. Hoberman, *Sport and Political Ideology*, pp. 232–33.

12. It also serves as an important corrective to more recent Marxist doctrines of sport, backed by the official communist parties of the Eastern bloc countries and in France by the French Communist party (PCF), which endorse high-performance sport and condemn the antisportive bent of the New Left. As noted, Andrzej Wohl's work is most exemplary of this approach to the

study of sport (see note 1, above). See in this regard Hoberman, *Sport and Political Ideology*, p. 238, and Hoberman's essay "Communist Sport Theory Today: The Case of Andrzej Wohl," *Arena Review* 4 (1980): 13–16.

13. Beamish, "Materialism and the Comprehension of Gender-Related Issues in Sport," p. 65.

14. Beamish, "The Materialist Approach to Sport Study," p. 55.

15. Karl Marx, *The Economic and Philosophic Manuscripts of 1844* (New York: International Publishers, 1972), pp. 113, 142.

16. Beamish, "Central Issues in the Materialist Study of Sport as a Cultural Practice," p. 38; idem, "The Materialist Approach to Sport Study," p. 65.

17. Brohm, *Sport: A Prison of Measured Time*, pp. 69, 136–37; Rigauer, *Sport and Work*, p. 89.

18. Rigauer, *Sport and Work*, p. 11.

19. T. R. Young, "The Sociology of Sport: A Critical Overview," *Arena Review* 8 (1984): 7.

20. At times Hoch comes close to holding such a view of sport. See *Rip Off the Big Game*, p. 101.

21. Beamish's misgivings about abstract treatments of labor and sport are scattered throughout his writings. In particular, see his essay "The Materialist Approach to Sport Study," pp. 57, 60–61, 68.

22. Beamish, "Understanding Labor as a Concept for the Study of Sport," p. 359.

23. Ibid., p. 358.

24. Hoch, *Rip Off the Big Game*, pp. 100–101.

25. Beamish, "The Materialist Approach to Sport Study," p. 66; idem, "Understanding Labor as a Concept for the Study of Sport," p. 357.

26. Rigauer, *Sport and Work*, pp. 9–10.

27. Brohm, *Sport: A Prison of Measured Time*, p. 40.

28. Beamish, "Central Issues in the Materialist Study of Sport as a Cultural Practice," p. 38.

29. McMurtry, "The Illusions of a Football Fan," p. 11.

30. Brohm, *Sport: A Prison of Measured Time*, p. 137.

31. Rigauer, *Sport and Work*, p. 1. See also Jürgen Habermas's essay "Soziologische Notizen zum Verhältnis von Arbeit und Freizeit," in *Konkrete Vernunft*, ed. G. Funke (Bonn, 1958), pp. 219–31.

32. Rigauer, *Sport and Work*, pp. 27–29, 77; Beamish, "Central Issues in the Materialist Study of Sport as a Cultural Practice," p. 40.

33. Brohm, *Sport: A Prison of Measured Time*, p. 5; Rigauer, *Sport and Work*, pp. 18, 107; Beamish, "Central Issues in the Materialist Study of Sport as a Cultural Practice," p. 40.

34. Brohm, *Sport: A Prison of Measured Time*, p. 40.

35. Rigauer, *Sport and Work*, pp. 23–24, 32–33, 50–51, 56–57, 59.

36. As Brohm argues, "The practice of competitive sport is everywhere governed by the *same* international federations, the *same* rules, the *same* techniques, and the *same* training methods." *Sport: A Prison of Measured Time*, p. 62.

37. Theodor Adorno, *Prisms* (Cambridge, Mass.: MIT Press, 1982), p. 91.

38. Rigauer, *Sport and Work,* p. 100.

39. Brohm, *Sport: A Prison of Measured Time,* p. 4.

40. Ibid., p. 178.

41. Ibid., p. 76.

42. Ibid.

43. Lipsky, *How We Play the Game,* pp. 126–27.

44. Rigauer, *Sport and Work,* p. 83.

45. Ibid., pp. 7–8, 85.

46. Ibid., p. 87.

47. Brohm, *Sport: A Prison of Measured Time,* pp. 3–4.

48. Ibid., pp. 26, 178; Rigauer, *Sport and Work,* p. 99.

49. Lipsky, *How We Play the Game,* pp. 39–40.

50. Ibid., p. 45.

51. Ibid., p. 56. In a similar vein, Young maintains that there is an important link between the mythic underside of sport and the profit motive of private capital. See his essay "The Sociology of Sport," p. 8.

52. Rigauer, *Sport and Work,* p. 111.

53. Hoch, *Rip Off the Big Game,* p. 10. Brohm is equally forceful in his claim that "it is just as naïve to try to rid sport of its negative aspects as to try and democratise the bourgeois or Stalinist state," whence he concludes the necessity of smashing the "present day body of society" and its dominant form of bodily activity. Brohm, *Sport: A Prison of Measured Time,* p. 34.

54. Brohm, *Sport a Prison of Measured Time,* pp. 63–64. The hard line the New Left takes here is reminiscent of the Red Sport International's (RSI) similar hard-line opposition to any attempt to form an independent sporting movement within capitalist society. The RSI and the Lucerne Sport International (LSI) made up the two rival factions of the workers' sport associations in the early 1920s. To members of the RSI, the very idea of promoting sport as a separate cultural movement, which was a major aim of the LSI, was anathema. The sport movement, they argued, must be completely subordinated to the revolutionary goals of the political and trade-union movements. On this point, see Steinberg, "The Workers' Sport Internationals, 1920–28," p. 240.

55. Rigauer, *Sport and Work,* pp. 104–5.

56. Ibid., p. 105.

57. Ibid., pp. 103–4. The New Left's aversion to competition and its preference for cooperation in sport is echoed in Balbus's analysis as well. See Balbus, "Politics as Sports," p. 79.

58. Rigauer, *Sport and Work,* p. 110.

59. Herbert Marcuse, *An Essay on Liberation* (Boston: Beacon Press, 1969), p. 21. When I pressed Rigauer on this very point in my conversations with him in the spring of 1988, he was unable to come up with anything more definitive than what he wrote in *Sport and Work.*

60. Brohm, *Sport: A Prison of Measured Time,* p. 52.

61. Ibid., p. 142.

62. Hoberman, *Sport and Political Ideology*, p. 235.

63. Guttmann's criticisms in this regard can be found in his following books and essays: *Sports Spectators* (New York: Columbia University Press, 1986), pp. 150–53; *From Ritual to Record: The Nature of Modern Sports* (New York: Columbia University Press, 1978), pp. 79–80; "Introduction" to Rigauer's *Sport and Work*, p. xxvi.

64. See Guttmann, *From Ritual to Record*, pp. 69–71. Further, although Lenk has offered many cogent criticisms of the New Left's conceptual effort to connect sport with alienated labor (indeed, many of them are quite formidable), his claim that the Left's disparagement of achievement behavior imperils the survival of human civilization itself—by, among other things, discouraging the adequate production of foodstuffs to meet the needs of a precipitously growing population—is clearly preposterous. Even a cursory review of this admittedly complicated and vexing issue reveals that the problem of world hunger today is almost exclusively a distribution problem, not a production problem. Furthermore, Lenk's central argument against the Left's reduction of sport to the alienated, compulsory achievement model, that the literally "herculean" demands and virtual absolute commitment required of top-level athletes today precludes the possibility of forcefully extracting a top-flight performance from them, is simply a bad argument. Though it may be true that such requirements would make it more difficult to compel such a performance than it would, to exact a rudimentary task like marching, it does not follow that it would make it impossible to coerce a high-quality performance of this sort. Simply put, the execution of a highly skilled performance that requires a significant degree of dedication does not logically entail, as Lenk insinuates, an unforced or an intrinsically valued performance. See his book *Social Philosophy of Athletics* (Champaign, Ill.: Stipes, 1979), pp. 2–3, 93, 95.

65. Beamish, "Central Issues in the Materialist Study of Sport as a Cultural Practice," p. 35.

66. Beamish, "Understanding Labor as a Concept for the Study of Sport," p. 359.

67. Marx, *Economic and Philosophic Manuscripts of 1844*, p. 136.

68. Karl Marx, *Capital, Volume 1* (New York: International Publishers, 1967), p. 177.

69. Karl Marx, *Grundrisse* (New York: Vintage Books, 1973), p. 611.

70. Marx, *Capital, Volume 1*, p. 41.

71. Ibid., pp. 42–43, 183–84; Karl Marx, *Capital, Volume 3* (New York: International Publishers, 1977), p. 825; idem, *Grundrisse*, p. 311.

72. My argument is based entirely on Bernard Suits's account of games. See his book *The Grasshopper: Games, Life and Utopia* (Toronto: University of Toronto Press, 1978), chapter 3.

73. Ibid., p. 144.

74. See Lenk, *Social Philosophy of Athletics*, p. 105; Rigauer, *Sport and Work*, pp. 108–9.

75. See Raymond Williams, *Marxism and Literature* (Oxford: Oxford University Press, 1977), p. 104.

76. See Henning Eichberg, *Der Weg des Sports in die industrielle Zivilisation*

(Baden-Baden: Nomos, 1973), p. 87; Wilhem Hopf, *Kritik der Sportsoziologie* (Lollar/Lahn: Aschenbach, 1979), pp. 78–79; Hoberman, *Sport and Political Ideology*, pp. 241–42.

77. This is, for instance, precisely the question Guttmann puts to Rigauer's claim that sport and work are structurally identical, which, incidentally, Rigauer doesn't answer to his satisfaction. See Guttmann's introduction to Rigauer's *Sport and Work*, pp. xxii–xxiv.

78. McMurtry, "The Illusions of a Football Fan," p. 11.

79. Gruneau, *Class, Sports, and Social Development* (Amherst: University of Massachusetts Press, 1983), p. 37.

80. G. A. Cohen, *Karl Marx's Theory of History: A Defence* (Oxford: Oxford University Press, 1978), p. 30. My argument in this context is heavily indebted to Cohen's penetrating analysis, and is, in fact, merely a gloss on his more extended argument.

81. Marx, *Economic and Philosophic Manuscripts of 1844*, 136. Beamish's rendering of the labor-sport connection cannot be similarly rehabilitated because it precludes any way of distinguishing sport from labor.

82. Again I must acknowledge my debt to Cohen. See especially chapters 9 and 10 of his book *Karl Marx's Theory of History*. Those who blanch at the claim that Marx employed functional arguments in his theoretical arsenal, and who consider the very idea heretical, no doubt do so because they link such arguments to the theory of functionalism. That theory has been roundly attacked by Marxists because they regard its chief claim that all elements of social life support and reinforce each other, and the social totality of which they are a part, to be both false and quietistic in its implications. But as Cohen argues, there is no necessary link between functional arguments and the theory of functionalism as such. The central thesis of the theory of functionalism, noted above, does not in itself commit one to functional arguments. More important, all hint of conservatism is purged from functional arguments when they are tied, as Marx ties them, to a theory that asserts that as society develops it unleashes a power (the productive forces) that will eventually lead to its own undoing. See Cohen, *Karl Marx's Theory of History*, pp. 283–84.

83. Ibid., pp. 252–53.

84. Theodor Adorno, *Introduction to the Sociology of Music* (New York: Seabury Press, 1976), p. 50.

85. McMurtry, "The Illusions of a Football Fan," pp. 11–12.

86. Gruneau, *Class, Sports, and Social Development*, p. 89. The failure of the New Left to engage seriously the questions of social class, Gruneau further contends, explains why its account of sport is skewed so heavily in a deterministic direction, and why it gives short shrift to the question of human agency.

87. Jürgen Habermas, *Knowledge and Human Interests* (Boston: Beacon Press, 1971), p. 51.

88. Cohen takes this argument in a different direction. See his *Karl Marx's Theory of History*, p. 281.

89. See, for example, Hoch, *Rip Off the Big Game*, pp. 12–14; Brohm, *Sport: A Prison of Measured Time*, pp. 66–70.

90. Rigauer, *Sport and Work*, pp. 17–18; Brohm, *Sport: A Prison of Measured Time*, pp. 67–69.

91. Brohm, *Sport: A Prison of Measured Time*, p. 67.

92. Beamish, "Understanding Labor as a Concept for the Study of Sport," p. 362. There is, however, one rather puzzling feature about Beamish's above point that deserves comment. This concerns his rather condescending reference to "merely expressing [humanist conceptions] in abstract, philosophical discourse." If his apparent displeasure with philosophical discourse in this regard has only to do with the torturously slow and often circuitous manner in which abstractly gleaned verities are put into practice, or never find their way into practice at all, or with sterile philosophical debates that have little to do with the concerns of human life, then his condescension is understandable, if not justified. If, however, there is implicit in his remark a certain rancor toward the abstractness of philosophical discourse itself, then it is hard to know what to make of it. The insight that labor is at bottom a primary and creative way in which human beings "externalize" their innermost capacities, and so cannot be reduced to wage labor (to name but only one humanist conception), is fully apparent only if we avail ourselves, as Marx did, of a philosophical consideration of the necessary and sufficient conditions of labor per se, of labor abstracted from its particular social instances. If it is objected that this is only a theoretical abstraction, then the objection must be conceded at once; for labor makes its appearance in the real world only in some particular social form or other. But I hasten to add two points. First, to consider sport only in its socially determinate form is no less an abstraction; that is, labor can no more make its appearance in the real world absent its natural form—the form that qualifies it as a laboring activity in the first place—than it can absent its social form. Second, to indulge in the kinds of abstractions we have been discussing is, after all, what theory is all about. To deny this is to confuse theory for practice, an intellectual construction with the slice of experience it is meant to explain. To denigrate it is to betray a thinly veiled aversion to theory, which far from benefiting practice may well impoverish it by depriving practice of a theory to guide it toward a rational society.

93. Marx, *Poverty of Philosophy*, p. 149, as quoted in Cohen's *Karl Marx's Theory of History*, p. 89.

94. Cohen, *Karl Marx's Theory of History*, p. 92.

95. As Adorno has felicitously put it, "whether one can talk of ideology depends directly upon whether one can distinguish between illusion and essence, and is . . . a central piece of sociological doctrine extending into all ramifications of the subject." "Introduction," *The Positivist Dispute in German Sociology* (London: Heineman, 1977), p. 2. I will soften this claim somewhat in the subsequent chapter.

96. Beamish, "Sport and the Logic of Capitalism," pp. 181–82.

97. I owe this point to Bernard Suits. See his essay "The Elements of Sport," in *Philosophic Inquiry in Sport*, ed. William J. Morgan and Klaus V. Meier (Champaign, Ill.: Human Kinetics, 1988), p. 43.

98. To paraphrase Novak, the appeal of sport on our "species being," on

our innermost nature, is its infrastructure, and business is its superstructure. See Michael Novak, *The Joy of Sports* (New York: Basic Books, 1976), p. 297.

99. McMurtry, "The Illusions of a Football Fan," pp. 13–14.

100. Lenk's arguments against the New Left's monolithic conception of achievement along the lines of the compulsory model, and against the subsumption of sport under that model, gain their currency here. *Social Philosophy of Athletics*, pp. 2–3, 8.

101. Christopher Lasch, *The Culture of Narcissism* (New York: Warner, 1979), p. 84.

102. As will be made clear later, I do accept that part of the New Left's argument that claims that the emancipation of sport must be tied to major changes in society as we presently know it. The sort of changes I have in mind correspond to a democratic-socialist model, as I will set forth later.

103. Rigauer, *Sport and Work*, p. 111.

104. I will argue in a later chapter that the Left's confusion of certain material properties of sport with social ones is not a simple cognitive mistake but betrays a particular ideological view of sport and its proper place in the social world. The claim that this error is ideologically backed represents a new twist on an old Marxist saw; it is the confusion of social properties with material ones that occupied Marx's principal attention, and which continues to receive the brunt of attention of contemporary Marxist ideology critics— the claim that the social features of alienated labor are natural to labor itself is the standard case in this regard. Yet, the inversion of this confusion, at least in terms of its status as a cognitive error, was not unknown to Marx. This is evident in his criticism of Fourier's attempt to turn work into play, an attempt, Marx argued, that was doomed to failure because it ignored the different material properties that mark work off from play. Marx, *Grundrisse*, pp. 611, 712. Fourier's misguided presumption, according to Marx, was that these differences were socially based, and so could be dissolved by appropriate social changes. In any event, the error can occur in either direction. I will later argue that the apparent shift of direction here indicates an important change in the ideological temperament of advanced capitalist society.

105. Guttmann, *From Ritual to Record*, p. 80; Gruneau, *Class, Sports, and Social Development*, p. 38.

106. John Hoberman, *The Olympic Crisis: Sport, Politics and the Moral Order* (New York: Aristide D. Caratzas, 1986), p. 111; see also Guttmann, *From Ritual to Record*, p. 88.

107. Marx, *Capital, Volume 3*, p. 820.

108. See Hoberman, *Sport and Political Ideology*, pp. 143–44. Hoberman recounts that, on the Fascist side of the equation, Mussolini "dreamed of having his ministers hurdle through flaming hoops while newsreel cameras rolled." Ibid., p. 61.

109. Rigauer, *Sport and Work*, pp. 33, 37. He also makes a similar concession on p. 78.

110. See William J. Morgan, "The Lived Time Dimensions of Sportive Training," *Journal of the Philosophy of Sport* 5 (1978): 12–26.

TWO

Hegemony Theory of Sport

While some variant of the New Left theory of sport discussed in Chapter 1 continues to hold sway in Europe, particularly in Germany and France, such is not the case in England and North America. There, on the contrary, hegemony theory has achieved intellectual dominion in critical considerations of sport. It is no exaggeration to refer to hegemony theory in this context as the received critical view of sport.

The parentage of hegemony sport theory is somewhat mixed. There is, not surprisingly, a strong European bloodline, which includes the pivotal work of the Italian Marxist Antonio Gramsci, the whole European tradition of class theory, and to some lesser extent the writings of the French historian and theorist Michel Foucault and the French sociologist Pierre Bourdieu.[1] It is to England, however, and to the English tradition of cultural studies in general and the Birmingham Centre for Contemporary Cultural Studies (CCCS) in particular that hegemony sport theory traces its chief progenitors. Foremost among them were three major texts: Richard Hoggart's *Uses of Literacy*, Raymond Williams's *Culture and Society*, and E. P. Thompson's *Making of the English Working Class*.[2] More particularly, it was Williams's anthropological, rather than literary, reading of culture as a "whole way of life" and Thompson's accent on working-class culture that proved most decisive in the development of hegemony sport theory.

It wasn't until the early 1980s, however, some thirty years after the cultural studies movement burst upon the scene, that hegemony theory made its decisive appearance in the field of critical sport studies. The canonical texts in this regard were Richard Gruneau's *Class, Sports, and Social Development* and John Hargreaves's *Sport, Power, and Culture*.[3] While Gruneau's book laid out the theoretical underpinnings of hegemony sport theory, Hargreaves's chronicled the historical rise and fall of hegemonic processes in the world of sport. In the relatively short period since the publication of the first of these texts, hegemony theory has established itself as a force to be reckoned with in sport theory. Hegemony theory is so entrenched that my treatment of it must encompass a wide range of theorists all of whom have at one time or another embraced it. A select list would include the works of John Clarke, Philip Corrigan, Chas Critcher, Peter Donnelly, Stephen Hardy, Robert Hollands, Alan Ingham, Jim McKay, Bryan Palmer, Alan Tomlinson, and David Whitson.[4]

Critical Program

The critical agenda of hegemony sport theory was defined by its broadly based criticism of established social theories of sport. That criticism followed three different lines: a critique of positivistically oriented modern social theories of sport, a critique of "long-standing" conservative and liberal-idealist theories of sport, and a critique of orthodox, structuralist, and avant-garde variants of Marxist sport theory.

The hegemonic critique of modern social theory shows rather clearly its partiality for the classical tradition of sociology. It was because modern social theory had turned its back on the encyclopedic sweep and historically centered focus of classical sociology, in a self-conscious and introspective effort to advance sociology as a distinct subject matter and method of inquiry, that hegemonists found fault with it. Two problematic developments in modern social theory, Gruneau argues, followed on the heels of that break with the classical sociological tradition: the turn to formal social theories such as Talcott Parson's *The Structure of Social Action* that attempted to spin out abstract theories of action, and the opposite but equally ill-advised resorting to subjectively rooted theories of society modeled after phenomenology and ethnography.[5] To remedy the former, Gruneau advocates a return to historical concerns, a focus on "lived experience" as opposed to formal abstractions, and a broadening of social inquiry beyond empirical analysis. To remedy the latter, Gruneau urges more simply that social theorists abandon crude voluntaristic accounts of the social construction of everyday life and concentrate on the larger, more pressing questions of social development.[6] Both remedies underscore hegemonists' efforts to resurrect classical sociology's emphasis on the essential unity of critical, interpretative, and empirical analyses, and to redeem the basic questions they posed about freedom and human capabilities and how these are either thwarted or advanced by changing social circumstances.

The second critique of idealistic theories of sport has a more familiar ring to it if only because it did not originate with hegemony theory. It is rather common to virtually all currents of Marxist thought as well as to empirically oriented forms of social inquiry. But hegemonists take up this critique with renewed vigor. They reject outright the idealistic tactic of separating sport, by a metaphysical sleight of hand, from the rest of social reality, and regard its claim that sport is an economically and politically unspoiled sphere of human life as a vapid, meaningless fiction. The mistaken manner of idealist thought has to do, on their account, with its false and duplicitous transposition of the materialist character of sport into an abstract form, which, by the magic of abstract definition, turns sport into an unfailing handmaiden of freedom and an equally unfailing enemy of unfreedom. The deleterious effects of this transposition are as obvious as they are ominous: it deflects attention from the material features of sport to its formal, expressive features; it casts problems of social development into spiritual rather than material terms; and it contributes to the overall reification of sport by estranging it from its active history.[7] The antidote for these sorts of idealistic excesses is equally obvious: a strong dose of materialism combined with historical acumen.

The third critique of existing Marxist theories of sport more precisely situates hegemony theory's place within this critical circle. The main focus of its attack in this regard is the New Left's treatment of sport, which is criticized mainly for its reductionist manner. Specifically, the New Left is accused of operating with a narrowly conceived base-superstructure interpretative model, which consigns virtually all determining power to the productive forces of society.[8] This sort of view prompts the simple, but false, conclusion that sport is merely a reflection of society's dominant productive forces, that sport is essentially an integrative mechanism of the status quo. The New Left is further criticized in this vein for separating sport and kindred forms of cultural production from the material base of society, thereby reproducing the same kind of split between sport and social reality so characteristic of idealistic forms of analysis.[9]

As indicated, however, the New Left is not the only target of the hegemonists' critique of Marxist sport theory. The structural, Althusserian brand of Marxist thought, which gained currency among cultural studies enthusiasts in the early 1970s, is also singled out for criticism. It is criticized by hegemonists on two principal grounds: that it underplays the determinative power of human agency, and that it misconstrues the relative autonomy of sport in functionalist terms—that is, the so-called autonomy of sport is linked exclusively to its ability to reproduce the social totality.[10] Finally, the Frankfurt school variety of Marxism, which refers in the main to the collective work of Adorno, Horkheimer, and Marcuse, and which so influenced the radical critics of the 1960s and 1970s, is criticized by hegemony theory for its simplistic equation of popular culture with mass culture, and for its depiction of the latter as a site of deception, pacification, and diversion.[11]

There is a common thread running through all these criticisms of Marxist treatments of sport: all of the above theories are guilty in one way or another of exaggerating the structural constraints (whether economic or cultural) on human agency with the unfortunate result that sport is adjudged little more than a staging ground for the inculcation of the prevailing ways of life and values of society at large. Enthusiasm and interest in sport is regarded as social pathology, as a symptom of cultural malaise. The solution proposed by hegemonists for these errant Marxist views is to steer their attention to the neglected but equally important productive relations of society, in particular, to issues of social class and class struggle. It is because the above theories give short shrift to class inequality and class contestation, they argue, that the Left has been unduly dismissive of the emancipatory potential of cultural practices like sport.[12]

Major Arguments

The foregoing discussion provides a backdrop against which to probe in a more substantive manner into the core of hegemony sport theory. Perhaps it is best to begin precisely where the hegemonists themselves begin: namely, with the so-called paradoxy of sport. Sport, as Gruneau for one sees it, is riddled by fundamental and apparently irrevocable contradictions.[13] Chief among these is sport's uncanny ability to cloak itself in an aura of unreality despite its obvious, and increasingly conspicuous, ties to larger society. The contradictory cultural status of sport is further underscored by the peculiar way in which the rules that are supposed to separate sport from social reality plunge it ever more deeply into the prevailing logic of that social reality, and by the utter seriousness given in sport to tasks that are devoid of any apparent social utility. The list of contradictions could no doubt be extended, but the central point to be made here, according to Gruneau, is that it is these sorts of contrasts and tensions, not the growing social, economic, and political influence of sport (and quantitative assessments of such influence), that should command the attention of critical theory. Its attention in this regard should focus on the connection between the "internal" contradictions of sport and the larger social contradictions and patterns of social development in society. This requires, as a minimal condition, that the discussion of the paradoxy of sport be moved from the realm of philosophical discourse, which needlessly mystifies and reifies sport, to the material realm of sociological discourse about sport and social reality.[14]

When we demystify sport's curious weaving together of seeming opposites into a coherent cultural form, what emerges is the hegemonists' seminal notion of sport as a social practice. To say that sport is a social practice is to say that it occupies no privileged place or high ground, that it is through and through a socially constructed and historically grounded affair. It is not separate from, prior to, or generative of human experience, but rather is constitutive of human experience. Put simply, sport is one specific way in which we make and remake ourselves as individual and collective agents, and in which we make and remake the social world that surrounds us. As such, its meanings and structures are connected in an indissoluble way to the "raw" experiences of material history.[15]

The hegemonists' rendering of sport as a social practice obviously precludes any regard for it as a "transhistorical essence," as some sort of sleek, transcendent metaphysical form. Nor does it allow for the view that sport answers some deep-seated transhistorical need. Hegemonists also reject interpreting sports as cultural texts, as metasocial stories and commentaries we tell and offer up about ourselves. The cultural-text thesis erroneously supposes, they argue, that sports can somehow be raised above the practical social reality they constitute, and represent that reality.[16] Hegemonists are further indisposed to the sort of argument that Simmel and others have proposed, which, while sympathetic to the view that social forms such as play are constituted out of the materials of life, argue that such forms can develop into autonomous forms complete with their own constitutive logic.[17] All such claims are regarded by hegemonists as just so much idealistic fluff, and are discredited because they violate the strictures of their conception of sport as a social practice. That conception of sport regards any abstract appeal to sport (for example, as a form of play or freedom) as incompatible with its social grounding. Hegemonists thus share with New Left theorists a contempt for abstract treatments of sport and argue, more forcefully, that the so-termed formal properties of sport can scarcely be conceived of (thought of) independently of lived social experience at any given historical moment.[18]

The hegemonists' reading of sport as social practice not only rules out any attempt to raise sport above the historical fray of life, but rejects as well any attempt to reduce it to a separate material reality. Contra Marx then, hegemonists treat the social predicates of sport as material ones and its material predicates as social ones. This shift in vocabulary betrays a wholesale departure from the base-superstructure model of Marxist thought. Sport is no longer to be explained in the manner in which Neo-Marxists such as Rigauer and Brohm explain it, as a superstructural activity that stands in some dependent relation to a separate material base. To think in this way is, as noted earlier, to ape an idealist mode of thought in the guise of a materialistic one. More to the point, to think in this manner—to begin one's analysis with the presumption that cultural forms can be treated as discrete categories, and then to try to find some way to grasp the relation between and among these cultural forms—is itself, hegemonists argue, a cognitive mistake and illusion.

All such attempts mistakenly confuse abstract representations of experience with experience itself, denuding cultural forms of their irreducible material reality by treating them as abstract categories. This cognitive misconstrual of the terms of lived experience, they argue further, conceals the "radical interaction" that occurs among social practices and that frustrates efforts to separate practices and their effects from each other.[19] The proper course of thought in this regard is to match the pervasive intersection of social practices in lived experience with a "totalizing" movement in thought. This leads hegemony theorists not so much to a rethinking of the superstructure as to its dissolution in favor of a much-expanded conception of the material base, one that regards any and all ways that human beings produce (either in interaction with others or with nature) the conditions of their life as belonging to the productive forces of society.[20]

It is easy to see how in this scheme—in which there are no second-rate (in the sense of materially deficient) practices, only an ensemble of inextricably linked social activities that collectively define the material conditions of life—sport qualifies as a form of material praxis. It so qualifies because it constitutes a concrete way that we produce and reproduce the means of our life and our social being. Sport is not then a "natural" byproduct of human experience, but a skilled accomplishment of practical life by which we define who we are and what kind of life we wish to live. So understood, it is apparent that the founding rules and logic of sport cannot be partitioned off, without loss of intelligibility, from the founding rules and logic of larger society. They are all of the same piece and so occupy the same space as all the other social practices of life that make up the material wellspring of society. It follows, therefore, that a study of sport in and for itself is not only a conceptual blunder but a fundamental irrelevancy.[21]

For hegemonists, then, sport is a material, productive activity, one that can be placed neither above nor below its basic materiality. But sport can be, and is, more precisely delineated in hegemony theory. The material praxis of sport is itself, hegemonists argue, an amalgam of socially structured possibilities and human agency. Hence, any theoretical consideration of sport must account for both of these elements if it is to avoid a one-sided analysis. Though I will discuss each of these features of sport separately, beginning with the notion of social structure, it is important to keep in mind that they stand in an intimate and sensitive dialectical relation to one another.

Hegemonists speak of social structures in essentially two senses. First, there are structures that refer to a set of habitual or institutionalized social practices that assume a systemic existence beyond the actions of any one individual. Second, there are structures that refer to deeper, abstract relations that shape social practices, such as the constitutive logic of language or a particular measure of human production.[22] Though what "deeper" and "abstract" mean in this second sense is never specified as such, presumably these terms indicate a difference in degree, rather than kind, from structures of the first, more ostensibly social sense. In any event, it is to structures of the first, institutionalized sense that hegemonists refer in analyzing social practices like sport.

More specifically, social structures figure in the constitution of social practices in a dual way: as the *medium* of their constitution and at the same time as the reproduced *outcome* of human agency.[23] This duality shows the folly of trying to divorce them from, or reduce them to, the terms of human agency. Structures are not the aggregate sum of individual acts, nor are they structurally independent and determinative of such acts. Rather, they are historically constituted actions of collectivities that bind the way we act in the social world. That means that although we produce and make our social actions, we never do so at our simple discretion.[24] The practices we produce are all subject to, and guided by, established and regularized patterns of action. These patterns are variously modulated by rules, resources, traditions, and organizations. Each of these sets out limits that constrain, rather than absolutely determine (given their rootedness in human agency), what we can and cannot do. They induce us to act in certain ways and impress upon us that social actions have to be done in accordance with what is regarded to be the "normal," "expected," and "official" way to do and value them.

The more specific social structuration of sport is treated by Gruneau and others as a function of its institutionalization. Gruneau defines the notion of an institution in a straightforward sociological way as a distinct pattern of social interaction "whose structural features represent recognized, established, and legitimated ways of pursuing some activity."[25] Applied to sport, institutionalization is defined as a process by which *a* way of engaging in and valuing sport becomes *the* way of engaging in and valuing sport. This involves, among other things, the formalization of the boundaries of sport and the codification of its rules, which are designed to ensure the ascendancy of the dominant way of playing the game over alternative ways. Indeed, the intended effect of the institutionalization process is to sanction the dominant moment of sport as its proper, universal one and to discredit alternative moments as illicit ones. Further, this process of privileging one moment of sport over another reflects the influence of certain groups who have a vested interest in its perpetuation and preservation. That interest, considered in the context of the social development and institutionalization of Western sports, reveals a distinctive pattern in which the structuring of sport has moved from the control of individual players to the restricted corporate control of select and quasi-autonomous formal organizations.[26]

Gruneau argues further that one can discern within the institutionalization of modern, Western sport the imposition of two formal limits (institutional structures) on the social practice of sport. The first limit he identifies is a technical one, and it functions by placing constraints on what one can do as a player in the game as specified by its established rules (for example, one cannot pass the ball beyond the line of scrimmage in Canadian or American football). The second limit he cites is a moral one, and it functions by limiting what one is allowed to do in a proprietary sense (for example, it is considered morally impermissible to injure deliberately one's opponent in certain sports). Gruneau recasts this distinction between technical and moral limits in accordance with John Searle's distinction between constitutive and regulative rules. In this revised form, technical limits are defined as constitutive rules upon which sport is structured as a social possibility. In the absence of these rules, sport would cease to exist as an identifiable piece of behavior, as a type of social action. The moral limits of sport, in turn, are refashioned as regulative rules whose presence, while not crucial to the fundamental structure of sport as such, are crucial to its execution. Finally, following Taylor's amendment of Searle's rendering of rules, Gruneau argues that the meaning of constitutive rules be extended to include *all* the rules of the social practices that make up the whole complex of society and that account for its production and reproduction.[27]

What is of particular note about Gruneau's analysis of the institutional structuration of sport is the broad manner in which he interprets its constitutive structures. This broad understanding explains his claim that the technical and moral limits specific to sport are neither innocent nor neutral, but are intimately bound up with its construction as a social practice, and with the creation of dominant interpretations of it. Moreover—and this is the key point—the constitutive limits and interpretations of sport are directly connected to, and implicated in, the constitutive limits and interpretations of society at large. All of this once again confirms, Gruneau argues, that the production and reproduction of sport cannot be severed from the production and reproduction of social reality.[28]

The discussion of the structuration of sport leads directly to a consideration of its second element, human agency. In a strict sense, of course, we have been talking about agency all along; one cannot speak, in hegemony theory at any rate, of social structures without speaking of the human agency that lies behind them. But agency is not to be understood here in any liberal sense. The liberal model of agency, hegemonists assert, is a narrowly circumscribed one that deals principally with matters of private choice in the marketplace and the political arena. It gives pride of place to "negative" freedom, to the ability of individuals to carry out their private economic projects and to exercise their personal political preferences without interference from other individuals or external groups and bodies (for example, the church or the state). Further, it is a model of agency that stresses "exit" over "voice."[29] The range of agency and power given to individual choosers in the market and in the voting booth is limited for the most part to their ability to abandon a product or political candidate or party.

The hegemonic notion of agency, by contrast, puts the accent on "voice" rather than "exit." It is not, as such, concerned with the exercise of private economic and political choices, but with who has collective control over the economy and polity, who makes the rules, who has the resources to do what, and who, ultimately, decides what can and cannot be done. Agency is measured here in terms of personal and collective empowerment, and freedom in terms of the capacity to realize personal and collective projects. The mere absence of constraint does not suffice on either accord of this hegemonic understanding of agency.

The hegemonic analysis of agency in sport, therefore, focuses on social groups and classes, and on individual action as it is framed by such social formations. More particularly, it studies collective human agency in terms of "relational" features of social class, which refer to the relative capacity of social groups to deploy rules, resources, and traditions in ways that further their particular interests.[30] The issue here is control: what social group(s) has shaped and structured sport into its modern, institutionalized form, and what is the meaning of this shaping and structuring for the production and reproduction of the social relations of capitalism.[31] This "relational" view of social class is to be contrasted with the "distributive" view, which emphasizes material and symbolic features of class that account for social ranking and inequality (for example, income, property, family status), and which when applied to sport shifts the attention to the opportunities available to people to participate in sport. Hegemonists regard this distributive interpretation of class—which is a commonplace of liberal analysis and which is frequently used to document an apparent increase in, and so an apparent democratization of, participation rates in modern sport—as not only a misleading index of class life in society but an incidental one. As Gruneau baldly puts it, the "whole issue of opportunities for *participation* is much less important than the question of opportunities for *control*, and the accompanying problems of the differential resources available to define and structure sport itself."[32]

The study of social-class relations and interrelationships is for hegemony theory the thread that ties the question of agency to that of structural development and social change. One can approach the agency question in this relational way by discussing the options and responses available to individual and collective agents in light of established institutional structures of sport. Thus, one can point out that agents can exert pressures against such structures, or that agents can modify such structures to accommodate their own peculiar interests, or finally that agents can find new options by acting through and within such structures.[33] While this approach is not without some merit, it is, Gruneau argues, a rather stiff and mechanical way to study agency, and, more important, it leaves unearthed the agency that informs the actual structuration of sport itself. By studying the latter, we can get a sense of the agency that lies behind the present institutionalization of sport, and so we can better understand precisely what pressures agents might be able to exert against this dominant moment of sport.

In trying to understand this "sedimented," "repressed" agency, however, it should be observed that the specific resources agents can individually or collectively bring to bear on their lives are not randomly distributed but are the products of specific historical systems of domination. These systems distribute resources in ways that give certain individuals and groups a disproportionate advantage in shaping social action, and in deflecting and/or incorporating challenges to their self-serving arrangement of the social terrain. In capitalist society, the allocation and strategic deployment of such resources is directed by rather precise, socially constituted rules. These include centrally the rules that govern the rational organization of the labor process, the rights to property, the creation of surplus value, and the marketability of educational credentials.[34]

The rule-governed allocation of these social resources, however, is never a one-sided affair. It is not the work of any one social group to the exclusion of all others. It is rather a negotiated outcome of class struggle over how sport and the other forms of social life are to be defined and conducted. Here we finally meet up with the notion that doubles both as the namesake of hegemony theory and as its guiding axiom: that systems of social domination can best be explained in terms of hegemonic processes of class contestation. What this notion is supposed to convey is that the social development of sport cannot be attributed to any single process or social class, nor can it be assigned to any conspiracy theory of bourgeois despotism, nor finally can it be passed off as the ineluctable outcome of historical destiny.[35] Rather, it can only be adequately explained by virtue of the patterned interaction that occurs between the dominant and subordinate classes.

More specifically, hegemony refers to all the ways in which the dominant class extends its sphere of influence over other classes and social groups.[36] That sphere of influence encompasses quite literally the "whole of living," the transformation and refashioning of the ways of life, the mores and customs, and the modes of conceptualization that make up the form and substance of any social order. Hegemony is achieved, it is argued, when there is effective *self-identification* from all quarters and all relevant parties with the hegemonic forms. This "internalized socialization" is, Williams points out, generally a positive one, but if that is not possible, it comes to rest on a resigned "recognition of the inevitable and the necessary."[37]

Obviously, this process of hegemonic domination favors the dominant class and so the prevailing productive and social systems of life.

That advantage is owed to several factors. For one, the dominant class has superior resources and has certain strategic advantages in mobilizing those resources. For another, the ruling class has control over mechanisms of incorporation in society, and so it is able, for example, to tie learning mechanisms in education to a select range of class-inspired meanings and values. Finally, the dominant class sets the terms and establishes the context within which any negotiation with the underclasses can and will occur.

However considerable its advantages may be in this regard, it is just as obvious that the prevailing class cannot go it alone in these matters. Its very dominance is contingent on its securing if not the consent then at least the cooperation and compliance of the subordinate classes. This means that interclass interaction, negotiation, and even contestation are inescapable and, therefore, indispensable elements of any attempt to achieve hegemony. Hegemonist theorists are quick to point out that this process of interclass negotiation is never a passive process, but an active, ongoing one that must be continuously renewed, limited, altered, and changed.[38]

The resilience, vitality, and unpredictable character of the hegemonic process of class interaction derives from a number of sources. On the one hand, it can be traced to a certain impotence in the ruling class itself. It is evident that no one class, however entrenched or powerful, can exhaust and/or control all the social resources of life. Short of a monopoly then, the dominant class cannot keep agents from reflecting on their lot in life, from wanting to expand their powers and better themselves, and from constituting their identities in ever new ways. It also follows that the dominant class cannot prevent the underclasses from establishing their own social enclaves of meaning and their own renegade cultural forms.

The vitality of class negotiation also derives more centrally from the lived experience of subordinate groups themselves. Hegemonists maintain as a general proposition that the way one sees, experiences, and values the world is a function of one's class position. Put in terms of our present discussion, that means that the lived experience of members of dominated social groups varies in important ways from, and stands in an oblique relation to, that of their social "betters." Williams calls these autonomous snippets of underclass experience "structures of feeling," and he argues that they constitute an important source of resistance and opposition to the status quo.[39] As forms of practical consciousness that are actually lived out and not simply thought, they are always different from the official conscious experience and formal beliefs of society.

Whatever the source or character of these various strands of class interaction and contestation, they collectively confirm that one can find at any given moment in larger society alternative and even oppositional forms of social life that are class-specific. Since the dominant class cannot treat any threats to its dominance lightly, it can do little else but negotiate with, and make concessions to, agents of subordinate groups. Two points follow from the above. First, while it is true that the upper class has the greater power and wherewithal to shape life in its own image, it is patently false that agency always works from the top down.[40] Second, hegemony is built as much through contradiction as it is through reflection, correspondence, and similarity.[41]

The Emancipatory Potential of Sport

The issue that now must be squarely faced is what sort of emancipatory capacity, if any, can be claimed for sport under the aegis of hegemony theory. Does sport, in short, enslave or liberate us? Does it serve the interests of social reproduction or those of progressive social change? Does sport advance the cause of freedom or the cause of social domination and control?

These are difficult but important questions. However, at least two important clues to answering them can be gleaned from our prior discussion of the social constitution of sport. The first clue suggests *how* any question regarding the emancipatory status of sport must be answered, and the second relatedly suggests *where* one must look to answer such a question.

It is important to recognize at the outset that the *how* specified in this instance is an epistemological and a normative one. It is the *how* that crops up in the following two questions: How do we *know* whether sport is a liberating force, and how do we *assess* (judge) its emancipatory pedigree? The answer given by hegemonists in both cases is a decidedly historical one. They are quite certain that this is the only way in which we can know and judge any social practice. Resorting to theoretical abstractions here, as we have seen, is ruled out because they necessarily falsify the terms of lived experience. Put differently, hegemonists contend that there are simply no "natural starting points" beyond the ken of social life with which we can anchor our knowledge claims and our value judgments. Therefore, all that is gained by "naturalizing" social practices such as sport is to explain away the complex and contradictory historical processes that constitute them.[42]

We have no choice then but to turn to history to decide whether and in what sense sport opens up or closes down possibilities for human expression. That historical turn requires that we evaluate sport in the context of the historical struggle over the resources and rules of social life.[43] More particularly, it requires that we play off against each other human capacities and the social (institutional) forms that frame them. By simply asking whether this or that institutional form disables or enables this or that capacity, we can determine whether the regulated and expected ways in which social actions have to be institutionally carried out are justified or not. This normative task can be accomplished, Corrigan assures us, without imputing any essentialistic character or meaning to human capacities.[44]

In arguing that sport can be known and evaluated only historically, hegemonists have also answered the *where* question as well; where we are to look in considering the emancipatory credentials of sport is to its social-historical constitution. We are to look to its social constitution because sport is not an abstract thing but a concrete social practice. Its status as a social practice rules out, it is argued, not only an abstract search for its ennobling features, but any immanent reading of sport as well. It rules out such an immanent inspection of sport because it flies in the face of its social constitution, of its rootedness in the social constitution of larger society. There are, hegemonists stoutly insist, no *a priori* or otherwise inherent properties of sport that make it a utopian or subversive form of life. That sport lacks any such redeeming internal qualities also precludes any counterfactual appeal to such supposed qualities, any appeal, that is, to some internal core of sport as a regulative emancipatory ideal. This appeal must fail because it falsely presumes that sport has such a core and because it confuses metaphorical assertions (promises) with actual states of affairs.[45]

An immanent consideration of the emancipatory potential of sport must give way, therefore, to an exoteric one that takes into account the social facts of the production of sport as a form of life, and so its material couplet of agency and structure. Two important rules of thumb figure into such an analysis. First, sport will be found to be a liberating force only if the agents in the course of that practice *could have acted differently*, and, more important, if the agents that engage in that practice also control it.[46] Second, the more institutionalized a sport or any other practice under the sway of capitalism is, the less likely it will be controlled by those who actually engage in it, and the less likely it will be found liberating.

A hegemonic strategy for assessing sport easily follows from the above. To begin with, it will not center on a search for stuctureless instances of sport, for pure agency. That is ruled out not only because it violates hegemonists' positive conception of freedom, but because it also violates their central premise that even the most rudimentary social actions are bounded by structures: there are, as they see it, simply no unstructured social acts. The strategy will center, therefore, on a search for structures in sport that either facilitate or thwart agency in the sense specified earlier. That entails a careful consideration of different levels of agency/structure in sport.

In this regard, Gruneau broadly distinguishes between informal, noninstitutionalized forms of play and formal, institutionalized forms of sport. Not surprisingly, Gruneau is rather generous in his appraisal of the former, for he finds play a far more liberating than constraining form of life. He does so on two grounds. First, the limits associated with play are those that are essential to its accomplishment as a social action. Second, the limits of play are open-ended ones that are receptive to the will and actions of the agents that engage them. While the unintended consequences of the structured actions of play are more difficult to discern and evaluate, it can scarcely be denied, Gruneau argues, that play extends our freedom in ways that many if not most of our social practices do not.[47]

Gruneau's assessment of the institutional realm of games and sports is far more critical than it is praiseworthy. In hegemony theory, as noted above, institutionalization is virtually synonymous with incorporation. More particularly, the structures of sport are found wanting in two respects. First, those structures have less to do with the accomplishment of sport as a social action, a social practice, than they do with its accomplishment as an institutional form of capitalist society. It could hardly be otherwise, since Gruneau holds that the structural limits of sport are bound up with the institutional limits that contour and shape all other forms of life within capitalist society. Second, it follows that the limits of sport are not open-ended ones, that they are enacted not at the discretion of the agents (players) themselves, but at the discretion and interests of those members of the dominant class who define precisely what they are and what social significance they have. Contrary to the positive finding regarding play, sport is adjudged far more constraining than it is liberating. It is free only in the weak, liberal sense of negative freedom, in the paltry sense that players may accept or reject these limits as conditions of their involvement in sport.[48]

While there is general agreement in the hegemonist camp with Gruneau's treatment of play, there is plainly disagreement with his largely negative treatment of sport. Ingham and Hardy in particular accuse Gruneau of conflating different levels of agency/structure in sport, of collapsing an important qualitative distinction between "recreational sport" (which for them runs the gamut from pure play to institutionalized games and certain commercialized forms of sport) and professional sport.[49] Though Gruneau's unflattering assessment of the structural limits of institutionalized sport readily applies to the realm of professional sport, they argue, it does not do justice to the kinds of structures one typically finds in recreational sport. These structures, by contrast, are only marginally affected by the economic imperatives and constraints that weigh so on professional sport, and are, resultantly, more open-ended and more hospitable to the expression and control of the agents who engage in them. Thus, while professional sport dramatizes the power and control of capital over consumption (monopoly) and labor (monosopony), recreational sport dramatizes struggles of incorporation and resistance, and gives off mixed messages regarding the moral and political use and regulation of space and time.[50]

Ingham and Hardy's critical emendation of Gruneau's analysis is an important one, if only because it alerts us to the variegated structuration of sport, but one may quarrel with their contention that his treatment of institutional sport applies principally to professional sport. It is apparent that many of the institutionalized versions of so-termed recreational sport are as structurally constrained as their professional counterparts. On that basis, Ingham and Hardy's strategy of tracking down less structurally encumbered, and so apparently more liberating, forms of sport may be problematic if, as appears to be the case, it involves simply writing off the whole realm of institutional sport as a virtual lost cause. To concede such would be clearly to give away too much. That is why it is important to remember that while Gruneau held no illusions about the ennobling possibilities of formally organized sports, he never gave up on them altogether. He consistently maintained that it was both reasonable and prudent to search for traces of freedom within the cracks and crevices of its institutional framework, and that such a search was a legitimate part of any inquiry into the emancipatory rank of sport.

What exactly is entailed by such a search? What sorts of gaps and openings are we to be on the lookout for? Quite plainly, if the major structures of institutional sport are inscribed with the signature of the dominant class and its prevailing systems of social relations, then a search for fractures within this framework must be directed to enclaves of meaning, value, and experience that reflect the desires and interests of the underclasses, and/or those of the fractions of the ruling class that oppose the dominant moment of sport. These sorts of experience and repositories of meaning, therefore, must be brought to light in order to register the forms of knowledge and cultural production they contain that challenge the dominant institutions and discourses of sport.[51]

Precisely what kinds of alternative meanings and experiences can, however, be teased out of the dominant moment of sport? It is customary for hegemonists to cite in such cases the "residual" and "emergent" elements of sport. The residual elements refer to older, but not archaic, class practices that while formed in the past are still active in its current production as a cultural form. They are part of the baggage of any hegemonic process, and they comprise whole slices of experience and meaning that the dominant class variously opposes, represses, undervalues, neglects, or simply ignores.[52] There is, according to Gruneau, a wide array of such elements in sport that act as surviving pressures against its modern technical and instrumental bent. Some of the more salient of these include the ethos of fair play, the spontaneous enjoyment of sport, the qualitative appreciation of sport performances, the persistence of an ascriptively oriented, noninstrumental amateur code, and working-class traditions of sport participation that trade on socialist notions of class solidarity.[53] While any of these lingering class practices are capable of escalating, either individually or collectively, into self-conscious political protests and/ or oppositional practices, at the very least they count as forms of resistance to hegemonic assimilation and as buffers against assaults made on the traditional integrity of sporting practices.

Besides the residual elements of institutionalized sport, there are emergent elements as well. As the name implies, these elements refer to new meanings, values, and class practices that are not merely novel acts of cultural production but oppositional ones. They arise, as do their residual counterparts, from the dominant moment of sport, as bits and pieces of class practices that the dominant culture variously ignores, privatizes, or generalizes as natural.[54] Examples of such elements are harder to come by in the world of sport, but they include the black movement, the women's movement, and the "new games" movement in sport, all of which tried to develop alternative ways of doing sport that were more congenial to self-expression and human civility.[55]

The persistence of old class practices and the emergence of new ones originate out of, and receive their sustenance from, the hegemonic processes that make up the institutional form of sport. As such, the search for residual and emergent enabling forces within this institutional form necessarily refers us back to these processes themselves.

Hegemonists argue that the apparent success the dominant culture has had in constructing and reconstructing cultural forms of the likes of sport to suit their own interests and needs should not lull us into a false sense that subordinate social groups have been hopelessly pacified in perpetuity or that the sharp edges that define hegemonic confrontation have been irrevocably softened. They maintain further that such complacency is false precisely because the consensual foundation upon which the legitimacy of the dominant moment of sport rests is an "extremely fragile," contradictory, and unstable one.[56] There is every reason regarding the present situation of sport, therefore, for *"making hope practical, rather than despair convincing."*[57]

The sources of this hegemonic instability with respect to institutional sport are manifold. One such source stems directly from the way in which liberal democratic capitalist societies are structurally constituted and ordered. Evidently, the partitions and walls erected by liberal democracies—which insulate, for example, the private from the public spheres of life and perhaps more centrally the individual from society—are not merely ideological fabrications. Hence, as Palmer argues, they afford individual agents from subordinate groups a small measure of self-determination out of which various challenges to the standing of sport can be mounted.[58]

Another source of instability derives more centrally from the terms that underlie the institutionalization of sport itself. Indeed, it arises out of the very conditions of agency upon which the dominant moment of sport seeks to build its legitimacy. Those conditions pivot about a conception of sport as a practice centered on the pursuit of personal mastery in which opportunities for creative and dramatic self-expression, and, more generally, for fun and excitement, are crucial. What is so unsettling about these kinds of qualities of human agency, argues Gruneau, is that they are utterly capricious and fickle, and so they can quite easily reverse their meanings in ways that make them problematic for the status quo. As such, they provide at best a "shaky foundation" for the hegemony of institutional sport, and one doubtless in which the dominant culture can take little solace.[59]

Yet another source of hegemonic instability springs from the class-based dynamics of human agency. The collective meanings and values of the dominant moment of sport are always, as noted previously, differentially experienced and interpreted by agents from subordinate groups. However entangled the constitutive technical and moral structures of institutional sport may be in the constitutive structures of the dominant culture, the social possibilities and meanings of life expressed in sport are mediated by their reconstituted expression in the diverse cultural forms of the underclasses.[60] It is simply naive, therefore, as Bourdieu insists, to suppose that all practitioners of formally organized sport confer the same meaning on their practice, or even, strictly speaking, that they are engaged in the same practice.[61] All of this suggests once again that institutional sport is not the barren wasteland of unfreedom that some members of the Left have made it out to be.

These various fractures in the formal infrastructure of sport all speak in one way or another to the resiliency of human agency, to its ability to survive in the small and delicate spaces ceded to it by the dominant culture. More specifically, they testify to the oppositional potential that resides within even the more forbidding institutions of capitalist society. While these institutions are not bound together by anything so tenuous as a gossamer thread, what does bind and hold them together can be breached. The message this bodes for considerations of so-called "official" sport, hegemonists maintain, is clear: members of the working class and other disenfranchised social groups are quite capable of penetrating the dominant moment of sport and using it for their own purposes. This fact deserves, as Gruneau argues, far more attention and consideration than it has thus far received in the critical literature on sport.[62]

As upbeat and "cautiously" optimistic as the hegemonic theoretical appraisal of the emancipatory capacities of sport is, it is overshadowed by the hegemonists' sober historical findings on this matter. To say that these findings are discouraging is to engage in understatement. In a nutshell, they suggest that the working class and other subordinate social groups have been largely co-opted by the ruling class, that indeed we can regard that incorporation as a virtual *fait accompli.* Since in hegemony theory virtually everything—from the possibility of social change in general to the capacity of social practices to assume an oppositional posture—depends on the vitality of class conflict and the resiliency of human agency, that finding is a rather crushing one.[63]

In this regard their findings show convincingly that the history of the North American labor movement has been one of interclass collaboration and negotiation rather than class conflict. Although the working class consorted with its "superiors," and so largely conformed to the social conditions under which its members had to live and labor, this does not mean that they completely endorsed those conditions. But it does mean, and this is bad enough, that they tacitly accepted the essential structures of capitalism in order to acquire a middle-class standard of living.[64] Moreover, on those infrequent occasions when they did clash with the ruling class their response was more often than not "inadequate," "haphazard," and in the main uncritical. However exciting these episodic clashes might have been, they almost always ended in clear victories for their employers and the state.[65]

The ineffectuality of the working class in mounting a significant challenge to the social relations of capitalism largely explains, hegemonists argue further, its quiescence in the realm of sport as well. In order to ignite class struggle in any specific sphere of life, and in order for any such localized struggle to succeed, there must be some general climate of class discontent and resistance that can be tapped into and that can fan the flames of social change. There was apparently no such climate to nurture resistance to the status quo, which only made the working class more vulnerable to the hegemonic onslaught of the dominant moment of sport. There were not only few alternatives to institutional sport, but scarcely any challenges made against its dominance. Far from being the delicate and fragile thing that hegemonists have theoretically portrayed it to be, "official" sport has proved itself a virtual juggernaut crushing thus far every rival to its dominion.[66]

So the working-class attachment to sport, hegemonists dutifully report, evidently worked for rather than against capitalism. Its actions seemed to be driven more by the desire for amusement than by the desire to confront its subordinate position in the social system of sport. That the "good times" it sought in sport contributed to and reproduced the "bad" conditions of its existence appeared to be of little concern to the working class.[67] Even in those instances where it was able to penetrate partially the shell of institutional sport, it failed to act against it or even to understand fully that the sports it patronized were quite literally out of its control.[68]

The picture this historical evidence paints is not a pretty one, but it is a clear one: sport is no longer, if it ever was, a site of class and cultural contestation.[69] So hegemonists are pressed into the hardly optimistic conclusion that the limits and pressures of institutional sport are now widely regarded by subordinate groups as the limits and pressures of everyday experience and common sense.[70] Indeed, if there is any disagreement or conflict over the nature and meaning of institutional sport today, it is a disagreement waged not between classes but within the fractions of the privileged class; the conflict is one that involves a hopeless struggle of nineteenth-century ideals of amateur sport against the remorseless logic of twentieth-century ideals of technical-instrumental sport.[71] What is perhaps most problematic about this historical state of affairs for social critics of all stripes, hegemonists point out further, is that the working class was won over to the dominant moment of sport, rather than forced or manipulated into it.[72]

Ideology Critique

The hegemonist sketch of sport as a social practice that is intimately bound up with the social resources and structures of larger society makes it an adversary of all idealist-tending theories of sport. What makes its aversion to idealism an ideological matter, however, is its conviction that its own account of the social rootedness of sport is a true and correct one, and that idealism's denial of this rootedness serves the interests of social domination. In this conviction, of course, it joins hands with the New Left, who also targeted idealism as its main ideological opponent. Therefore, it stands to reason that much of what the hegemonists have to say on this score will not be altogether new, though it will be more sophisticated and substantial.

One caveat before I proceed: Though the New Left and hegemony theory share in idealism a common foe, it is no secret that the latter camp has linked the former to idealism in its misguided attempt to reduce sport to a separate material reality.[73] I bring this criticism up again only to make the point that hegemonists, contra their treatment of idealism proper, ventured no ideological conjecture about this linkage. They were evidently of the view that the New Left had committed a simple, though unfortunate, cognitive mistake, that its reductionistic understanding of sport could not be traced to any discernible interest in social domination. It was rather the attempt to place sport above, rather than below, its basic materiality—the attempt to idealize its social constitution—that aroused their ideological suspicion.[74] Put differently, it was the tendency to associate sport with immaterial play, as opposed to material work, that led hegemonists to believe that in this instance at least they were dealing with more than a cognitive mistake.

Once again play turns up as the main ideological culprit in the critique of modern sport. There are in this regard two features of the play theory of sport that are especially offensive to hegemonists. The first concerns its *modus operandi*. The dissociation of sport from its constitutive historical setting and its association with the ephemeral realm of play is accomplished, hegemonists argue, by use of counterfactual abstractions that create boundaries between sport and social reality where there are none. The second odious feature of this theory is that by making play homologous with sport it turns sport into a universal forum for creative self-expression and freedom. In both cases, hegemonists argue, the social facts concerning the constitution of sport have been significantly altered.

We have yet to specify what is ideologically problematic about this errant theory of sport. Here hegemonists respond in three characteristic ways. Their first response focuses on the intended point of the conceptual separation of sport from social reality, which is, they submit, to idealize the liberating capacity of sport. By depicting sport as an idyllic oasis in an otherwise barren social desert, people are encouraged to give themselves over to half-truths, myths, and airy metaphors that bear little resemblance to the real world. One is induced, in other words, to romanticize the abstract limits of sport as enabling ones. But this only leads, Gruneau contends, to a confusion of vague promissory notes for actual states of affairs, and to, what is much worse, a celebration and adulation of sportive ways of life that are beyond the social reach and that operate against the material interests of most human agents.

The hegemonists' second line of response is that the play theory of sport conflates two kinds of freedom. There is first of all the more narrow notion of freedom from necessity, which refers specifically to the way that the rules of particular social practices allow them to be conducted on their own terms, for their own sake. Here freedom is secured by submitting to established rules that literally make possible one's engagement in that practice. There is second a much broader notion of social and political freedom whose attainment may well require one to challenge, contest, or otherwise break existing rules.[75] What is both mistaken and ideological about the idealist conflation of these two senses of freedom is that it wrongly and dangerously supposes that compliance with the rules that facilitates freedom from necessity *ipso facto* facilitates political freedom. It suggests that people are only truly free when they submit to existing rules and structures, that, in other words, freedom is always vested in a certain form of unfreedom, and so that acts of rule breaking are by definition unfree ones.

The hegemonists' third line of response builds on the second and argues that the ill-conceived notion of freedom employed in idealistic renderings of sport is used as a prop to support the larger notion that the liberal society in which we live is a free and progressive one. By passing off sport as a showcase of freedom, by highlighting the apparent greater opportunities people now have to participate in sport, by showing that people really do enjoy equal opportunity in sport and that rewards are commensurate to effort, and by drawing attention to the ever-rising standards of performance in sport, ideologues seek to vindicate not only sport but the society that supposedly makes all this possible.[76] The claim pressed here is a fairly simple one; if freedom, genuine achievement, and meritocracy flourish within sport, then they cannot, it is asserted, be unknown to the larger society that nurtures and sustains them. The basic problem, hegemonists hasten to point out, is that these alleged ennobling features of sport are myths more than they are social facts, and, therefore, whatever homilies they are supposed to convey about liberal society are not to be taken seriously. Suffice it to say, we should be leery of any such resorting to sport as a legitimation device for society, and more generally of any effort to connect idealistic analyses of sport and culture with liberal theoretical and political frameworks.

Critical Analysis

In contrast to the rather heated critical reception of New Left sport theory, hegemony sport theory has had a rather easy time of it. Indeed there have been few critics of its treatment of sport. This must be attributed in large measure to the potency of hegemony theory itself,[77] a far more sophisticated, rich, and powerful theory than its Neo-Marxist predecessor. Alas, it is not an unproblematic theory. Indeed, I shall argue that it is fraught with conceptual problems that can be traced to the shaky epistemological and normative grounds on which it rests. In particular, I will argue that hegemony theory fails to do justice to the manifold social constitution of sport, conflates the social practice of sport with its institutionalization, and advances an account of the emancipatory potential of sport that it cannot critically deliver.

The major problem with the hegemonic account of sport concerns the broad manner in which it construes the social production of sport. It is committed to the view that the social constitution of sport is irrevocably and irreducibly bound up with the constitution of all other social practices and with social reality itself. Such a capacious view follows as a matter of course from the previously noted revision of the Marxist base-superstucture schema, a revision that consisted for the most part in the emptying of the cultural superstructure of society into its material infrastructure. What we get by dumping cultural forms of life into material, productive ones is precisely the indissoluble connection between cultural production and material production—and by extension, sport and material social reality—posited by hegemonists. Sport turns out to be simply one instantiation of the general interpenetration of cultural and material life.

In this view, therefore, there can be no privileged places in the social totality. As such, the space sport occupies in the ensemble of social relations cannot be distinguished, save conceptually,[78] from the space occupied by any other social practice. It is in this strict sense that the founding rules, structures, meanings, and metaphoric qualities of sport are said by hegemonists to be radically implicated in those of larger society.

Hegemony theory thus leaves us with the following disjunction: either sport is a social practice whose constitution is of the same piece as that of social reality, or it is, as idealists say of it, a form of life that arises naturally out of social interaction as some sort of universal manifestation of the human spirit. The latter claim is plainly false. As hegemonists correctly point out, it cannot survive even a prima facie consideration of the social facts of the case. We are left, they suggest, with the former claim as the only defensible and plausible account of sport.

The cogency of hegemonist sport theory rests squarely on whether the above disjunction is an exhaustive one. I maintain that it is not. Thus, while I concur with that theory's rejection of the idealistic portrayal of sport as a natural product of consciousness, I remain unconvinced that this refutation entails anything like the account of sport advanced by hegemony theory. On the contrary, I hold that the undifferentiated way in which hegemonists depict the social constitution of sport glosses over the variegated and complex nature of its actual social constitution. Further, I will suggest that something like Simmel's account of sport, which holds that sport is a concrete emanation of social life that develops its own autonomous form and constitutive logic, is closer to the truth. The view of sport I am urging, then, is one that doesn't flinch from Rorty's supposition that "there is nothing deep down inside us except what we have put there ourselves, no criterion that we have not created in the course of creating a practice";[79] my view insists only that what we put into the social landscape we put into it in more or less complicated and enduring ways, and that sport must be counted among the more complicated and enduring products of social life. What it does reject outright is the hegemonic charge that arguing on behalf of the autonomy of sport, of its separateness from other social practices, commits one *ipso facto* to an idealistic frame of reference. That charge is itself an unfortunate and unimaginative byproduct of the above false disjunction that needlessly confounds and conceals the social facts behind sport's separateness from and complicity in larger society.[80]

What, then, is problematic about the hegemonic account of the social constitution of sport? The answer has to do with the way it treats the constitutive structures of sport. It was Gruneau who argued that the "technical" and "moral" limits of sport could be rendered in the idiom of Searle's distinction between the constitutive and regulative rules of games.[81] It was Gruneau again who argued that Searle's treatment of constitutive rules could be extended, pace Taylor, to include all social practices and the production and reproduction of society itself. Thus Gruneau believed that Taylor's injunction to expand the notion of constitutive rules in this manner leads precisely to the broad view of the social production of sport he endorses throughout his book: that the constitutive structures of sport are neither innocent nor neutral and that such structures are "clearly connected" to the larger structures of social reality. The apparent inseparability of the social constitution of sport and society rests, therefore, on this argumentative base.

I would argue that Taylor and Gruneau are not making parallel moves here. Indeed, I would claim, more strongly, that Gruneau's understanding of Taylor's injunction was mistaken, as was his understanding of Searle's interpretation of constitutive rules. This claim requires that we determine what, after all, Taylor intended by his suggestion that the notion of constitutive rules be applied across the board to a variety of social practices. The answer, I believe, is simply that a wide assortment of human practices that have apparently no clearly defined rules could nonetheless be profitably understood as rule-governed activities.[82] In making this suggestion Taylor was merely amplifying, not augmenting, Searle's own account when the latter argued that "sometimes in order to explain adequately a piece of human behavior we have to suppose that it was done in accordance with a rule, even though the agent himself may not be able to state the rule and may not even be conscious of the fact that he is acting in accordance with the rule."[83]

There is not the slightest hint in either of their above premises that this extended use of the notion of constitutive rules entails or otherwise implies, as Gruneau argues, that the constitution of any social practice is irreducibly tied to the constitution of any other social practice. I hasten to emphasize here that there could not be such a hint precisely because Taylor's and Searle's understanding of constitutive rules not only does not support Gruneau's account of the social constitution of sport, but operates at cross-purposes to that account.

I can illustrate my point with an example drawn from Peter Winch. Imagine, Winch supposes, a man—let us call him A—who writes the following figures on a blackboard: 1 3 5 7. A asks B to continue the series. B, with no apparent reason to be suspicious or skeptical, writes 9 11 13 15. But A rejects this as a continuation of the series and says that it goes as follows: 1 3 5 7 1 3 5 7 9 11 13 15 9 11 13 15. A then asks B again to continue the series from this point. Given the more complex character of the series, B has a variety of responses to choose from. Let us suppose he makes a choice and that A again refuses to accept it and offers another continuation of his own. And let us suppose that this goes on for quite some time with the same result in each case. Undoubtedly at some point, Winch insists, B would say to A, with perfect justification, that he was not following a mathematical rule at all, even though all the continuations A made could be brought under some sort of rule or other. In other words, Winch concludes, "A was following a rule; but his rule was: always to substitute a continuation different from the one suggested by B at every stage. And though this is a perfectly good rule of its kind, it does not belong to arithmetic."[84]

The moral to be derived from this tale concerns the quite distinct specifications of behavior that follow from the invocation of constitutive rules and how understanding those rules is indispensable to understanding what those pieces of behavior are all about. It is the peculiar nature of such rules when applied to social practices that they introduce distinctions where there otherwise would be none. Indeed, constitutive rules quite literally found the distinctions they draw so that we are able to distinguish in the above an arithmetical practice from an idiosyncratic one. It is just this function of distinguishing and of marking off forms of behavior that both Searle and Taylor underscore when they speak of constitutive rules. Thus Searle contends that "constitutive rules constitute an activity the existence of which is logically dependent on the rules."[85] He argues further that acting in accordance with the constitutive rules of a practice must be understood in a quite specific way that makes clear the aim of that practice.[86] Finally, he argues persuasively that the creation of constitutive rules creates the possibility of new forms of behavior in a nontrivial sense.[87]

If the above account of the constitutive rules of social practices is a plausible one, and I believe that it is, then it follows that such rules do the very opposite of what Gruneau suggested they do. That is, they mark off, rather than bind together, social practices from each other and their immediate social context. Thus the constitutive rules of, let us say, chess carry with them no direct implication for those of, let us say, soccer or any other practice. It could scarcely be any other way since such rules always stand in an internal relation to the practices they found. It is the constitutive rules of a practice that make it what it fundamentally is, and that endow it with whatever intelligibility and modicum of rationality it may possess.

What is true in general of the constitutive rules of social practices is true in particular of the founding rules of the social practices that fall under the rubric of sport. These likewise function in a quite singular and discriminating way, and, in particular, establish the peculiar kind of rationality that obtains in sporting practices. The special nature of these rules, as noted in Chapter 1, has to do with the curious restrictions they place on the means we may use to realize sportive goals. Such rules always prohibit the most expedient and direct way to achieve the goal in favor of some less expedient and indirect way to achieve it. Hence, in sport the permitted means for achieving the goal are always narrower in scope than the possible means. It is, therefore, useful but proscribed to trip one's opponent in a footrace. Of course, it hardly needs repeating that arbitrarily restricting the available means to a goal, while a perfectly rational thing to do in a sportive game, is a quite irrational thing to do in everyday life.

Two points follow from the above. First, the constitutive rules of sporting practices really do partition them off from the whole round of social life just as the constitutive rules of other social practices partition them off. Second, in order to grasp the social constitution of sport at this fundamental level we need to see and understand how it is different from everything else in the social landscape, how its logic of action contrasts with that of other social practices.

At the same time, understanding the distinctive logic of sport's constitution does not require that its social fabric be denied. Sport is not, as hegemonists correctly observe, a natural emanation of the human spirit. The constitutive rules of sport, and any other practice, are neither historically arbitrary nor socially inexplicable. These rules are fashioned, like everything else, out of the social and historical stuff of life itself. That sport has clear historical and social precedents cannot, and on my account need not, be denied. The sport of jousting, for example, has an obvious historical relation to feudalism. It is not surprising that such a sport would enjoy wide popularity in social conditions bordering on virtual anarchy in which military actions figure prominently. There is therefore an obvious correspondence between the sports we engage in and find alluring, and the social conditions in which we live. Moreover, many sports have their roots in the practical world. Sports such as diving, skiing, skating, and footracing originally served practical needs and so fell squarely within the province of everyday social life.[88]

None of this, of course, detracts from the basic point I have been making all along regarding the differentiating capacity of the constitutive rules of sport. I am committed to the view that such rules are both socially based and autonomous. Hence, whatever social or historical analogues a sporting practice might have, the fact remains—and it is indeed a social fact that I refer to here—that sport is neither exhausted by, nor is capable of, being reduced to its social context. That it cannot be so treated has directly to do with the way that the constitutive rules of a sport separate it from its social context. Thus, while the moves made in military jousting (riding, charging, delivering a blow with a long, crude instrument) bear an impressive resemblance to those of sporting jousting, and while the moves made in, say, fleeing an enemy (striding, pacing, passing) strikingly resemble those of footracing, the incorporation of these moves into a sporting context strips them of their social logic (their instrumental orientation) and alters their status as social ends (valued ends worthy of pursuit). It will no longer suffice, therefore, simply to unseat one's opponent in the sport of jousting, or simply to outdistance one's pursuer in a footrace. Rather, one must now pursue ends that include a quite precise, if not peculiar, specification of the manner in which they are to be attained. Thus, the end sought in footracing is to outdistance one's pursuer by, among other things, staying on the track. It is only when otherwise prosaic aims are refashioned in this way to make them sufficiently challenging that players find them worthy of pursuit.[89]

It may be appropriate to claim then that the medieval sport of jousting intimates a certain military posture toward life and that the contemporary sport of football intimates a certain violent posture toward life. It may be further appropriate to track these respective dispositions back to the social conditions whence they sprang. But it won't do to claim that jousting is *fundamentally* a feudalistic practice, or alternatively that jousting is "indissolubly" connected to feudalism; nor can we say that football is essentially a capitalist practice, or alternatively that football is "indissolubly" connected to capitalism.[90] To assert such is to ignore the way in which these fragments of social life, once incorporated into a sportive setting, are stripped of their instrumental demeanor and everyday significance and endowed with a life and meaning of their own. It is to ignore, in short, the important wedge driven between sport and its social context by its constitutive rules.

Thus I find the hegemonic argument that the social production of sport is inseparably linked to the social production and reproduction of general social life to be a seriously flawed one.[91] Moreover, it is a view that ensnares itself once again, though in its own inimitable way, in the various conundrums that make up the queer doctrine of what we, after Suits, have called "radical instrumentalism." In peddling the fused account of the social constitution of sport and the whole round of social life that it does, hegemony theory assumes a certain level of commensurability and equivalence between the goals and rational manner of life and the goals and rational manner of sportive practices. We have every reason to be suspicious of this. By tying sport too closely to the rest of life, hegemonists would have us believe that one may treat a goal in life as if it were a goal in a game and vice versa. But, I submit, such a belief is plainly false and only succeeds in trivializing both life and sport.

The implausibility of this belief is apparent no matter how one pitches it. For the sake of argument, let us begin with the former case. Let us suppose that a certain fireman treats the task of saving a child on the second floor of a burning house as if it were a goal in a game.[92] So understood, the fireman would forsake the usual means used to secure the safety of the child, say by using a ladder, in favor of some more challenging way, say by using a pole vault. But to construe his task in this way is to surely misconstrue, in this case rather poignantly, what being a fireman is all about. It is a salient fact about life, but not about games, that goals and ends are valued and found sufficiently challenging in themselves quite apart from any arbitrary introduction of obstacles to their accomplishment. Thus, to regard saving a child as a valuable end only if there is some contrived obstacle to its achievement is to trivialize what a fireman does, and doubtless more important, to make a mockery of the value of human life itself.

The same may be said of those who treat goals in games as if they were goals in life. Let us now suppose, less fancifully to be sure, that a golfer treats her task of putting a ball into a hole as if it were a goal in life. So understood, such a player would resort to any possible, not just permitted, means to realize her goal. But to construe her task in this way is to misconstrue what being a golfer is all about. It is a salient fact about games, but not life, that goals in themselves are considered insignificant; it is only when unnecessary obstacles are placed in their path that players find them sufficiently challenging to pursue. Therefore, to regard putting a ball in a hole as itself the valued end sought in golf is to trivialize golf, and more important, to make a mockery of what sporting practices like golf are all about.

To summarize, I have been arguing that a reckoning of the constitutive structures of sport as a social practice does not convey the expansive treatment of the social constitution of sport offered by hegemonists. On the contrary, I have claimed that it suggests a much more defined, quite precise rendering of the social production of sport. At the same time, I have taken pains to show that such an account does not require resorting to a reductive concept of the social, nor does it depend on some idealistic ploy. It does require the recognition that the specification of the constitutive rules of sport implicates a fundamental layer of its social constitution that must be clearly distinguished from other layers and social facts about it. This is in keeping with my earlier claim that sport is a complex social practice, which is simply another way of saying that it is produced in a socially variegated, manifold manner.

However, my earlier characterization of sport as a complex practice must be modified in one important respect. Previously, using Marx's vocabulary, I characterized sport as an amalgam of material and social properties.[93] By material properties I meant those properties of sport that are specified by its constitutive rules and that define its peculiar rationality. By social properties I meant those properties of sport that are specified by its immediate social setting and that define its particular historical significance as a form of commodity sport. I now wish to amend, but not to dissolve, this distinction by differentiating between the constitutive and the contingent *social* properties of sport. On this reading the constitutive properties of sport (now construed as basic social rather than natural properties) refer, as before, to its constitutive rules and logic, and its contingent properties refer, again as before, to its social context. While the contingent properties of sport make up an important part of its social constitution, they are neither a necessary nor a sufficient part of that constitution. Sport, that is, can very well exist in their absence, though, of course, it could not exist in the absence of its constitutive elements. Put more precisely, and in our earlier idiom, sport or commodity sport is not commodity sport by virtue of what is necessary and sufficient to make it sport. All of this confirms my central criticism of hegemony sport theory: it confuses the contingent features of sport's social production with its constitutive ones and so falsely presumes that sport cannot be separated from its social context.

This brings me to my second criticism of hegemony theory: it confuses the social practice of sport with the social institution of sport. My argument here is that while hegemony theory purports to give an account of sport as a practice, what it actually gives is an account of its institutional normalization. There is, to be sure, an obvious and important connection between this latter criticism and my first criticism of hegemony theory. My earlier criticism that hegemony theory glosses over the manifold social constitution of sport—more particularly, that it confounds the contingent for the constitutive features of sport's production—can be traced to its present confusion regarding the practice and institution of sport.

What precisely is this distinction that hegemonists have supposedly botched? In other words, just how are we to draw the line between social practices and institutions? Perhaps even more fundamentally, why would we even want to make such a distinction in the first place? Isn't the drawing of such lines, and the making of such distinctions, as hegemonists generally intimate, a confusion in its own right of lived experience with its abstract reconstruction?

Since the answer to the latter question sets up an answer to the former one, I will begin with it. The best way to answer that question is simply to point out that the distinction in question is in fact crucial to the whole hegemonic account of sport as it is to a comprehensive understanding of sport. An argument, of course, must be made for that assertion, but for now it is important to note that it is Gruneau himself who introduced, albeit in a confused way, the couplet of social practice and institution to the discussion of sport. In doing so he appeared to be following a rather well-established precedent in hegemonic thought. Hegemonists are not at all adverse to distinguishing between institutions and other sorts of social entities and arrangements. Raymond Williams, for instance, was fond of distinguishing between social "formations" (social movements and tendencies found in intellectual, artistic, philosophical, and scientific circles) and the institutions of larger society.[94] As we have seen, it is a virtual mainstay of hegemony theory to differentiate sharply between various forms of social being and life, usually along class lines, and their institutional counterparts.

So the distinction between the practice and institution of sport does not appear to be problematic in itself, and is in any event not unknown to hegemony sport theory. We know, then, where to look to answer our first question. The germ of this distinction, where to draw the line between a social practice and institution, is supplied by hegemony theory itself. However, the problem, as noted above, is that hegemonists more often than not blur and distort this line of demarcation. Hence, one cannot simply lift this distinction from their various pronouncements about it; rather it must be carefully teased out of their theory. I propose to do just that.

When hegemonists refer to sport as a social practice they most often mean that sport is exclusively a product of our social being, that it enjoys no natural or transhistorical status.[95] But it is not this notion of practice, and the by now well-worn contrast it sets up between socially grounded forms of lived experience and their illicit cognitive surrogates, that we are after now. Rather the notion of practice at issue here is the one that Gruneau alludes to in certain select instances when he talks about games and sports as formally bounded activities whose rules and structures are designed to ensure its separation from necessity.[96] It is this sense of practice, in which sport is understood as a discrete form of life that founds and specifies definite and rather exotic ways of behaving and acting in the world, that comes closest to what Searle and Taylor mean when they talk about particular social practices and their constitutive rules. It is, in short, the very singular and distinctive notion of sport as an autonomous and separable practice that I refer to in my first criticism of hegemony theory. It is this sense of practice, moreover, that sets up the sought-after contrast to the correlative notion of institution as revealed in Gruneau's largely correct observation that the social significance of the founding rules of the social practice of sport depend in part on whether they "become institutionalized features of social life," that is, on whether sport as a social practice is made over as an institution.[97]

Before proceeding, we must specify our above reference to institution. Fortunately, hegemonists have a quite clear—and for our purposes a quite consistent and relevant—view of what an institution is. As recounted above, it is a straightforward sociological conception that refers to the underlying patterns and characteristic forms of organization by which the ensemble of practices that make up society at any given time are ordered and assigned a range of social meanings. More specifically, institutions represent recognized, established, and legitimated ways of pursuing practices that reflect the social biases and interests of specific social groups. By mobilizing those biases and interests in particular ways, the official and dominant way of doing sport, culled from the various ways in which it could be done, is produced. In the particular case of modern, Western sport, that process of institutionalization has led, as previously noted, to the burgeoning of formal bureaucratic bodies in whose name virtually all legislative and judicial regulatory offices have been vested.[98]

The above distinction between the practice and the institution of sport is, I reiterate, a cleaner and more sharply differentiated one than anything available in the hegemonic literature itself. If it were not, then both of my criticisms of hegemony theory to this point would have missed their mark. That they have not is owed to two points. The first, which vindicates my earlier assertion, is that hegemony theory must presuppose something very much like the practice-institution distinction above. To speak of institutions, as hegemonists do, as legitimating devices that formalize and objectify particular ways of doing some activity or other requires for its very intelligibility that what is formalized already exist. Institutions, in other words, sanction and regulate preexisting practices, practices whose existence is logically independent of their (sanctioning and regulating) resources and rules. The second point is that while this distinction is crucial to hegemony theory, it systematically and routinely violates it.

It violates this distinction in a variety of related ways. Perhaps foremost in this regard is that it talks about the practice of sport in terms that bespeak its institutionalization. A case in point is Gruneau's central claim that the constitutive structures of sport as a social practice are indissolubly connected to those that govern the whole round of social life. While this is a perfectly appropriate way to talk about institutions, whose sphere of influence spans the whole ensemble of existing social practices, it is an inappropriate way to talk about discrete social practices. It glosses over, as I noted in my first criticism, the very distinguishing marks that make a social practice the particular and unique practice that it is. In the language of the present discussion, that means that we must be careful to single out the constitutive elements that separate practices from each other, from the broader constitutive institutional structures that, at another level, bind them together.

The practice-institution distinction is further compromised by Gruneau's puzzling claim that games and sports are "by their very nature . . . institutionally defined social practices."[99] While Gruneau invokes this distinction to make his point here, the way he ties each element in the distinction together renders it suspect. Admittedly what Gruneau means by this claim is difficult to say, but there are at least two ways one could read it, and either one, I contend, is problematic.

On one reading we could interpret Gruneau to be saying that by some endogenous logic, or internal inertia, every sporting practice seeks, if not demands, an institutional form. While it is true that every practice, no less sport, requires some sort of institutional support, it is clearly preposterous to claim that sporting practices on their own accord aspire after an institutional status, that they crave some kind of institutional anchor. Moreover, the empirical evidence, which contains plenty of examples of sports that are largely unadorned by institutional trappings, weighs in heavily against any such view.[100]

A second reading suggests that what Gruneau had in mind here was that sports are institutional reproductions of play, that sports, in other words, are institutional embodiments of playful practice. Though the quotation from Gruneau above does not say that in so many words, its context does at least imply such a reading. Further, Gruneau did quite explicitly at times refer to sport as an "institutional [version] of playful action."[101] The implication here is that sport is preeminently an institution as opposed to a practice, and that the antecedent activity it objectifies is not, therefore, sport but play. The notion that formal, organized sport is somehow grounded in play is the very view that Ingham and Hardy attribute, though in a different context, to Gruneau: "it is not so much sport but the residual, assertive-expressive essence of play that [for Gruneau] provides the key [to the emancipation of subordinate groups].[102]

While at times Gruneau does appear to assume such a view of sport, it is clearly incompatible with the basic thrust of his theory. For one thing, such a view flies in the face of his repeated insistence that sport is indeed a bona fide social practice. For another, to argue that play is somehow the uncontaminated core of sport, and that, by implication, play can be cut loose from its institutional moorings and put to use as a regulative ideal to evaluate the moral and cultural fitness of sport at any given time, is to replicate the conservative view of sport. As Gruneau's criticisms of Huizinga and Lasch make abundantly clear, he cannot abide by any theory of sport that trades on some version of "the debasement of play" theme.[103]

The third, and clearly the most egregious, way in which hegemony theory does violence to the practice-institution distinction lies in Gruneau's contention that the limits and constitutive structures that frame games and sports are themselves institutional ones.[104] This is indeed a radical claim. To allege such is to assert considerably more than that the constitutive structures of sport as a practice are indissolubly connected to those of its institution; it is effectively to subsume the former under the latter. It is, in other words, to treat the constitutive rules upon which sport is structured as a social possibility as synonymous with those upon which it is structured as an institution. What gets lost in this virtual dissolution of any meaningful distinction between the practice and institution of sport is the sense of sport as a separate, rationally differentiated sphere of life. In its stead we get a rather clear picture of the institutional facts of its social constitution that confirms its direct and undeniable links to the broader limits of social reality. The only problem, of course, is that it presents a one-sided, not to say vexing, picture of the social facts of sport's production.[105]

Just why Gruneau and other hegemonists have succumbed to this confusion of social practices and institutions is hard to say. Perhaps they simply overreacted to the idealistic excesses of much of the critical literature on sport. Or it might just be, as Jeffrey Stout has argued, that sociologists "barely know how to talk about social practices . . . at all" given their preoccupation with institutional matters and concerns.[106] There is also the possibility that Gruneau for one may have been misled by Searle's more basic philosophical conception of an institution. I am referring here to Searle's famous distinction between "brute" facts, which are essentially physical facts, knowledge of which is garnered by simple empirical observations that record our sense experiences (for example, this stone is next to that stone), and "institutional" facts, which are essentially social facts, knowledge of which is garnered by citing the appropriate set of constitutive rules that underlie a given human institution (for example, the Dodgers beat the Braves 5 to 4).[107] It is clear that what Searle calls an institution is what Taylor, Gruneau (in specific cases), and I each call a practice. As such, it has little to do, given the epistemological use Searle makes of it to broadly mark off social from natural facts, with what sociologists, and what hegemonists after them, call institutions.

In any case, what is clear is that hegemonists violate, if not annul, their own distinction between practices and institutions. What account they provide of sport, therefore, as I argue above, is not of sport as a social practice but of sport as a social institution. As we shall see in an ensuing chapter, however, once that account is untangled from the mistakes and confusions discussed above, it proves to be a very useful and cogent reckoning of the broader ways in which sport is constituted in society.

My third criticism of hegemony sport theory takes me in a different direction. It has to do with the attempt by adherents of this theory to spin out a critical social theory of sport that is neither unduly optimistic (in the manner of idealism's voluntaristic excesses) nor unduly pessimistic (in the manner of the New Left's deterministic excesses). Hegemonists wanted, in short, to make room for human agency in their theory; they wanted to demonstrate that it was not a dead issue; that it had not succumbed to class co-optation or mass deception; that human beings were, after all, not mere dupes of the social orders to which they belong. Moreover, they sought to bring attention to the vibrancy of human agency without mitigating the social and historical constraints that limit what we can and cannot do. The point was not to deny or otherwise circumvent those constraints but to study and analyze them in the effort to find crevices within which freedom and reason could make a difference. Too little attention, they contended, had been paid by leftist critics to the resiliency of agency and the emancipatory prowess of sport. Preoccupied as such critics were with the ways in which sport mirrored the productive forces and relations of capitalism, they overlooked, or blithely dismissed, the ability of human agents to see through the dominant moment of sport.

Raymond Williams's exhortation to make "hope practical rather than despair convincing" was, therefore, their exhortation. But, I reiterate, theirs was a principled optimism, not an unbridled one. They were well aware of the opposite, and no less erroneous, tendency: the inclination to find resistance to the status quo everywhere. Indeed, they were openly contemptuous of critics who, stunned by the major economic and political defeats represented by the triumph of Reganism and Thatcherism, sought to compensate by finding resistance even in the most innocuous expressions of popular culture. They regarded such efforts, as well as their guiding exhortation "pessimism of the intellect, optimism of the will," as little more than exercises in cultural apologetics.[108] What hegemonists advocated instead was a "cautious" optimism, one that stressed that the moment of resistance must be understood in the way that it both opposes and is contained by hegemony.[109]

The "cautious" optimism espoused by hegemony theory is certainly a noble and laudable aim, and a welcome departure from the often simple-minded determinism practiced by the New Left. I have no bone to pick with this critical aim nor the program that undergirds it. Rather, my criticism concerns hegemony theory's apparent failure to carry it through. I argue that when we critically examine the various claims hegemonists make for emancipatory agency in sport, they don't stand up. I argue further that whatever optimism outlasts that critique is anything but cautious. I conclude, therefore, that hegemony theory leaves us with a social theory of sport that is every bit as gloomy, dismal, and deterministic as its New Left counterpart. Indeed, far from making hope practical, I claim that what hegemony theory actually achieves, if its account is to be believed, is an explanation of the staying power of capitalism, of the resilience not of human agency but of capitalist forces of containment.

I would like to begin my criticism with what I take to be a striking, though perhaps not surprising, omission in the hegemonic consideration of human agency. I am referring here to the liberal model of agency, to its conception of freedom as essentially a matter of free choice. What I find curious about this omission is that while hegemony theory takes great pains, as we shall see, to tease out the various levels of individual and collective agency, and discusses the nuances of each at some length, it has next to nothing to say about individual choice. Gruneau explains the lacuna this way: "the whole issue of opportunities for *participation*," he contends, "is much less important than the question of opportunities for *control*."[110] In other words, whatever choice an individual makes and is allowed to make is less significant than who controls and structures the activities that individual chooses. The "who" that does the controlling and structuring in such instances is always some collective body or other—it is naive to believe that individuals qua individuals could ever hold let alone exercise the requisite controlling power. Gruneau thus regards questions about opportunities for involvement in sport as "benign" ones, which if given too much prominence, as liberal ideologues are wont to do, lead to falsely optimistic accounts of the democratization of sport and of capitalist society.[111]

We can agree in principle with Gruneau that control is more important than choice, and "voice" more important than "exit." We can also agree that certain liberal theorists, but not all, frequently make too much of the latter, and that at times they even seem to hold that negative freedom is the only kind of freedom there is, or the only kind of freedom worth hanging on to and defending. We can agree with all of this and yet still question whether the issue of freedom of choice is a "benign" one. We can question further whether the hegemonic privileging of positive over negative freedom, like its liberal opposite, misses the larger point that one kind of freedom is as indispensable to human emancipation as the other, that, indeed, positive freedom presupposes in some important way negative freedom and vice versa.

There are two reasons why hegemonists, parroting classical Marxists, think that putting the issue in the way I do above is mistaken. Those two reasons pick out two things about the liberal model of free agency that hegemonists find particularly offensive. The first is that liberal theorists treat individuals as single, discrete atoms, not as members of some social group. The second is that liberals seek to establish freedom of choice by setting up partitions, for example, the separation of state and church and the separation of state and educational institutions. It is only by building walls of this sort, liberals maintain, that individuals can freely express their religious beliefs without outside interference, and that intellectuals can freely take up and espouse heretical (nonconventional) views without fear of political retribution.

Hegemonists regard both prongs of the liberal model as shams. For one thing, they regard individuals foremost as members of social groups to which they belong by virtue of the social relations that obtain in larger society. Individuals are construed, to use Marx's language, as "personifications of economic categories, the bearers of particular class relations and interests."[112] For another, the walls upon which liberalism anchors its notion of freedom are considered both porous and false. The fact is, hegemonists insist, that today religious creeds are just finessed so that they mesh with the ideological requirements of capitalism, and that present-day educational institutions are little more than upscale factories for the production of the managerial ranks of the capitalist work force.[113] It could scarcely be any other way since Marxists are typically predisposed to regard separate spheres of life as passive reflections of others, and hegemonists to only a slightly different view that distinct spheres of life are at best active reproductions of others.[114]

But, I maintain, we have reason to be suspicious of hegemony's denigration of negative freedom. We have good grounds for treating that denigration, which it shares with classical Marxism, as a vice rather than a virtue, as a fundamental weakness rather than a strength. I believe we are justified to suppose so for at least three reasons.

First, by trivializing the importance of privacy and individual liberty, hegemony theory, like Marxism, makes itself an easy target of state despotism, of the ill winds of totalitarianism and its grotesque offspring, fascism. Rosa Luxemburg was not unaware of this when she wrote of the Russian revolution that "the remedy which Trotsky and Lenin have found, the elimination of democracy as such, is worse than the disease it is supposed to cure."[115] Horkheimer was also aware of this suspect vulnerability when he wrote in the late sixties, apparently still convinced of the lingering potency of fascism, that "to protect, preserve, and, where possible, extend the limited and ephemeral freedom of the individual in the face of the growing threat to it is far more urgent a task than to issue abstract denunciations of it or to endanger it by actions that have no hope of success."[116]

Second, by failing to incorporate individual choice within their conceptual grid of human agency and freedom, hegemonists underestimate the importance of microsocial features for macrosocial activity. What is worse, in doing so they sever an important link between social outcomes and individual action, and so leave unaccounted for an entire layer of agency and action whose explanatory force is not insubstantial. What hegemony theory fails to see, therefore, is that, as Elster puts it, social phenomena are explicable in ways that bear crucially on the properties, goals, beliefs, actions, and wills of individuals.[117]

Finally, in undervaluing the import of individual liberty, hegemony theory has slighted its own program of human emancipation. It can be persuasively argued not only that freedom of choice is important in its own right as a goal of emancipation, but that hegemony's, and certainly Marxism's, notion of individual and collective self-determination requires, in ways not fully understood by either, a "protected space" by which meaningful choices can be made.[118] No matter how porous some of the liberal partitions might turn out to be, we would be ill-advised to scrap them altogether, if, that is, emancipation were our stated aim. Saying that commits us at least in principle to conceding some limited value to the existing divisions within liberal society. As Walzer poignantly puts it, "no one who has lived in an illiberal state is going to accept this devaluation of the range of liberal freedoms."[119] The tumultuous events of 1989 and 1991 poignantly confirm Walzer's point. To this, I would only add that no one who lives in a liberal state but who has, for whatever reason, been denied the privileges and protections accorded therein, is likely either to trivialize or otherwise deny those individual liberties.

A final curiosity about this point should be noted. This concerns a certain inverted analogue apparent between liberalism and hegemonism. Just as liberal theory's overestimation of negative freedom induces an inflated and overly optimistic picture of democratic tendencies in sport and society, hegemony theory's underestimation of negative freedom induces an equally inflated and overly optimistic picture of the emancipatory prospects of its designated liberating agent, the working class. I have in mind here Bryan Palmer's daring claim that a robust racism and sexism evident among many members of Canada's white working force registered a significant resistance to capitalism and, in his words, a "struggle to resecure some of the territory lost to an adversary they no longer see." While Palmer on the one hand deplores such racism and sexism, on the other he baldly asserts that in order to be responsive to the workers' challenge to capitalism in such instances we must "look past [any] superficial stance of indignation."[120] Though Palmer's argument is not wildly implausible, it misses its mark and is, shall we say, a trifle perverse. Two points are germane here. First, an expression of moral indignation in the face of overt cases of racist and/or sexist behavior is anything but superficial. Second, Palmer's suggestion that we just "look past" such instances in the effort to wring from a generally unobliging working class an emancipatory moment is not likely to succeed, as he himself concedes in his ensuing remarks, and can hardly be passed off as an example of the kind of "cautious" optimism championed by hegemony theory.[121]

Aside from this omission of individual agency, however, hegemony theory has done a reasonably good job of identifying the various levels of human agency that are operative in social life. Since my next set of criticisms directly concerns that categorization of human agency, I first want to carefully reconstruct what hegemonists have to say about this matter.

For present purposes then we can discern five important levels and/or senses of agency in the hegemonic literature. They include the following:

1. The privately accommodative. This comprises the personal goals and aims that inform the day-to-day actions of our lives: who we intend to marry; what house we're going to buy; whether or not we're going to have children; and, in the realm of leisure, what sports we play or observe as spectators. All of these are private projects, which, though momentous in their own right, are entirely inscribed within existing social relations and so typically reproduce them.

2. The privately oppositional. This also includes our personal goals and aims, but in this case our private projects run counter to existing social relations. This is accomplished through expressing discontent with dominant institutions and cultural forms by searching for alternatives within one's private life or one's family, or within some local group or other. The possibilities here are too numerous to cite in detail but may involve private acts of political dissent (individual acts of protest and defiance), or individual moral expressions, or local ecological acts of nurturance and concern. In the case of sport, the possibilities are once again legion but center on the private and local pursuit of recreational sports, which run the gamut from "pure" play to the private appropriation of more highly organized sports to countercultural activities like the New Games movement. Though these acts take issue with existing social relations, their individual and local character ensures that they too fall within the bounds of prevailing social relations, and so are largely reproductive in their overall effect.

3. The collectively accommodative. This takes in the bulk of public actions that occur in the mainstream of everyday life. They include collective projects that typically affirm established institutions: parades, celebrations, conventions, public-relations exercises, and the like. Since these sorts of projects take

their cue directly from existing social relations, they are re-productive in a quite active and strong sense.

4. The collectively oppositional. This accounts for those public actions that contest the status quo. These sorts of collective projects represent "counterhegemonic" assertions that are based in a recognized opposition of interest. They include various forms of social and political protest, which frequently center on disputes concerning the distribution of goods and services. In the realm of sport, the most obvious examples are the political protests that took place in Mexico in 1968 and in Munich in 1972. The use of sport as a form of resistance to colonial rule, as apparent, for example, in the Balinese cock-fight, would also count as a form of collective opposition. While these kinds of public actions are rooted in conflict, they are not subversive in any deeper sense; that is, they do not seek to transform the social relations that bind them, but only to redress, within those very social relations, whatever injustices or grievances their enactors have suffered. In this sense then, they have quite obvious and important reproductive effects.

5. The radically transformative. This encompasses radical, collective attempts to transform existing social structures. These attempts are not simple cases of conflict but rather concerted, conscious efforts to dismantle one social order in favor of another. This is the rarest and most exceptional form of agency, because, obviously enough, revolutions are quite rare and exceptional historical events.[122]

The kind of agency that hegemonists brand as oppositional—and are keen to draw attention to because it has been covered over by both idealist and Neo-Marxist theories of sport—is the privately and collectively oppositional (categories 2 and 4 above). We can then simply dispense with further consideration of the privately and collectively accommodative realms of agency (categories 1 and 3 above), which have nothing centrally to do with the hegemonic case for reviving optimism in the vitality of human agency. Once we do so, however, a certain problem in the hegemonic account of oppositional agency becomes apparent. That problem concerns a discrepancy between the kind of agency that hegemonists on the one hand endorse and celebrate as oppositional, and on the other, once they get around to an historical evaluation, reproach as lacking transformative import.

That is to say, their dismal historical prognosis regarding the radical potential of the oppositional agency displayed by the working class (which requires something approaching the level 5 variety) is prefigured in their championing of a form of agency that was from the very outset deficient in radical prowess (which operates, that is, at the level 2 and level 4 variety). Hegemony theory thus falls prey to its own devices by sanctioning a level of agency that is out of step with its professed interest in social transformation. As such, the optimism it confidently, though not incautiously, exudes in the prospects of such a transformation appears at best misplaced, at worst, groundless.

What we have here is not some virulent form of agency whose radical potential was somehow thwarted or neutralized by a counterhegemonic parry from the dominant class, nor a form of agency whose resistance to the status quo represents also a "paradoxical cultural insertion into the hegemony of capitalist life."[123] On the contrary, what we have here is a form of opposition that harbors its moment of containment within itself, one that is, therefore, already effectively incorporated. If we can call acts of this sort oppositional—and I am insinuating that hegemonists stretch their case here or at very least equivocate—then they are acts whose insertion into the dominant hegemony is preestablished rather than paradoxical.

All that hegemony theory manages to show regarding so-called oppositional agency in sport, therefore, is its largely conformist and ineffectual manner, and, by extension, the largely conservative aspirations and allegiances of the subordinate groups that engage in such agency.[124] Its proponents thus fail to provide the necessary evidence to support their optimism that oppositional agency in sport, or anywhere else in the social terrain for that matter, will eventuate in the kind of social transformation that they envisage is required to produce a fully humane society. If anything, the large gap in hegemony theory's conceptual grid between actions at levels 2 and 4 and those at level 5 gives the impression that radical agency is a rather esoteric form of action and experience that only rears its head in actual revolutionary periods. Its historical findings that even level 2 and level 4 oppositional actions have been for the most part muted in sport only cement this impression. Hence, I concur—with one important qualification—with Rojek's following indictment of the work of the Centre for Contemporary Cultural Studies' (CCCS) on leisure and sport, which I hereby extend to the whole corpus of hegemony sport theory, "in letters which spell out the bleakest proofs of the prophecies of Frankfurt Marxism, the work of the Centre reveals in the 'subtext' of its research a view of the working class as effectively integrated into the system."[125]

The one important qualification is that I hold the shortcomings of hegemony theory's treatment of agency to be deeply rooted ones that implicate some of its sacred theoretical pillars. One of those pillars involves a left-wing version of the argument that someone's own vocabulary (and the set of experiences it captures) is always the best vocabulary for understanding what he or she is up to; that the subject's own explanation of what he or she is doing is the one that we want to explain those actions.[126] In leftist guise, this epistemological act of privileging the subject takes on a grander scope and argues that the subject's own account of his or her behavior is not only the best account of what he or she is up to, but is also the best account available of the world about us. The subject in this case is the collective one of the working class, or some other specified group, and the world in this case is the social world. The privileging of the working class comes in this regard to the view that because it occupies a special position in the social world it is best equipped to understand how that world actually works. This claim comes, of course, with a practical twist; the special vantage point of the working class not only ensures that it is its vocabulary, repertoire of experiences, and actions that we need to tap in order to grasp the contradictions of the social world, but that it is its vocabulary, experiences, and actions that we need to put to use to resolve those social contradictions. That is why the theoretical comprehension of the social world and the practical understanding and actualization of its transformation necessitates, in this argument, an internal explanation of the special position of the working class.

The classical Marxian version of this argument, which was itself a refurbished rendition of Vico's famous dictum *verum et factum convertuntur* (the true and the made are convertible), singled out the working class because of its key position in the material production of the social world. It argued that the working class is in a unique position to know the social world, and to come to recognize itself in it, because it quite literally made that world through its collective labor. It argued further that because the bourgeoisie plays only a parasitic role in the production of the world, it is incapable of fully knowing that world, and so it is condemned to a reified and fragmented understanding of it.[127]

Hegemony theory offers a rather simple variant of this argument. In this case, however, the special position of the working class is not confined to its pivotal role in the material production of society, to its labor—for hegemonists, it will be remembered, recognize no meaningful distinction between material and cultural production—but extends to the whole production of society. What is special about the working class in this expanded sense is its unique vantage point in the negotiation processes that constitute larger society. All such hegemonic negotiations must be filtered through the working class and win its support if the dominant class expects to be able to govern society. So the dominant class is quite literally "forced to renegotiate continually the terms upon which consent for [its] rule could be sustained."[128] As a result, the working class finds itself in the enviable position of not only being able to see the social world in its own light, but of being able to interpret and reconstitute the collective meanings of cultural forms like sport on its own terms.[129]

What are we to make of these sorts of epistemologically privileging arguments? Rorty has argued more generally that it is a mistake to think that a subject's own account of its behavior and actions is in any sense privileged. Sometimes such self-accounts are quite adequate and sometimes the other "person's, or culture's, explanation of what it's up to is so primitive, or so nutty, that we brush it aside."[130] In the case of the hegemonic version of this argument, we argued that the working class's perspective on the social world, however viewed, is inadequate.

But, as intimated above, it cuts more deeply than this. This is because the apparent shortcomings of the working class put into question not just its adequacy as an *explanans* of the social world, but its supposed special position and central role in the production of society. As Elster writes, "There is no reason to suppose that beliefs shaped by a social position tend to serve the interests of the persons in that position" or endow those persons with any special insight, theoretical or practical, into the workings of the social world about them.[131] In fact, there is every reason to believe, from the available historical evidence alone, the very opposite: that the working class's position in the production of the social world is an important source of its own ideological delusion and of its production of its own social repression. Moreover, there is every reason to believe, again from the same historical evidence, that its implication in its own repression accomplishes its submission to the status quo more effectively than if that submission were directed exclusively from above by the ideological decrees of its bourgeois rulers.[132]

That the various failings of subordinate groups to see through the dominant moment of sport and construct genuine alternatives to it can be attributed at least in part to their complicity in their own false consciousness is a point we owe once again to hegemonists. Thus Palmer notes that "in an active if not autonomous sense, [workers] create forms of interaction and consciousness that reproduce the directives of a larger and impersonal *system* of oppression and exploitation."[133] Hollands observes how various workers' practices such as "doubling up" (hurrying the pace of production in order to create breaks of from fifteen to twenty seconds) and "making out" (the skillful engagement and completion of tasks over and above quota rates), which ostensibly were attempts by workers to gain some measure of control over their work, in fact "only represent[ed] a moment in the continued production of capitalist relations." That management actively sought to facilitate such workers' tactics, Hollands further observes, by enhancing their position in production (by, among other things, increasing worker autonomy, encouraging individualism, and relaxing inspection of piecework on the shop floor), only underscores the major point at issue here.[134] In the case of sport, Hargreaves avers that the accommodation of the working class to official sport was "to a large extent self-imposed," and exemplifies "how it renders itself subordinate . . . by relatively autonomous processes."[135]

While hegemonists, not surprisingly, continue to interpret the working class's production of its own servitude in terms amenable to their basic theory—arguing that such production is simultaneously both a form of resistance to and affirmation of the status quo,[136] its complicity in its own domination is sufficiently clear to cut through any such theoretical subterfuge. Still, Hargreaves and other hegemonists have a legitimate point when they retort that the accommodation of the working class to dominant cultural forms such as sport is "never merely a matter of self-imposition" but involves the complicity of the dominant class as well. But its legitimacy is more far reaching than Hargreaves and his compatriots are willing to concede. What makes this point legitimate about the dominant class is what makes the hegemonist claim about the special position of the underclass illegitimate. The alleged special position of the working class turns out once again to be not so special after all. Indeed, what hegemony theory really establishes is its relative inferiority and impotence in the general scheme of things.

I should mention, however, that the problem of explaining the alleged privileged vantage point of the working class in the face of its manifest impotence is not unique to hegemony theory. Indeed, it originates with classical Marxism itself. It was, as we have seen, a centerpiece of Marx's theory that the proletariat was uniquely situated to know and change the social world because it quite literally made that world. At the same time, Marx harbored no illusions about the capacity of the bourgeoisie to check the proletariat's radical potential by variously immiserating it, keeping it in a backward and immature theoretical and practical condition, and generally concealing its central role in the production of the world. The question arises then of how to square the favored material position of the working class with its obvious dependence on, and subservience to, the bourgeoisie. For Marx the answer was by recourse to a triggering device, that is, to the clash between the productive forces and the productive relations of a society. Marx held that when the productive forces outstrip the productive relations (as happens, for example, when the development of the productive forces in capitalism is constricted by its profit motive), the dominant class will no longer be able to contain the proletariat. From here, according to Marx, it is but a short step to socialism.

Whether Marx's resorting to this triggering mechanism resolves the above antinomy is a hotly debated and much disputed topic in leftist circles these days. While it is an enormously important question, it need not detain us at present. I mention it only to make my point that while hegemony theory might have had good reasons to jettison the base-superstructure paradigm of classical Marxism, that move left it without any device or way of resolving the above antinomy. There is nothing in hegemony theory, I hasten to add, that takes the place of this paradigm, or that explains how the working class might overcome its dominion, how, in other words, its oppositional agency might escalate into radical agency—nothing, that is, save the assurance hegemonists offer that the working class is capable of such agency.

But the replacement of the base-superstructure scheme with the negotiating scheme of hegemonic class conflict and confrontation gives us an additional reason to question that assurance. While it is true that everything must be filtered through the working class in such negotiations, it is also true that what gets filtered through it is controlled by someone else. And while it is true, as Raymond Williams tells us, that no dominant culture can exhaust all human practice, energy, and intention, it is also true, as Williams admits, that "advanced capitalism, because of changes in the social character of labour, in the social character of communications, and in the social character of decision-making, . . . reaches much further than ever before . . . into hitherto 'reserved' or 'resigned' areas of experience and practice and meaning."[137] While it is further true that the consent of the working class must be obtained in order for the dominant class to retain its dominant position in the social world, that consent is always secured in a way that disadvantages the former.

What I offer above are not casual assertions but rather the very conditions that hegemonists tell us govern any class negotiation process. They argue that it is the dominant class that sets the terms and the agenda for class negotiation, and that establishes the "outer limits" and the "horizon of thought" within which such negotiations take place.[138] That means that while workers have varying influence and control over particular items that come up for negotiation, they have no influence and control over who presides over these deliberations. Said otherwise, what is not open for negotiation, and what is never a negotiable item in such proceedings, is the advantaged position of the dominant class itself. On the contrary, it is the presumption of that class advantage that pervades every facet of the dickering process. It follows as a matter of course, therefore, that while various forms of oppositional agency by subordinate groups may be actuated in these class deliberations, and additional ones may be finessed as outcomes, no such case can be made for radical agency. That option is simply ruled out by the superior position enjoyed by the dominant class, and so it is not a negotiating ploy that would be available to any subordinate group. Of course, it is not as if subordinate groups are in any position to wring such concessions from their rulers. That is why Clement's question to Gruneau—"how does Gruneau propose to test his proposition that when a subordinate group is in a position to challenge a dominant group as a result of some change in historical circumstances there is a tendency for the forms of cultural expression of the subordinate to take on a transformative rather than a reproductive character,"[139] which is in one sense well conceived—ultimately misses its mark. The subordinate group, according to the very terms of hegemonic negotiation, is never in a position to challenge the dominant group in this transformative sense, which explains why even its oppositional initiatives turn out to be reproductive ones.

I contend, therefore, that hegemony sport theory has failed to resolve what Raymond Williams regards as the "major theoretical problem" facing any theory of this sort: "to distinguish between alternative and oppositional initiatives and contributions which are made within or against a specific hegemony . . . and other kinds of initiative and contribution which are irreducible to the terms of the original . . . and are in that sense independent."[140] Its failure in this regard is certainly not one of nerve or of critical intelligence, but of theoretical commitment. Hegemony theory's commitment to the class negotiation scheme accounts for its inability to pick out instances of oppositional agency in sport that are not of the intrahegemonic variety. It is its commitment to this scheme that explains hegemony theory's inability to realize its own project, one unredeemed in New Left sport theory, to revive and recapture the resilience of agency in cultural forms like sport. By turning up only intrahegemonic forms of resistance to officially sanctioned sport—forms of resistance that contain their own neutralizing antidote—hegemonists succeed in demonstrating not the robustness of human agency but the manifest power of the dominant culture to produce and limit its own forms of counterculture.[141] One may attempt to extract a moment of optimism from the otherwise dismal historical prognosis of sport that the hegemonists offer by appealing to their theory of class negotiation, but that attempt will fail; for, I maintain, that theory confirms in the main their grim historical assessment.

Williams and other hegemonists have objected that breaks beyond the established hegemony have in fact occurred, and that such breaks have at times led to genuine revolutionary activity. If so, one might object further that it would clearly be wrong to overlook such breaks and succumb to the view that the cultural process is merely adaptive, extensive, and incorporative.[142] I fully concur. But my criticism of hegemony theory does not commit me to denying such breaks or to holding that the cultural process is an essentially incorporative one. On the contrary, my criticism is only that hegemony theory is unable to account for or otherwise explain breakthroughs of this extrahegemonic character. In all such independent, autonomous breaks (such as the break that led from feudalism to capitalism), a dominant group loses its grip on its advantaged position and is supplanted by a new group that stakes out its own advantaged position. It is just this loss of dominance, this fall from favor, that is nowhere explained in the class negotiation terms of hegemony theory. Indeed, that theory is based on the supposition that class deliberations take place between a dominant party and a subordinate party. What hegemony theory explains is not the ascendance of a party to a dominant position or the fall of a party to a subordinate position, but the negotiations that occur between an already dominant party and an already subordinate party. Further, since all such negotiations presume that the advantaged position of the dominant class is exempted from the bargaining process, social transitions in which dominance changes hands between parties must be attributed to something else besides interclass hegemonic negotiations.[143]

In summary, one could say that hegemony theory is unable to account for extrahegemonic social transformations in the way that classical Marxism is able to, or thinks itself able to, explain such social shifts. In this respect at least, the explanatory scope and prowess of hegemony theory is out of step with the main problematic that confronts Western Marxism today: finding some way out of capitalism and into socialism. It is better equipped to explain what impedes such a transformation than what might accomplish it. At its best, then, hegemony theory provides a powerful explanation of the daily detail, of the interior, intrahegemonic conflicts, struggles, and proceedings that are necessary to hold together any dominant social order. It opens our eyes to the hustle and bustle and fury of activity that underlies the construction and maintenance of any status quo. But it can't open our eyes to autonomous acts and projects that exceed and defy the established hegemony, because it cannot see them or make them out for what they are.

What remains in hegemony theory's conceptual arsenal is the argument that the hegemonic process is an extremely delicate, fragile, and unstable one. This argument takes its point of departure not from any special position or potency allegedly held by some subordinate group or other, but from the character of sportive agency itself and from the limited position and potency of the dominant group in class negotiations. It directly attacks, therefore, the major premise of my above criticism that the dominant party holds a distinct and considerable advantage over all other parties in such deliberations. It does so in order to recoup for its theory of class negotiations a radical promise and potential that I have denied it possesses to this point.

As I indicate above, hegemonists offer two versions of this argument. The first, and more particular one, argues that the very conditions of agency upon which the dominant class seeks to build its hegemony over sport challenges that hegemony.[144] So elements of sportive agency such as fun, fantasy, and excitement are claimed to be easily reversible in their effect, providing at best a precarious ground for the dominant class to solidify its hold on institutional sport. The second, and more general one, simply claims that the accomplishment of any hegemonic consensus is "extremely fragile" because the capacity of the dominant class to command such consent is limited. It is because that class is unable to impose its will over subordinate groups as it pleases, therefore, that all "dominant social relations and alliances in capitalist liberal democracies" are said to be unstable.[145]

I contend that both versions of this argument are suspect. To begin with the first, the claim that the special conditions of sportive agency are recalcitrant to hegemonic penetration flies in the face of all the available conceptual and historical evidence. Indeed, there is every reason to suppose, on the basis of that evidence, that elements such as fun and excitement lend themselves rather easily to manipulation and control. Tomlinson convincingly argues, for instance, that the workers' hedonistic predilection for sport has more often than not contributed to the reproduction of the status quo than its ruin. By indulging themselves in the "good times" provided by sport and other forms of popular culture, he argues, they have contributed to the production of "bad times."[146] Further, Hargreaves observes that the working class's preoccupation with entertainment and amusement spectacles often has a depoliticizing effect, making it especially vulnerable to exploitation by commercial interests.[147] So the appeal to the hedonistic elements of sportive agency to weaken the grip of the dominant culture's hold over the hegemonic process does not appear to be a very promising one.

That leaves us with the second, general claim regarding the fragility of the hegemonic process itself, and so of the dominant culture's control over this process. This argument fails, however, because it is a simple tautology. In this respect, MacAloon was correct in his harsh assessment of hegemony theory as short on real theory and long on "tautological labeling and description."[148] The claim that hegemonic forms of consensus are inherently unstable is a tautological description of what MacIntyre refers to as the "pervasive unpredictability in human life [that] renders all our plans and projects permanently vulnerable and fragile."[149] Once we uncouple the tautology from the putative facts about social life it describes, I argue, any argumentative force or charm it might have is dissipated as well.

What hegemony theory's tautology comes to is something like the following. Each contending social party in hegemonic negotiations tries to impose its interests, plans, and projects on the other, or, what is the same thing, seeks to embody its projects in the social world. An important way in which social groups attempt to foist their projects on the social world is by making predictable as much of that world as possible. Indeed, much of the utility of the social sciences (particularly administrative and management theory)—and shall we say much of their inflated status—derives from this point. It is also the case, however, that each of the contending parties seeks to make itself opaque and unpredictable to the others. So each tries not to disclose too much about itself in order to elude the generalizations used by the others to render its behavior predictable, in short, to control it. So there is a rather complex social dynamic that attaches itself to class negotiations in which each party attempts to make the other predictable at the same time that it attempts to make itself unpredictable.

It is, of course, a commonplace of hegemony theory that the dominant party has the upper hand in this process of rendering behavior alternately predictable and unpredictable, and so it is better able to disguise itself and to make transparent the actions of subordinate parties. But if the above account of class negotiations is an accurate one, then it follows that the generalizations the dominant class uses to decipher the behavior and actions of the underclasses have limited predictive power. They will never be able, therefore, to render the behavior of their subordinates completely transparent, and so they will never be able to control them completely. The putative facts regarding social interaction between groups in various states of dependency show, then, that complete control by one group over another is a social fiction. They show that the best-laid plans and the most carefully managed and informed projects of even the most powerful groups in society are fallible and subject to countervailing pressures that in the long run might well overturn them.

If this is indeed what hegemony theory's tautology concerning the fragility of class negotiation comes to, as I maintain, then it fails to disarm my criticism that the hegemonic theory of class negotiation is preeminently a theory of social containment as opposed to social transformation. That fragility demonstrates the inability of one group to exert absolute control over another. It rules out, in other words, the kind of totalitarian control and social order described by Aldous Huxley and George Orwell. But what it doesn't rule out or otherwise impugn are the more modest forms of control and domination that preoccupy hegemony theory: the prospect, for example, that a social group or class with a greater concentration of resources may well be able to have its way, to control (in the sense of shape and limit) less advantaged groups for a significant period of time. While it does rule out the likelihood that a totalitarian society could survive in the long run, it doesn't rule out the likelihood of its doing so in the short run. This is significant because, as MacIntyre poignantly observes, "we need to remember . . . the voices from Auschwitz and Gulag Archipelago which tell us just how long that [short] run is."[150] So the appeal made by hegemonists to the fragility of class consensus to buttress the radical promise of the hegemonic process cannot succeed, and when carefully unpacked, it seems to be a rather disingenuous claim.

My final major criticism of hegemony theory concerns its normative dimension. That dimension is, of course, an integral feature of its theory. What marks off a critically oriented social theory from other forms of social inquiry is its interest in evaluating the slice of social life it otherwise tries to explain and interpret. Hegemony theory is certainly no different in this respect, so it too is interested in securing some vantage point by which it can criticize social reality. To pull off that feat, however, it has to have recourse to critical standards and principles that are not themselves implicated or otherwise mired in that social order, that, in other words, are beyond ideological reproach. It has to be able, therefore, to distinguish the true from the false, the correct from the incorrect, the right from the wrong, the legitimate from the illegitimate.

The approach hegemonists use to ground their normative canons of criticism is, as discussed above, an historical one. Their turn to history is driven by the simple premise that there is no other place on which to found our justificatory efforts. They stoutly insist that there are no abstract, ahistorical, invariant standards that we might appeal to here to bail us out. It is mere folly, therefore, to engage in some search for the hidden essence of sport in order to back up our criticisms of institutional sport. All we have are the historical and social facts of the case, and it is out of these facts and these alone that we must construct our critique of "official" sport.

One might object at this point, however, that in dismissing the possibility of justifying a critique of dominant sport and culture on universal grounds, hegemonists commit themselves to a form of relativism that threatens their own critical project. If there are indeed no invariant features of sport that we can petition in this regard, then it follows, according to this argument, that any evaluation or critical assessment of sport is as good as any other. In other words, absent an ultimate justification anything else we might turn up to justify our critical efforts will turn out to be utterly arbitrary and capricious. So hegemonists find themselves, the argument continues, in the untenable if not absurd position of holding a particular view (that standards of truth and rightness are relative to certain historical contexts and social conventions) while at the same time holding that no point of view is more right or justified than another. This whole manner of argument is self-refuting, as Putnam's following quip felicitously shows: "if any point of view is as good as any other, then why isn't the point of view that relativism is false as good as any other?"[151]

But this is not the sort of relativist view that hegemony theory holds, or, if Rorty is to be believed,[152] that anyone holds. What hegemonists hold is not that there is no such thing as right or wrong (that all principles, standards, views, and beliefs are merely matters of personal taste or opinion), but that what is right or wrong, true or false, is always relative to some specifiable set of circumstances. It is the view that John Dewey called "objective relativism," which asserts that truth and critical judgment are indeed objective determinations, but that their reach extends no further than the relevant social conventions. This view also distinguishes itself from the above extreme brand of relativism in holding that societies that share the same material and cultural circumstances will also share the same social standards and principles of judgment, and so can be similarly evaluated.

But this raises the whole issue of just what social conventions and norms, according to hegemony theory, constitute our critical judgments about sport. What norms, in short, are available to us that provide an objective and valid assessment of sport? The answer that hegemonists give to this question, it will be remembered, is that the appropriate norms can be read off of certain forms of oppositional agency practiced by certain subordinate groups in society. It is the forms of agency unleashed in these social enclaves that furnish us with the critical standards we need to evaluate the dominant social forms of sport and of culture. All that is required, Corrigan reminds us, is that we contrast the former with the latter, that we ask whether this or that form of agency is enabled or constrained by this or that institutional form.

It is this feature of hegemony theory's normative account, and not its supposed relativist commitments, that I find problematic. My criticism of this account will follow two lines, both of which are anticipated by my previous criticisms of hegemony theory. I will argue first that the separation of social forms and human capacities required by that account violates a fundamental tenet of hegemony theory that forbids such a move. I will argue second that the oppositional agency that can be attributed to subordinate groups like the working class is not up to the normative task set for it by hegemony theory.

My first criticism refers to hegemony theory's commitment to what we earlier called "radical interactionism": that the social constitution of any one cultural form is implicated in the constitution of all other cultural forms and of social reality itself. This thesis, I claim, which is really a thesis of radical contextualism, rules out any effort to separate the context of social constitution from the facts of human agency, to include the capacities that underlie the latter. That does not mean, of course, that we cannot conceptually distinguish and talk about human capacities apart from the social forms that spawned them, but it does clearly mean that we cannot contrast them in the strong normative sense implied here. We cannot so contrast them because hegemony theory's strong contextualist thesis commits it to the view that social forms are logically prior to human capacities. The logical priority of social forms means straightforwardly that we have the kinds of capacities and abilities we have precisely because we have the kinds of social forms that we have.

Corrigan's normative gambit of pairing off human capacities against their social forms actually mimics, I argue, a legitimation tactic frequently used by certain bourgeois liberal theorists. It is a favorite ploy of such liberals, in order to promote their own agenda of individualistic concerns, to deny that social forms have the binding logical force attributed to them above. That is to say, it is because liberals are committed to the quite different view that human capacities are logically prior to social forms that they typically view the individual's entry into social life as (ideally) a voluntary act made by (potentially) rational individuals with prior interests who ask the question "What kind of social contract with others is it reasonable for me to enter into?"[153] My claim then is that such liberals are being quite consistent when they argue this way, but that hegemonists most decidedly are not.

It is important to unpack what it means to say that social forms are logically prior to human capacities in order to see how far off course hegemonists stray when they are wittingly or unwittingly led to deny this. There are two senses in which such forms may be said to be logically prior. The first is the conceptual sense that the human capacities we have and enjoy presuppose the existence of quite specific social, cultural, and historical arrangements. The point here is that it would be conceptually impossible to have these sorts of capacities if we did not have these sorts of particular cultural arrangements. The second is the causal sense that the social forms we inherit shape and mold whatever capacities we may possess. The point here is that we wouldn't have the capacities we do unless they were caused by these social forms. In either sense, then, capacities cannot be meaningfully detached from their forms.

However, there is at least one way to ascribe some independence to human capacities in the hegemonic causal account without denying their social grounding. That account argues that although social forms cause capacities in the sense of shaping them, they do not absolutely determine them. Rather, the causal effect of social forms is more limiting than determining, which means that it is certainly possible that a capacity or form of agency unleashed by a social form may well exceed its grasp and even turn against it. Against this it might be argued, and has been argued by hegemonists and liberals alike,[154] that the kinds of institutional forms one finds in liberal democratic societies are designed to function in such a way that at least some of the capacities they give rise to will elude their social spell. If so, then hegemony theory's watered-down causal account offers little consolation for its normative account, since the transcendent capacities that emerge from institutional forms in this sense are just the ones enabled by those forms. But that still doesn't preclude the possibility that at least some kinds of capacities that are not directly enabled by their institutional forms might nonetheless arise from those forms in an oppositional manner.

Unfortunately, it is just this sort of possibility that seems to be ruled out, or at least severely limited, by my second criticism. That criticism suggests that it is problematic to ascribe some sort of constitutive status to the perceptions, beliefs, outlooks, and vantage points of the subordinate groups that inhabit the social world. It is problematic to do so for precisely the reason discussed earlier that the disadvantaged position of subordinate parties in their hegemonic negotiations with the dominant party is just that: a position of disadvantage that by and large confines their oppositional agency to the intrahegemonic level and makes them vulnerable, not immune, to ideological manipulation. Hence, the inability of hegemony theory to make good its claim regarding the privileged position of the working class— or, what comes to the same thing, its inability to advance a robust theory of social change—means that it has been unable to discover, authorize, or otherwise document the kinds of agency that would justify its cautious optimism about the fate of the social world, and the normative claims it makes on behalf of subordinate groups. It also means that the capacities and actions that, as it were, slip through the causal network of social forms are unlikely to alter to any appreciable degree the inferior bargaining position of the underclasses because they qualify more so as novel acts than oppositional ones.

Critical Appropriation of Hegemony Theory of Sport

As I suggested earlier, it is no accident that hegemony theory has achieved the intellectual prominence that it has in critical sport studies. It is, in short, a formidable social theory and has proved itself to be more than a worthy successor to its European Neo-Marxist counterpart. So when it comes to the question of what can be salvaged from this theory, the short answer is, quite a lot. But, of course, as my criticisms of hegemony theory suggest, that answer must be qualified. In this line, I am going to argue that hegemony sport theory can be successfully appropriated in two ways.

The first and more straightforward way requires no conceptual revision of any consequence to hegemony theory. I am thinking here especially of its important account of the institutionalization of sport and other cultural practices. The focus on how such social forms evolve, operate, change, and vary their meanings—what Corrigan calls "thick" descriptions and Foucault calls "eventalized" analyses—is an integral part of any critically oriented social theory, and one in which hegemony theory has much to offer. I also have in mind here its attention to the basic and daily detail of class life within capitalist society, and its vigilance regarding the activities of the underclasses. No critical theory of sport can simply ignore the dynamics of class life in modern society, and however unpromising the actions of subordinate groups may appear at present, that is no reason to write off such groups, or analyses in which they figure, in perpetuity. On both of these counts, therefore, hegemony theory deserves our critical acclaim if not assent.

The second, more fundamental way in which hegemony theory can be appropriated does, however, require a substantial revision of its conceptual framework. To demonstrate this I need to backtrack my argument somewhat. There are, I contend, two theoretical gambits or language games that run through hegemony sport theory. The major one involves its theory of radical "interactionism." In this theory, we get a broad and rather undifferentiated account of the social constitution of sport that links it indissolubly and irrevocably to the constitution of social reality. This is the source of its prohibition of any effort to extricate sport from its social setting, and of its refusal to privilege sport or any of the other social practices that make up the cultural realm of society.

The minor language game unaccountably reverses the above stricture against privileging social practices and accords certain practices like sport an honorific place in the social world on the basis of their alleged autonomous standing. In a manner of argument directly reminiscent of those of idealist theorists like Michael Novak, it is claimed that sport's form really is set apart by its constituting structures, and that the insulation of its form allows it to both suspend social reality and offer some dramatic commentary on it.[155] So viewed, sports become social texts that enable us to tell stories about ourselves in an exciting, imaginative, and lively venue that challenges our everyday significations and meanings.[156] What this revised social-text thesis of sport amounts to, therefore, is a new hegemonic emancipatory narrative that trades not on the vitality of class conflict and agency but on the tension between capitalist patterns of rationalization and the capacity of sport to dramatize basic features of social life.

I find this second language game of hegemony theory to be an intriguing one, and one that I will try to incorporate, with some important modifications, in my reconstructed theory of sport. But the more immediate and important point at issue here is that these two language games cannot be reconciled with each other. The first language game of radical "interactionism" operates at cross-purposes to the second language game of autonomous social texts. The reason why this is so is the very same one that hegemonists invoked earlier to discredit such dramatic theories of sport: that they all falsely presume, in a quasi-idealist manner, that sport can somehow be placed above its constitutive social reality and creatively represent that reality.[157] So the second gambit that hegemonists periodically flirt with requires making an argumentative move that is expressly forbidden by the first. There is then no way to get from one language game to the other. Indeed, if one chooses to play the first game what we end up with is not an optimistic view of sport as an autonomous practice but a pessimistic one based on its apparent inability to incite the right kind of oppositional agency among subordinate groups. I take, therefore, Critcher's following conclusion to be emblematic of the deep pessimism of this first gambit: "to look for alternative ideals implicitly critical of dominant values, we have to look outside of what we define as sport."[158]

That these two language games are fundamentally incompatible with one another is no doubt why Gruneau for one was clever enough to enframe them in a paradox. He begins and ends his book *Class, Sports, and Social Development* with the thesis of the basic paradoxy of sport. But we have good reason to be suspicious of this so-termed paradoxy. Just as the appeal to a god in Greek tragedy often signals the disclosure of an incoherence in its moral standards and vocabulary,[159] so, I maintain, the appeal to paradox in hegemony sport theory often signals the disclosure of an incoherence in its conceptual standards and vocabulary. To see this we need only recognize that to say that something is a paradox is to say both that it is a contradiction and that that contradiction is rationally inexplicable. But I submit that what we have in this instance is not a genuine paradox but a genuine contradiction. The alleged paradox of sport can be rationally explained as an ill-fated attempt to integrate two opposed language games, the consequence of which is, unsurprisingly, a bold-faced contradiction. What follows from this contradiction is not that sport itself is inexplicable, only sport taken up in this confused (pseudoparadoxical) way. That means that if we are going to be able to provide an adequate rational account of sport, then one of these language games must give way to the other. And what must give way, I argue, is the problematic radical interactionist strand of hegemony theory in favor of some critically fortified version of its autonomous strand.

NOTES

1. Antonio Gramsci, *Prison Notebooks* (New York: International, 1971); Anthony Giddens, *Studies in Social and Political Theory* (New York: Basic Books, 1977); Michel Foucault, *Discipline and Punish* (New York: Vintage Books, 1979); Pierre Bourdieu, *Distinction: A Social Critique of the Judgment of Taste* (Cambridge, Mass.: Harvard University Press, 1984). Of course, Giddens, Foucault, and Bourdieu are not themselves hegemonists.

2. R. Hoggart, *The Uses of Literacy* (London, 1977); Raymond Williams, *Culture and Society* (London: Penguin Books, 1961); E. P. Thompson, *The Making of the Working Class* (Hardmondsworth: Pelican Books, 1968).

3. Richard S. Gruneau, *Class, Sports, and Social Development* (Amherst: University of Massachusetts Press, 1983); John Hargreaves, *Sport, Power and Culture* (New York: St. Martin's, 1986).

4. John Clarke and Chas Critcher, *The Devil Makes Work* (London: Macmillan, 1985); Philip Corrigan, "The Politics of Feeling Good," in *Popular Cultures and Political Practices*, ed. Richard Gruneau (Toronto: Garamond Press, 1988), pp. 43–50; Chas Critcher, "Radical Theorists of Sport: The State of Play," *Sociology of Sport Journal* 3 (1986): 333–43; Peter Donnelly, "Sport as a Site for 'Popular' Resistance," in *Popular Cultures and Political Practices*, ed. Gruneau, pp. 69–82; Stephen Hardy and Alan Ingham, "Games, Structures, and Agency: Historians on the American Play Movement," *Journal of Social History* 17 (1983): 285–301; Robert Hollands, "Leisure, Work and Working-Class Cultures," in *Leisure, Sport and Working-Class Cultures*, ed. Hart Cantelon and Robert Hollands (Toronto: Garamond Press, 1988), pp. 17–39; Alan Ingham and Stephen Hardy, "Sport, Structuration, Subjugation and Hegemony," *Theory, Culture, and Society* 2 (1984): 85–103; Jim McKay, "Marxism as a Way of Seeing: Beyond the Limits of Current 'Critical' Approaches to Sport," *Sociology of Sport Journal* 3 (1986): 261–72; Bryan Palmer, "'What the Hell,'" in *Popular Culture and Political Practices*, ed. Richard Gruneau (Toronto: Garamond Press, 1988), pp. 33–42; Alan Tomlinson, "Good Times, Bad Times, and the Politics of Leisure," in *Leisure, Sport and Working Class Cultures*, ed. Cantelon and Hollands, pp. 41–64; David Whitson, "Structure, Agency, and the Sociology of Sport Debates," *Theory, Culture and Society* 3 (1986): 99–106. The books of Gruneau and Hargreaves mentioned above as well as their various overlapping essays belong here as well.

5. The criticism of ethnographic inquiry is not shared by Tomlinson, for one; he makes wide use of this approach in his work. See his "Good Times, Bad Times, and the Politics of Leisure," p. 44.

6. Gruneau, *Class, Sports, and Social Development*, pp. 9–15.

7. For the specifics of this critique of idealist theories of sport see Gruneau, *Class, Sports, and Social Development*, pp. 27–30, 44; Hargreaves, *Sport, Power and Culture*, p. 2; and Critcher, "Radical Theorists of Sport," p. 335.

8. Critcher, "Radical Theorists of Sport," p. 335; Gruneau, *Class, Sports, and Social Development*, p. 37; idem, "Freedom and Constraint: The Paradoxes of Play, Games, and Sports," *Journal of Sport History* 3 (Winter 1980): 73.

9. Gruneau, *Class, Sports, and Social Development*, p. 37.

10. Gruneau, "Sport and the Debate on the State," in *Sport, Culture, and the Modern State*, ed. Hart Cantelon and Richard Gruneau (Toronto: University of Toronto Press, 1982), p. 26.

11. Gruneau, "Introduction," in *Popular Cultures and Political Practices*, p. 14.

12. Gruneau, *Class, Sports, and Social Development*, pp. 38, 87.

13. Ibid., p. 17.

14. Ibid., pp. 17, 21.

15. Ibid., p. 28; Gruneau, "Sport and the Debate on the State," pp. 27, 28.

16. Gruneau, *Class, Sports, and Social Development*, p. 72.

17. Ibid., p. 171 n. 35.

18. Ibid., pp. 50–51.

19. Raymond Williams, *Marxism and Literature* (Oxford: Oxford University Press, 1977), pp. 80–81, 87. See also Stuart Hall, "Cultural Studies: Two Paradigms," in *Culture, Ideology and Social Process*, ed. Tony Bennett et al. (London: Open University Press, 1987), pp. 23, 26.

20. For the general argument to this effect see Williams, *Marxism and Literature*, p. 91, and for its application to sport see Gruneau, *Class, Sports, and Social Development*, p. 55. By in effect junking the base-superstructure schema of classical Marxism, Williams and his disciples took themselves to be faithfully executing Marx's injunction to make cultural history material. That injunction, they argued, was violated by consigning cultural life to the once-removed, secondary, and dependent sphere of the superstructure. For further discussion of this point see Williams, *Marxism and Literature*, pp. 18–19.

21. Gruneau, *Class, Sports, and Social Development*, p. 55, 61–62; Clarke and Critcher, *The Devil Makes Work*, p. xii; Hollands, "Leisure, Work and Working-Class Culture," pp. 17, 31.

22. Gruneau, *Class, Sports, and Social Development*, p. 165 n. 42.

23. See Giddens, *Studies in Social and Political Theory*, p. 130. For an adaptation of Giddens's theory of structures to sport, see Hardy and Ingham, "Games, Structures, and Agency," p. 286.

24. Gruneau, *Class, Sports, and Social Development*, pp. 55–56.

25. Ibid., p. 59.

26. Ibid., pp. 59, 142.

27. Ibid., pp. 60–61.

28. Ibid., pp. 61–62.

29. Samuel Bowles and Herbert Gintis, *Democracy and Capitalism* (New York: Basic Books, 1986), p. 127.

30. Gruneau, *Class, Sports, and Social Development*, pp. 65, 169 n. 22.

31. Ibid., p. 81.

32. Ibid., p. 129.

33. Ibid., p. 62.

34. Ibid., pp. 62, 65.

35. Hargreaves, *Sport, Power and Culture*, p. 208.

36. Gruneau, *Class, Sports, and Social Development*, p. 170 n. 27.

37. Williams, *Marxism and Literature*, p. 118.

38. Williams cautions in this regard that because of the dynamic character of hegemonic processes even the use of the concept of hegemony to refer to such processes can degenerate into an ossified abstraction. The remedy for this, Williams suggests, is to give the concept an adjectival rather than a nominal form, to speak, that is, of the hegemonic rather than hegemony. Katherine Gallagher discerns in this remedy a general rule for concept construction in hegemony theory. As she states, "Williams judges concepts according to the ease with which they can be converted into adjectival modifications of the one allowable [and least reified] noun in his lexicon, 'process.' . . . The more static, idealist, or deterministic a concept is, the more stubbornly nominal, the more dangerous it appears." "The New Materialism in Marxist Aesthetics," *Theory and Society* 9 (July 1980): 642–43. Whether or not Williams's preoccupation with adjectival forms amounts to, as Gallagher insinuates, a kind of "obsessive de-reification" is a matter for critical debate.

39. Williams, *Marxism and Literature*, pp. 130–33.

40. For a fuller discussion of this point and its implications for historiography see Hardy and Ingham, "Games, Structures, and Agency," p. 291.

41. Gruneau, *Class, Sports, and Social Development*, p. 149.

42. Hollands, "Leisure, Work and Working-Class Cultures," p. 30.

43. Gruneau, *Class, Sports, and Social Development*, p. 51.

44. Corrigan, "The Politics of Feeling Good," p. 45.

45. This is the basis of Gruneau's critique of conservative, idealist-tending theories of sport that appeal to sport's "playful essence" as a critical standard by which to judge its modern degradation. The problem with all such appeals, according to Gruneau, is that they abstractly separate play as an *ideal* from the real social process. *Class, Sports, and Social Development*, pp. 162–63 n. 24.

46. Ibid., p. 56.

47. Ibid., p. 58.

48. Ibid., pp. 58–59.

49. Ingham and Hardy, "Sport, Structuration, Subjugation and Hegemony," pp. 90–92. In fairness to Gruneau, however, he does insist that people can search for alternatives to institutional sport at the personal and local level, and that local sports have not been completely co-opted by the former. On this and related points see his *Class, Sports, and Social Development*, pp. 147, 151.

50. See Ingham and Hardy, "Sport, Structuration, Subjugation and Hegemony," pp. 92–93. Of further interest here is David Whitson's essay "Structure, Agency and the Sociology of Sport Debates," p. 100. This argument resembles to some extent Rigauer's argument that the less encumbered by rules a sporting activity is, the more free it is. See his *Sport and Work* (New York: Columbia University Press, 1981), p. 103.

51. See Corrigan, "The Politics of Feeling Good," p. 46.

52. Williams, *Marxism and Literature*, p. 122.

53. Gruneau, *Class, Sports, and Social Development*, pp. 145–46.

54. Williams, *Marxism and Literature*, pp. 125–26.

55. Other examples of emergent sporting practices would include countercultural recreational activities such as surfing, frisbee, and early "hot dog" skiing as well as high risk sports. All of these activities grew out of a disaffection with the overly organized and rather bland character of institutional sports. For a more detailed discussion of such sports see Peter Donnelly's essay "Sport as a Site for 'Popular' Resistance," p. 74.

56. Gruneau, *Class, Sports, and Social Development*, pp. 147–48, and *Popular Cultures and Political Practices*, p. 21.

57. Raymond Williams, *Towards 2000* (London: Chatto and Windus, 1982), as quoted in Corrigan's "The Politics of Feeling Good," p. 44.

58. Palmer, "What the Hell," pp. 40–41.

59. Gruneau, *Class, Sports, and Social Development*, p. 152.

60. Ibid., p. 148.

61. Bourdieu, *Distinction*, pp. 209–10. Bourdieu argues further along these lines that "tennis played in Bermuda shorts and a tee shirt, in a track suit or even swimming trunks, and Adidas running-shoes, is indeed another tennis, both in the way it is played and in the satisfaction it gives" (p. 212).

62. Gruneau, *Class, Sports, and Social Development*, p. 191 n. 128.

63. As I discuss above, hegemonists frequently resort to theoretical claims and pronouncements regarding the supposed fragile nature of all hegemonic compacts in order to offset the plainly pessimistic import of their historical findings. Whether or not their use of theory here as a kind of damage-control device succeeds is a matter for my subsequent critique of hegemony theory.

64. Gruneau, *Class, Sports, and Social Development*, p. 126.

65. Palmer, "What the Hell," pp. 36–37.

66. The most prominent victims of "official" sport include the previously mentioned black and women's sport movements as well as the more whimsical new games movement. None of these movements was apparently able to surmount the technocratic disposition, the rational utilitarian ethic, the market model of competition, and the linear conception of excellence that collectively comprise the dominant moment of sport. On the characterization of dominant sport see Gruneau, *Class, Sports, and Social Development*, pp. 135, 143, 152.

67. Tomlinson, "Good Times, Bad Times, and the Politics of Leisure," p. 59.

68. Gruneau, *Class, Sports, and Social Development*, p. 47.

69. Critcher, "Radical Theorists of Sport," p. 343.

70. Gruneau, *Class, Sports, and Social Development*, p. 145.

71. Critcher, "Radical Theorists of Sport," p. 340.

72. Hargreaves, *Sport, Power and Culture*, p. 7.

73. Gruneau, *Class, Sports, and Social Development*, p. 37. For a discussion of this point see p. 62, above.

74. That is not to say, however, that one couldn't make an ideological point of the New Left's reductionist tendency. One could focus, for example, as I

will do in Chapter 3, on the social interests served by the merger of sport and labor. But such an ideological tack, I argue here, is foreign to the conceptual arsenal of hegemony theory.

75. Gruneau, *Class, Sports, and Social Development*, p. 44.

76. Ibid., p. 139. See also Hargreaves, "Sport and Hegemony: Some Theoretical Problems," in *Sport, Culture, and the Modern State*, ed. Cantelon and Gruneau, p. 130, and Hargreaves, *Sport, Power and Culture*, pp. 111–12.

77. The scant criticism is also due, less grandly, to the still-marginal status of critical theory in North American sociological circles, and, ironically, to the absence of a critical tradition within hegemony theory itself. The two points are not unrelated. The marginal status of critical scholarship has apparently prompted hegemonists, and like-minded critical souls, to forestall significant criticism of each other's work in an effort to maintain a united front in their advocacy of a critical approach to the study of sport. The specter of critical theorists criticizing one another presumably threatens that unity and that advocacy. Since I hold the opposite view, that sober and well-grounded criticism (rational argumentation as opposed to bellicose saber-rattling) actually strengthens rather than weakens the efficacy of critical theory, I am encouraged by the increasingly critical tone of some of the more recent exchanges between, for example, feminists and hegemonists.

78. Even in this instance, as noted above, there are rather severe prescriptions regarding what can and cannot be abstractly marked off. See Gruneau, *Class, Sports, and Social Development*, pp. 50–51.

79. Richard Rorty, "Pragmatism and Philosophy," in *Consequences of Pragmatism* (Minneapolis: University of Minnesota Press, 1982), p. xlii.

80. My criticism of the unimaginative status of the hegemonist charge that the social genesis of sport nullifies its autonomous standing is analogous to Marx's criticism of the unimaginative status of "hitherto existing materialism's" claim that the "thing, reality, sensuousness" is essentially and merely an object as opposed to a form of *"human, sensuous, practice."* It is also worth noting in this regard that just as it was left up to idealism to develop the notion of sport as an autonomous practice, so it was left up to idealism, Marx argued, to conceive of the active side of the object. Idealism erred in both cases, of course, by only developing these notions abstractly. See Marx's "Theses on Feuerbach," in *Marx and Engels: Basic Writings of Politics and Philosophy*, ed. Lewis S. Feuer (New York: Anchor Books, 1959), p. 243.

81. Gruneau, *Class, Sports, and Social Development*, pp. 60–61. In this same passage, Gruneau already mistakenly refers to the regulative, moral limits of sport as its constitutive structures.

82. Charles Taylor, "Hermeneutics and Politics," in *Critical Sociology*, ed. Paul Connerton (New York: Penguin Books, 1976), p. 175.

83. John Searle, *Speech Acts* (Cambridge: Cambridge University Press, 1969), p. 42.

84. Peter Winch, *The Idea of a Social Science and Its Relation to Philosophy* (London: Routledge and Kegan Paul, 1977), p. 30. The more immediate and specific point Winch tried to make with this example was that the intelligi-

bility of the notion of "following a rule" requires, among other things, that others be able to fathom just what sort of rule one is following.

85. Searle, *Speech Acts,* p. 34.

86. Ibid.

87. Ibid., p. 35.

88. My argument here is a gloss of an argument I made in my essay "Radical Social Theory of Sport: A Critique and a Conceptual Emendation," *Sociology of Sport Journal* 2 (1985): 62–63.

89. Bernard Suits, "Sticky Wickedness: Games and Morality," *Dialogue* 21 (1982): 757.

90. The folly and unduly speculative nature of such arguments are apparent in the contradictory claims they often give rise to. For example, Novak claims that American football is essentially a "socialist" game and McMurtry claims that it is essentially a "capitalist" game. It is of course neither. See Michael Novak, *The Joy of Sports* (New York: Basic Books, 1976), p. 77; John McMurtry, "The Illusions of a Football Fan: A Reply to Michalos," *Journal of the Philosophy of Sport* 4 (1977): 11–14. For a fascinating, but no less speculative, account of the cultural configurations of European soccer and American baseball and football, see Andrei Markovits, "The Other 'American Exceptionalism'—Why Is There No Soccer in the United States?," pp. 125–50; and Charles Maier's "Comment on Andrei Markovits, 'The Other American Exceptionalism,'" pp. 151–54. Both of these essays were published in *Praxis International* 8:2 (July 1988).

91. The criticism I make of hegemony theory in this instance is not unknown in hegemonic circles. No less of a pivotal figure than Raymond Williams warned that "there is equal danger in an opposite kind of error, in which the generalizing and connecting impulse is so strong that we lose sight of real specificities and distinctions of practice, which are then neglected or reduced to simulations of more general forms." *Marxism and Literature,* p. 143; see also p. 93. There is little evidence, however, that Williams heeded his own warning. The reason why he didn't is attributable, no doubt, to his conviction that the practice of insulating social practices from one another was the main ideological tendency in capitalist society. My subsequent ideological argument will maintain just the opposite: that the changing tenor of the times encourages the practice of conflating social practices with one another.

92. I have borrowed this example and the general line of argument from Suits, "Sticky Wickedness," p. 757.

93. See Chapter 1, pp. 43–44.

94. Williams, *Marxism and Literature,* pp. 117, 119.

95. Gruneau, *Class, Sports, and Social Development,* pp. 50, 54.

96. Ibid., p. 58. Aside from other paradox-laden passages, this particular passage and snippets of other scattered passages are the closest Gruneau comes to this view.

97. Ibid., p. 59. In accord with my previous criticism, Gruneau does not quite say this as clearly as I intimate here.

98. Ibid., pp. 21–22, 59.

99. Ibid., p. 21.

100. Crew would be but one example. On this point, see David Halberstam's riveting account of this sport in his book *The Amateurs* (New York: Morrow, 1985).

101. Gruneau, *Class, Sports, and Social Development*, p. 59.

102. Ingham and Hardy, "Sport, Structuration, Subjugation and Hegemony," p. 89.

103. Gruneau, *Class, Sports, and Social Development*, pp. 25, 28, 162–63.

104. Gruneau is quite explicit on this point and argues that the technical and moral limits of sport are "those limits most commonly perceived as occurring *within* institutionalized games and sports." Ibid., p. 60.

105. What is vexing about this radical conflation of social practices and institutions is that it reduces talk about the latter to gibberish. As I argue above, institutions presuppose the prior existence of practices. In their absence, it is hard to make sense of just what an institution is supposed to be or do.

106. Jeffrey Stout, "Liberal Society and the Languages of Morals," *Soundings* 69 (Spring 1986): 55.

107. Searle, *Speech Acts*, pp. 50–53. The distinction between this philosophical sense of an institution and its sociological sense, which as I note above *largely* prefigures my distinction between a practice and an institution, can be traced to Arnold Gehlen's book *Urmensch und Spätkultur*. In this regard, Gehlen distinguished between the ordinary language sense of institution as the intentional foundation of an activity and/or project, and the Latin notion of institution (*institutio*, "custom") as the pre-given, habitual, unquestioned character of human behavior and action. I owe this point to Hans Blumenberg's essay "An Anthropological Approach to the Contemporary Significance of Rhetoric," in *After Philosophy: End or Transformation?* ed. Kenneth Baynes et al. (Cambridge, Mass.: MIT Press, 1987), p. 457.

108. Gruneau, "Introduction," *Popular Cultures and Political Practices*, p. 25.

109. Ibid., p. 27.

110. Gruneau, *Class, Sports, and Social Development*, p. 129.

111. Ibid., p. 82. The one exception to this omission of any reference to the liberal notion of choice and individual agency within the hegemonic camp is Palmer's concession that liberal institutions allow individuals a small measure of self-determination. But Palmer does little more than mention this point. See p. 77, above.

112. Karl Marx, *Capital, Vol. 1* (New York: Vintage, 1977), p. 92. In saying this, however, I am not saying that either Marx or hegemonists simply reduce individuals to their economic and social roles. They are always, of course, more than this, but they are more than this without shedding the social relations that they bear and exemplify.

113. On this point, see Michael Walzer, "Liberalism and the Art of Separation," *Political Theory* 12 (August 1984): 317. I will have considerably more to say about all of this in Chapter 5.

114. For a criticism of Marxism's aversion to liberal partitions and walls see Bowles and Gintis, *Democracy and Capitalism*, pp. 18–19.

115. Rosa Luxemburg, *The Russian Revolution: Leninism or Marxism* (Ann Arbor: University of Michigan Press, 1961), p. 62, as quoted in Max Horkheimer, *Critical Theory* (New York: Herder and Herder, 1972), p. viii.

116. Horkheimer, *Critical Theory*, p. viii. It should also be noted that Adorno was keenly aware of the threats to the individual posed by mass society and tirelessly searched for surviving traces of it that could withstand the integrative forces of advanced capitalism. Interestingly enough, one place where he found such traces of selfhood still largely intact was in the sphere of leisure. See his essay "Freizeit," *Gesammelte Schriften Vol. 10* (Frankfurt. Suhrkamp, 1983), p. 655. For an analysis of this and other features of Adorno's theory of sport see my essay "Adorno on Sport: The Case of the Fractured Dialectic," *Theory and Society* 17 (1988): 813–38. It is also noteworthy in this regard that Marxism's failure to seriously engage liberal notions of democracy and individual liberty has precipitated a wide ranging reassessment of liberal democracy in Western Marxist circles. Evidently, many of the theorists who work in these circles agree with Walter Adamson that "orthodox Marxism's single greatest embarrassment is not the failure of its historical predictions, or the reluctance of the working classes to follow its political lead, but its contempt for 'bourgeois' democracy." "Convergences in Recent Democratic Theory," *Theory and Society* 18 (January 1989): 126. For the attempt at some rapprochement between liberalism and Marxism in the so-called Budapest school of Marxism, see Ernesto Laclau and Chantal Mouffe's *Hegemony and Socialist Strategy: Toward a Radical Democratic Politics* (London: Verso, 1985); on the Frankfurt school see Jürgen Habermas's *The Theory of Communicative Action, Volume I* (Boston: Beacon Press, 1984), and on analytic Marxism see Jon Elster's brilliant book *Making Sense of Marx* (Cambridge: Cambridge University Press, 1987).

117. Jon Elster, "Belief, Bias and Ideology," in *Rationality and Relativism*, ed. Martin Hollis and Steven Lukes (Oxford: Basil Blackwell, 1982), p. 123.

118. Walzer argues for this very point and goes on to claim that critical theorists should enlist "liberal artfulness" regarding such things as "protected spaces" in the service of socialism. "Liberalism and the Art of Separation," p. 318. I fully concur with Walzer, and will make an argument to this effect in Chapter 5.

119. Walzer, "Liberalism and the Art of Separation," p. 320.

120. Palmer, "What the Hell," pp. 38–39.

121. I refer here to Gruneau's general endorsement of Palmer's essay, not to mention all the other essays that appear in his edited collection *Popular Cultures and Political Practices*, as representing the kind of "cautious" optimism that he approvingly associates with the Gramscian turn in analyses of popular cultures. See his "Introduction" to that volume, p. 27.

122. The above schema of hegemonic agency was distilled from the following sources: Hardy and Ingham, "Games, Structures, and Agency," pp. 292–93, 297; Gruneau, *Class, Sports, and Social Development*, pp. 148, 151; Ingham and Hardy, "Sport, Structuration, Subjugation and Hegemony," pp. 90–91; Donnelly, "Sport as a Site for 'Popular' Resistance," pp. 71, 74.

123. Gruneau, *Class, Sports, and Social Development*, p. 147.

124. The evidence amassed by hegemonists on this point is rather overwhelming. See Gruneau, *Class, Sports, and Social Development*, pp. 126–82; Hardy and Ingham, "Games, Structures, and Agency," pp. 293, 297; Hargreaves, *Sport, Power and Culture*, p. 67. Hegemonists' criticism of the ineffectual and largely reformist bent of the response of the working class to the dominant moment of sport, which led to democratic reforms that had little if any transformative effect, presages the larger point Bowles and Gintis have made regarding the mobilization of the working class in periods of social conflict. That point is, as they argue, that "where workers' movements have mobilized more than handfuls of isolated militants—as in England in the early nineteenth century, in Germany in the late nineteenth and early twentieth century, or in Italy or Spain in the twentieth century—their inspiration and their solidarity has been based more on the demand for democracy than for socialism." *Democracy and Capitalism*, p. 62.

125. Two further points follow from this one. First, notwithstanding the genuine historical sensitivity, if not ingenuity, hegemonists have displayed in their various considerations of sport, their seeming indifference to their own formidable pessimistic historical findings suggest simply another variation of what Clarke and Critcher aptly call the use of history to "dehistorize" leisure. *The Devil Makes Work*, p. 46. Second, the hegemonists attempted to allay certain misgivings that members of the so-called Frankfurt school had about the working class as an agent of social change by appealing principally to its penchant for engaging in oppositional agency of the level 2 and level 4 variety. This attempt is flawed because Horkheimer's and Adorno's doubts concerning the working class stemmed not from any simple-minded view that they were merely dupes of the system, passive receptacles of bourgeois ideological directives. (Though this is, unfortunately, the popular view of their position, it is in fact a caricatured view of their actual position.) Rather their doubts were historically well founded ones about whether or not the working class was capable of mounting a genuinely radical response to their bourgeois masters. Hegemonists offer precious little solace about this prospect.

126. For a particularly lucid account of this argument see Rorty, *Consequences of Pragmatism*, pp. 200–202.

127. See Martin Jay, *Fin de Siècle Socialism* (New York: Routledge, 1988), pp. 67–81.

128. Gruneau, "Introduction," *Popular Cultures and Political Practices*, p. 21.

129. Gruneau, *Class, Sports, and Social Development*, pp. 140, 148.

130. Rorty, *Consequences of Pragmatism*, p. 200. While Rorty argues that a person's, or group's, or culture's own account of itself does not warrant epistemological privilege, it does warrant moral privilege. As he provocatively puts it, "The reason why we invite the moronic psychopath to address the court before being sentenced is not that we hope for better explanations than expert testimony has offered. We do so because he is, after all, one of us. By asking for his own account, we hope to decrease our chances of acting badly" (p. 202).

131. Elster, "Belief, Bias and Ideology," p. 130.

132. For further examples of such see Elster, "Belief, Bias and Ideology," pp. 130–32.

133. Palmer, "What the Hell," p. 37.

134. Hollands, "Leisure, Work and Working-Class Cultures," p. 32.

135. Hargreaves, *Sport, Power and Culture*, p. 112.

136. Palmer, "What the Hell," p. 38. The larger point Palmer and other hegemonists attempt to make here is that paradox is one of the principal ways in which hegemony works itself out. I have been implying all along, however, that in this and other similar cases we are not dealing so much with an inexplicable paradox as we are with a quite explicable contradiction. The present contradiction is that one and the same act in one and the same sense can be both oppositional and affirmative. It is only by equivocating on what counts as an oppositional act, I argue, that hegemonists are able to finesse this and other blatant contradictions as paradoxes.

137. Williams, *Marxism and Literature*, pp. 125–26.

138. See Hardy and Ingham, "Games, Structures, and Agency," p. 249.

139. Wallace Clement, "Response to Gruneau and Taylor," in *Sport, Culture, and the Modern State*, ed. Cantelon and Gruneau, p. 100.

140. Williams, *Marxism and Literature*, p. 114.

141. Ibid.

142. Ibid.

143. My claim that hegemony theory is unable to account for extrahegemonic agency does not mean that it doesn't allow for the possibility of such agency. Its view that constraints on action are best conceived as limits rather than as absolute determinants clearly allows for the occurrence of such agency. But, I argue, the fact that such agency is conceivable in no way explains its actual occurrence in certain specified times or places.

144. Gruneau, *Class, Sports, and Social Development*, p. 152.

145. Ibid., p. 148.

146. Tomlinson, "Good Times, Bad Times, and the Politics of Leisure," pp. 59–61. Tomlinson rightly points out that the hedonistic tendencies of the working class are not altogether crass or blind ones, but spring in part from a sober and realistic reckoning of the limited opportunities they have to change things for the better.

147. Hargreaves, *Sport, Power and Culture*, pp. 82–83.

148. John J. MacAloon, "An Observer's View of Sport Sociology," *Sociology of Sport Journal* 4 (1987): 108.

149. Alaisdair MacIntyre, *After Virtue* (Notre Dame, Ind.: University of Notre Dame Press, 1984), p. 103. My following discussion of this point is also drawn from *After Virtue*, pp. 103–8.

150. MacIntyre, *After Virtue*, p. 106.

151. Hilary Putnam, *Reason, Truth and History* (Cambridge: Cambridge University Press, 1981), p. 119.

152. As Rorty argues, "relativism is the view that every belief on a certain topic, or perhaps about *any* topic, is as good as every other. No one holds this view." *Consequences of Pragmatism*, p. 166.

153. MacIntyre, *After Virtue*, p. 251.

154. For Palmer's version of this hegemonic argument see "What the Hell," pp. 40–41.

155. Gruneau, *Class, Sports, and Social Development*, pp. 149–50.

156. The apparent ability of sports, conceived as popular forms of theater, to communicate shared experiences and feelings in this way is why Hargreaves likens them to the great festivals of medieval Europe. See his "Sport and Hegemony: Some Theoretical Problems," in *Sport, Culture, and the Modern State*, ed. Cantelon and Gruneau, pp. 124–25. In an earlier essay, however, Hargreaves gave a less flattering assessment of the dramatic capacity of sport and claimed that it was sadly deficient to "purer" dramatic forms such as the cinema and the theater and that it encouraged escapism. In this regard, see his essay "The Political Economy of Mass Sport," in *Sport and Leisure in Contemporary Society*, ed. Stanley Parker (1975).

157. See Gruneau, *Class, Sports, and Social Development*, pp. 72. See also p. 64, above.

158. Critcher also puts it more cryptically: "the only way to reform sport is to convert it into something else that ceases to be sport." "Radical Theorists of Sport," pp. 340, 342.

159. I owe this point to MacIntyre, *After Virtue*, p. 132.

THREE

The Corruption of Sport and Its Ideological Distortion

In the previous chapters I have argued that both the New Left and hegemonist currents of critical sport theory are beset by serious conceptual errors. I now want to argue that those conceptual errors are socially backed ones, more specifically, that they are ideologically induced mistakes that derive whatever intelligibility they possess from a certain dominant, but false, picture of prevailing social reality. In particular, I will argue that the Left's conception of sport as radically continuous with its social setting seems plausible in an advanced capitalist society that seems bent on reducing everything that goes on within its borders to matters of money, status, and power. In claiming this, I am not only alleging that the beguiling force of the Left's errant conceptions of sport can be traced to this new integrationist phase of capitalist society and to the picture of social reality it fosters, but further that the way in which the institutions of that society are presently structured requires that we confound the character of sport and other social practices in just this radically contextualized way.

In order to support my claim that the Left's reductionist renderings of sport are ideologically grounded, however, I must first offer some account of the social forces that actually corrupt and undermine social practices like sport. It is only by way of such an account that I can specify in just what sense the Left's strong contextualist readings of sport go awry in their own assessment of those pathological forces, and in doing so, further their corrosive effect.

Social Practices, Social Institutions, and the Degradation of Sport

The assessment of the social influences that degrade human endeavors such as sport is made easier, if not surer, today by the remarkable unanimity among contemporary social and political theorists as to the larger social forces that degrade society as a whole. What makes this virtual unanimity all the more remarkable is that it comes from a politically and intellectually diverse band of thinkers a short list of which would include people such as Bellah, Bernstein, Dewey, Habermas, MacIntyre, Meilander, Rorty, Stout, Tawney, and Walzer.[1] One will find represented on this short list some liberal agitators, a couple of theologically inspired political critics, a well-known antimodernist Aristotelian, and the most famous living exponent of the so-called Frankfurt school of Marxism. What unites this curious assortment of social critics is the view that advanced capitalist societies suffer from a surfeit of the economic, from an unprecedented onslaught of market imperatives and influences that threaten to disrupt and overwhelm everything else it is that people do that might be properly described as noneconomic. These men are in full accord that the distinctive rationality, values, and aims of the market have exercised an untoward influence on the organization and conduct of modern life that exceeds its proper sphere of influence and worth.

As one might suspect, there are a myriad of theoretical idioms, at least as many as the theorists cited above, within which one might press this critique of contemporary capitalist society and its desecration of noneconomic human endeavors. One could, for example, pursue this criticism as Tawney does when he argues, "The burden of our civilization is not merely, as many suppose, that the product of industry is ill-distributed, or its conduct tyrannical, or its operation interrupted by embittered disagreements. It is that industry itself has come to hold a position of exclusive predominance among human interests, which no single interest, least of all the provision of the material means of existence, is fit to occupy."[2] Or one could adopt Habermas's denser theoretical prose and criticize contemporary capitalism for its "colonization" of the practices of the lifeworld by the systemic organizational and bureaucratic pressures it exerts upon them. In Habermasian language, then, what defiles human practices is the displacement of their inner logics and forms of consensual agreement by the "steering media" (principally money and power) of the capitalist economy and state, which imbue such practices with their own instrumental brand of rationality and administrative forms of coordinating action.[3]

For present purposes, however, I will frame my criticism of the lop-sided market orientation of late capitalism in terms of Alaisdair Mac-Intyre's idiom of social practices and institutions. I will do so because it is, in my estimation, the most perspicacious idiom we have at our disposal. Its perspicacity has to do in the main with its ability to grasp and explain what the Left's own inarticulate and blurred distinction between the practice of sport and its institutionalization is unable to grasp or explain fully: that while much of what is called sport these days is infected with the rational demeanor and ethic of the market, particularly the entertainment market, there is more to sport than is evident in its business side. That is, it captures the sense of former boxer Ken Norton's lament that boxing is a wonderful sport but a dirty business, and of Neil Postman's observation that despite sport's close association with the entertainment business it is still possible to attach virtues such as clarity, honesty, and excellence to its prac-tice.[4] However, what is most important about MacIntyre's rendering of the practice-institution distinction, and what prompts my present use of it, is that it is able to account for what is potentially corrupt-ing about the double standing (as business ventures and as endeav-ors geared toward excellence) of practices like sport. What is poten-tially corrupting about the double standing of these endeavors is that their business side may come to overshadow their practice side. This possibility is structurally rooted, MacIntyre argues, in the present ten-dentious relation that obtains between practices and institutions, which is itself rooted in the one-sided process of rationalization that has shaped advanced capitalist society. It is a well-entrenched tenden-cy of this rationalization process to supplant the logic and goods of practices with the logic and goods of institutions, which are them-selves modeled after business enterprises and driven, accordingly, by market interests.

Expressed in MacIntyre's vocabulary, then, what is pathological about late capitalist society is that it systematically and routinely usurps the logic and goods of practices by the logic and goods of institutions. So understood, everything depends on making clear the key terms of MacIntyre's distinction between practices and institutions.

By a social practice MacIntyre means something more than a mere aggregate of skillful actions framed by rules and a system of defined roles: a special kind of rule-governed activity defined by the standards of excellence and the internal goods that make it up. As he defines it then, a social practice is "any coherent and complex form of socially established cooperative activity through which goods internal to that form of activity are realized in the course of trying to achieve those standards of excellence, . . . with the result that human powers to achieve excellence, and human conceptions of the ends and goods involved, are systematically extended."[5] So understood, tic-tac-toe, throwing a football with skill, and planting turnips are not practices, but chess, football, architecture, music, painting, and science are practices. What apparently distinguishes the former from the latter is that activities such as tic-tac-toe are insufficiently complex and/or cooperative in their conduct and the kinds of excellence and goods they engage insufficiently sophisticated to count as practices in the relevant sense.

Two crucial elements of MacIntyre's definition of a practice distinguish it from other accounts of a practice and, most important, from the Left's own conception of a social practice. The first is the notion of internal goods. These sorts of goods are first and foremost social goods of a particular kind. They are not idiosyncratically held goods defined by our individual choices of them, nor are they merely mutually held goods defined by the culture, subculture, or particular group to which we belong. Rather, they are socially held goods that are defined by the particular practices that we take up. Their mutuality in this case is practice-specific as opposed to group-specific.

It is the practice-specific character of these social goods that warrants calling them, after MacIntyre, internal goods. These goods are internal to practices in two important senses: they cannot be achieved in any other way save by our engagement in said practices, and they can be recognized and specified as the particular goods that they are only by those who actually take up the practices in which they are embedded.[6] It follows, therefore, that only those who possess the requisite experience as participants in practices are fit to judge and otherwise assess their internal goods.

There are, additionally, two particular kinds of internal goods that are definitive of social practices. The first involves the standards of excellence of the practice itself, and of our attempt to measure up to and, if possible, surpass those standards. The second internal good of practices also derives from the pursuit of their standards of excellence. When we pursue such standards in a serious and committed way we are able to realize "the good of a certain kind of life" that is embodied in that pursuit, and that gives it its allure and charm.[7]

Both of these internal goods figure in our conception and experience of social practices, and play a large and indispensable role in shaping their rational complexion and demeanor. This can be seen quite clearly in the case of sport. The excellences that frame our sporting practices, and the good of the specific kinds of life that their pursuit discloses, provide their practitioners with a determinate reason to participate in them. Such a reason makes the attainment of their internal goods the foremost aim and purpose of their involvement. More specifically, they furnish a reason for taking up a practice such as soccer that makes the realization of the particular physical and strategic skills it calls for, and the practical judgment, competitive mettle, and challenges it requires, if not the whole, then certainly the main point of its practice.

What goes for soccer goes as well for all sporting and social practices. But, of course, there are goods of a different sort that can also be achieved by participating in practices. These goods have to do with the rewards that are often bestowed upon athletes and their counterparts for their distinguished accomplishments in practices. Since these goods, which run the gamut from materially valuable prizes to cash awards, and to a certain notoriety and even power that comes from being well known, are not specific to the practices in which they figure, they are best characterized as external goods. They are external goods in two relevant senses: there are always alternative ways of attaining such goods, and the attainment of such goods is never limited to participation in a particular practice.[8] Further, it follows from their external status that the link of such goods to practices such as sport is a contingent one that has more to do with the social circumstances in which such practices are conducted than with the actual practices themselves.[9]

So it is apparent that there are two kinds of goods that can be had by participating in practices like sport. Still, it is important not to obscure the important differences between them. The external goods that are awarded to athletes for their athletic achievements are not the same goods that are embodied in those achievements. The embodied goods have to do, as suggested above, with the pursuit of physical excellence that qualifies them as the particular athletic achievements they are. It is worth pointing out that for practitioners and other relevant participants at least the apparent incommensurability of these two kinds of goods is not, and typically has not been, treated as an idle intellectual curiosity, but rather as a pressing, and even at times an urgent, practical problem. The history of almost every sporting practice that we know anything definitive about is replete with arguments among its interested parties over whether the external goods that are meted out to successful athletes might impede, distract, or otherwise distort their quest for athletic excellence.

A second important difference between these two types of goods should also be noted here. This difference has to do with the reach and amplitude of the goods in question. With regard to external goods, that reach is largely confined to those who actually achieve them. When external goods are achieved they typically become someone's property and possession. So the more that someone achieves (acquires) of such goods the less there is for everyone else to achieve (acquire).[10] Though the internal goods of sport are also a product of the competition to excel, their reach is more diffuse. When new standards of excellence are attained in a sport, and new dimensions of the form of life intrinsic to that sport are realized, all members of that practice community benefit. So when Walter Camp and Amos Alonzo Stagg applied their agile minds and bodies to the game of football, and when Christy Matthewson and Honus Wagner unleashed their considerable skills in baseball, and when Suzanne Lenglen and Helen Wills raised the game of women's tennis to new levels and Mildred "Babe" Didrickson did the same for almost every sport she took up, all the members of their relevant sport communities gained from and were enriched by their achievements.

We have now to consider the second key element of MacIntyre's conception of a social practice. This second element concerns the notion of virtue whose employment, MacIntyre insists, is crucial to the realization of goods internal to practices. As he defines it, "a virtue is an acquired human quality the possession and exercise of which tends to enable us to achieve those goods which are internal to practices and lack of which effectively prevents us from achieving any such goods."[11] What MacIntyre is claiming here is that if one desires to achieve the standards of excellence and to grasp the kind of life peculiar to a practice, then one must be prepared to take whatever risks it requires, be willing to give "what is due to whom," be able to listen and constructively respond to criticism of one's shortcomings made by other knowledgeable practitioners, and be able to resist the allure of external goods. In short, one must be prepared to exercise virtues like courage, honesty, justice, and temperance.

What applies to social practices in general applies to sporting practices in particular. One can gain a sense of the excellences and kinds of life embedded in sporting practices only if one is virtuous in one's pursuit of those excellences and kinds of life. Of course, even though all sports excite some train of virtues, not all sports excite the same virtues, nor do they place the same emphasis on the virtues that they do share. High-risk sports like the luge and boxing, for example, emphasize courage, whereas sports that are less risky but more difficult to police, such as golf and marathon running, stress honesty. Nonetheless, it is not farfetched to suppose that some core set of virtues permeate all of our sporting practices. Justice and temperance come quickly to mind in this regard. So does a certain competitive mettle or fire, which seems crucial to sports of every stripe, and which has more to do with a refusal to give up even when all appears lost than it does with selfishly imposing one's will and desires upon others. Further, it may well be that competitiveness so understood incorporates hope as another key virtue of sports, where hope is best rendered, as Stout aptly puts it, as "the mean between despair and presumption."[12] Moreover, since athletic practitioners must depend on their teammates, game authorities, and even their opponents to supply them with the essential ingredients of a good sporting contest, it would appear that trust is another paramount virtue of athletic practices.

Whether we could add to this list of core virtues or not is, no doubt, a matter of conjecture. But what is not a matter of conjecture is the essential larger point that unless practitioners of sports and kindred endeavors are disposed to act in these virtuous ways, they will not be able to attain the goods that are internal to those practices, and, insofar as such goods supply us with reasons to take them up, they will jeopardize (as I shall comment upon more extensively) the very rational standing of those practices.

It is not a part of MacIntyre's argument that great pianists or athletes can't be mean-spirited individuals, individuals who lack many, if not all, of the virtues mentioned above. He readily concedes that, "where the virtues are required, the vices also may flourish."[13] But it is central to his argument that nonvirtuous pianists and athletes have to depend on the virtuous actions of others for their practices to flourish, and that such virtuous-deficient practitioners cannot themselves attain the goods internal to their respective practices.

Yet, it might be objected that the claim that gifted musicians and athletes that eschew virtues for vices in their practices are barred from attaining the goods internal to them is itself no more plausible than the claim that accomplished practitioners can't be wicked people. Highly skilled practitioners succeed more often than not in attaining the ends and goods they seek, and they appear to do so because of the great talents and skills they possess—quite apart, that is, from what virtues they may or may not have acquired in their training for a practice. In short, it is the relevant skills that practitioners possess, acquire, and refine that allow them to get what they want, and virtues seem to play no real, determinative role here. Indeed, a cynical observer of modern-day practices might claim that if indeed it takes something other than great skills for highly accomplished practitioners to achieve their ends, then that something has to do with a careful cultivation of the vices rather than the virtues. It seems evident these days that one is far more likely to acquire certain select vices than virtues in training for a practice, and for good reason since qualities such as ruthlessness better serve the ends that athletes and their compatriots typically seek.

But this objection suffers from a double confusion. First, it confuses the ends pursued by particular individuals with the excellences and forms of life peculiar to practices. Second, it confuses the relation between skills and the ends their successful exercise obtains with the relation between virtues and the goods internal to a practice their exercise realizes.[14] These confusions can be disentangled by way of an example. Imagine a supremely gifted, yet insufferably egocentric, athlete—say, a hundred-meter Olympic champion sprinter—who cares only about winning.[15] Since it is only winning that our hypothetical athlete cares about, and presumably the goods of money and prestige that invariably follow in its train, it is clear that the good she seeks has nothing essentially to do with sprinting as such—nothing to do, that is, with the good that is particular to sprinting and all other sports of this ilk. She could well achieve this good in any number of undertakings in which there is a competition for some prize and in which there are clear winners and losers, provided, of course, she possessed the relevant skills. So the good she pursues and achieves as her good is not the good particular to sprinting. Though her great skills, and perhaps even her egocentric manner, enable her to achieve the good that she does desire (winning and its associated rewards), they preclude her from obtaining the good peculiar to sprinting.

What our hypothetical Olympic-caliber sprinter lacks, then, is not technical skills, for she has these in abundance, nor a desire to win, for this is all she cares about, but a compelling reason to take up sprinting that makes the sort of life it exemplifies and the excellences and virtues that it demands of central importance to her own life. In order to make the good that is specific to sprinting her end and her good, she must do more than care about winning; she must, in other words, subordinate herself to its practice and temper her vices in whatever way the form of life intrinsic to sprinting requires. Without being truthful, just, and the like, the sort of human relationships it takes to sustain such practices would shrivel up and disappear. And when the virtues go, so do the practices that underwrite them and that give them their point.

Holding that virtues such as truth and justice stand in an internal relation to the goods that are specific to practices like sport does not commit one to a fixed, ahistorical conception of the virtues. It allows that these very virtues have themselves stood for different human qualities at different times and in different cultures. So it is, for example, that athletes of ancient Greece understood courage to be a martial virtue, one that they and their cultural peers believed not only sustained the athlete in his relentless pursuit of victory but the warrior in his unflinching desire to see the battle through to a successful conclusion. At the turn of the twentieth century, if historians such as Frederick Jackson Turner are to be believed, the virtues of temperance and honesty that were thought necessary to protect sport from unwholesome professional influences were linked to qualities such as "manliness and decency."[16] That few, if any, contemporary practitioners of sport would consider courage preeminently a martial virtue, or temperance preeminently a genteel one, is itself part of the historical lineage of the sporting virtues. That lineage suggests that while practices such as sport might flourish in cultures with very different codes of truth, honesty, justice and the like, they cannot flourish in cultures in which the virtues were not themselves esteemed, although, as MacIntyre suggests, "institutions and technical skills serving unified purposes might well continue to flourish."[17]

It is crucial to MacIntyre's account of practices that they not be confused with institutions. That is because the rational character and complexion of practices is of a different order than that of institutions, even though the material and financial well being of practices is contingent upon their corresponding institutions. Chess, football, chemistry, and medicine are practices; whereas chess clubs, the National Football League, laboratories, universities, and hospitals are institutions. Institutions, therefore, are typically large-scale organizations whose ostensible purpose is to oversee, nurture, regulate, and variously administer the particular practices that fall under their formal charge. As such, they are intimately involved with the legitimation of practices and the establishment of the bounds of what constitutes "normal" conduct within them, charged with raising the necessary capital to subsidize the practices they sponsor, structured in hierarchical terms of power and status, and wedded to a distribution scheme in which money, power, and status are dispensed as rewards for services rendered within both the organization and the practices they govern.

The kinds of goods that institutions deal in, therefore, are almost exclusively external ones. That entails, of course, that the money, power, and status that they wield and distribute in discharging their various bureaucratic functions are "exclusive" to those who handle these goods and to those to whom they are transferred, and that the more of these goods that are held by bureaucrats and dispensed to their designated recipients the less there are for others to use and dispose of.[18] That also means that the specific connection of external goods to practices is purely an artifact of their specific institutional make-up. While that connection is vital to the material sustenance of any practice, it remains, as any relation of goods external to a practice must, a contingent one. While practices require institutional backups, they may well exist and prosper in a variety of institutional settings.

The specific institutional setting that our present crop of practices find themselves bounded by, however, is an emotivist one through and through, which reflects the larger emotivist culture from which it takes its cue. Emotivism is the view that the particular ends that individuals, groups, and organizations pursue, and the beliefs, desires, values, and evaluative judgments that inform those ends, are all expressions of subjective taste and preference (in the case of groups and organizations, of course, those individual expressions are merely summed to reflect our aggregate desires).[19] Since they are treated as nothing more than expressions of subjective preference and inclination, they are thought to be beyond rational reflection and adjudication. That is to say, they are considered to be neither true nor false. What their expression reflects, therefore, is simply our arbitrary decision to hold certain ends, values, and beliefs as worth holding, as possessing some modicum of meaning and validity by virtue of our decision to treat them as such.

As social embodiments of our emotivist culture, institutions likewise treat the ends that govern their actions, as well as the beliefs and evaluative judgments that undergird them, as mere subjective preferences. The only status that ends have for institutions, therefore, is as givens whose legitimacy is presumed to be self-conferred. To ask or require of institutions that they consider whether the particular ends they embrace are worth embracing is to fail to understand both the nature of our institutions and the ends that drive them. Ends are not the sort of things that can be rationally legitimated, but only accepted as the subjective preferences that they are; and institutions are not in the business of deciphering the worth of the ends we hold, but only of the effectiveness of the means we employ to satisfy them. So while a consideration of the ends that shape the conduct of institutions lies outside of their rational compass, the assessment of the most efficient means to realize them does not. The rationality of institutions is, therefore, a means-based rather than an ends-based rationality, a fact that is readily apparent in the calculated manner in which they dispose of their central bureaucratic tasks.

The instrumental rational calculus of institutions and their emotivist bearing is especially evident in their capitalization of practices. In order to underwrite the often heavy costs of staging practices, institutions typically act like markets. As such, they become "want-regarding" institutions that respond to what might be best described as "effective demand."[20] That means that they are responsive to preferences if and only if they are backed up by the ability to pay for those preferences. So when, for example, athletic institutions seek patrons to subsidize their programs, and when they package athletic events to suit the tastes of consumers willing to pay for their "product," they are quite deliberately and self-consciously functioning as markets. In either case, no distinction is made between reflective desires that can be supported by reasons and principles, and matters of personal taste that cannot so be supported but only accepted for the personal preferences that they are. This is because markets are oblivious to any such distinctions and are not inclined to regard the preferences of any one individual to be less worthy of satisfaction than those of any other individual, provided, of course, that each can pay for his or her contribution to the athletic department and/or for admission to the game. In conforming to market principles, institutions betray their emotivist bent by reducing the interests of the sporting public to self-justifying consumer interests that it is not in their specific province to question, and about which it is in general fruitless to deliberate.

The instrumental predilections and emotivist leanings of institutions are also apparent in the formal manner in which they conduct themselves and preside over the practices that fall under their jurisdiction. Once again the ends that are attached to institutions, arbitrarily but quite resolutely, are treated as givens to be followed rather than questioned. And once again the means that are supposed to deliver those ends are treated as the proper focus of their deliberative proceedings. Here, however, efficiency has centrally to do with getting people to do what the leaders and managers of institutions tell them to do. It is the job of bureaucratic managers to organize their human resources in the most effective way to achieve the organizations' ends. That is what they are supposed to be good at, and that is the way that they derive and justify the authority they possess.

But in appealing to their capacity to maneuver subordinates into "compliant forms of behavior to legitimate their authority," the authority bureaucratic managers and their counterparts claim shows itself to be nothing other than the exercise of successful power. That is, it is premised on the negation of the distinction between power and authority, which is itself premised on the negation of the distinction between manipulative and nonmanipulative social relations.[21] Bureaucratic authorities are able to pass off their manipulation of people to get what they want in the morally neutral terms of bureaucratic expertise precisely because they regard such self-interested behavior to be beyond moral reproach. They are able to regard it as such because they are emotivists, that is, because they believe there are no objective normative standards of rationality that govern social interaction. It follows, therefore, that the only conceivable point of our social dealings with others is to persuade them to accept beliefs and values that are congenial to our own. So there appears to be nothing morally dubious about bureaucrats who treat subordinates in self-interested ways, and who claim a special facility in doing so.

The rational and emotivist predispositions of our present institutions obviously make them ill-suited as habitats for the development of the virtues. Indeed, their fixation on external goods and their calculative weighing of the instrumental consequences of their actions afford practically no room for the virtues. This is so because the virtues dispose, if not require, us to act without regard for the instrumental effects of our actions, a quality that hardly endears them to organizations that gauge their effectiveness by their success in achieving the external goods that give them their point and purpose. It is little wonder then why the pursuit of wealth, fame, and power in our society today is thought to be incompatible with the exercise of virtues such as honesty, justice, and temperance. Given the market and emotivist slant of our current institutions, it is unlikely that that incompatibility will diminish appreciably or be overturned in the near future.

It is apparent from our brief sketch of MacIntyre's distinction that practices are particularly susceptible to corruption by their institutions. There is a built-in tension between the two such that the virtuous pursuit of the goods internal to practices is always vulnerable to usurpation by the nonvirtuous, acquisitive, and calculating manner of institutions, of organizations that estimate their entire worth by the wealth they are able to command and the power they are able to wield. If MacIntyre (not to mention all of the other social critics mentioned above) is to be believed, this is the fate apparently that has befallen our present regime of social practices, which stand in a relation of dominion to the institutions that govern them from on high.

The dominion institutions currently hold over practices, and the tensions it creates between them, is rather easily illustrated in the case of sport. Indeed, it comprises the better part of what Lasch terms the steady submission of sport to the "demands of everyday life."[22] The quest for excellence embedded in the ways of life that constitute our modern sporting practices has been regularly subjected to institutionally sponsored commercial and bureaucratic pressures dating back to the late nineteenth century. That was about the period in which wealthy factory owners began to band together into professional sport franchises and to apply their managerial savvy to the conduct and promotion of sports, turning many into profitable business enterprises. Rules were changed and styles of play altered to suit the tastes of paying customers, and self-discipline was replaced with managerial discipline. Under the aegis of that discipline, professional sports owners were able to keep a tight rein on their players, even off the playing fields—it seems that players had no lives of their own that were considered separate from their athletic lives, and that rein grew tighter as owners flexed their legal muscles by signing players to exclusive contracts that reserved their services in perpetuity to particular athletic franchises (the infamous reserve clause).[23] With the recent advent of free agency and the astronomical salaries (paid to players of even marginal ability) that followed in its wake, many of these earlier harsh managerial constraints were simply discarded. But that only strengthened the hand of market forces in sport and their bureaucratic direction. While players could now offer their services directly to the highest bidders, who were only too happy to oblige, their mobility and market potential was restricted, with few notable exceptions, to one league. So the captains of the athletic industry and their bureaucratic surrogates were able to maintain significant monopolistic control over their product, and by playing this truncated market to their advantage (by, among other things, inserting performance clauses into players' contracts) were able to deepen and solidify their hold on professional sports at the same time that they relaxed their former heavy-handed, disciplinary treatment of them.[24]

The institutional oversight of collegiate and so-called amateur sports reveals much the same picture. If they differ at all from their professional counterparts, they differ only in degree, not kind. The name of the game here is also money and power and their effective control and use. So most of these athletic institutions are preoccupied with the same bureaucratic and market concerns that dominate the agenda of professional sports; most regularly and without apparent duress or regret follow these bureaucratic and economic mandates even when their effects on the games themselves, which they are ostensibly pledged to safeguard, appear foreboding. Hence, while the National Collegiate Athletic Association (NCAA) proudly touts its efforts to stem the professionalization of college athletes, it scarcely questions the rectitude of universities staging massive athletic spectacles to the larger public, nor does it consider the possible ramifications of such on the conduct of sport as a practice. To make matters worse, our legal institutions, which are supposed to function as a court of last appeal in regulating practices like sport, particularly in those instances where their host institutions fail them, seem unwilling or unable to curb the enormous economic appetite and bureaucratic temperament of our athletic institutions, and often appeal, as Feinman observes, "to actual commercial behavior for quasi-objective norms on which to base [their] judicial decisions" about sportive matters.[25]

It is this uneasy, downright unsavory relation between our practices and institutions that accounts for, as Stout puts it, "many of the most deeply felt problems of our society,"[26] and certainly most of the deep-seated problems that plague contemporary sport. But if this is so, and I am on record for thinking that it is so, then it is important to be clear about what makes this "uneasy" relation a corrupting one. What precisely is it about the present structural makeup of our institutional settings that can be said to desecrate the practice of sport, music, medicine, and the like?

Perhaps it is best to begin with what *isn't* corrupting about the current sway our institutions enjoy, and gladly exercise, over our practices. In this respect, it is not, as some suppose, merely because institutions control the financing of practices, nor that they dole out cash prizes or other monetarily valuable fare for distinguished performances in practices, that they can be said to defile practices. While it is true that, among the external goods that institutions regularly dabble in, money is the most notorious in arranging what Walzer refers to as "scandalous couplings between people and goods"[27]—or in our case, practices and goods—there is a sense in which this is what money is supposed to do, and that in playing the part of the "universal panderer" it fulfills a valuable role in society. There is nothing inherently perverse in putting up the capital for a venture one believes in, or for being paid, and in even being paid handsomely, for doing something supremely well, just as there is nothing inherently perverse in wanting to buy this book or that painting. This sort of capitalization and exchange of money for accomplished performances or goods is not only convenient for all concerned, but an important ingredient of the life we share with others. It reflects, as Walzer argues, "our sense of the great variety of desirable things,"[28] causes, and performances, and so in itself is neither to be despised nor subject to moral or political reproach.

However, what is degrading about the manner in which institutions finance practices, and about the way in which they dangle external goods in front of the eyes of practitioners and lord their power and status over them and the practices they partake of, is the social dominance they accord such goods and bureaucratic power in contemporary society. Money and power can be said to be dominant goods when they are able to command a wide range of other goods to which they have no intrinsic connection, when, that is, they can be converted into other goods without regard for their "intrinsic meanings." Illicit conversions of goods of this sort involve the invasion of one sphere of life and set of goods by another, alien sphere of life and set of goods. As Walzer forcefully argues, "to convert one good into another, when there is no intrinsic connection between the two, is to invade the sphere."[29] So the dominant status of goods such as money and power is a function of their ready convertibility into other goods, which, in turn, is a function of their ability to cross, and intrude upon, spheres of life to which they have no internal, substantive relation.

Put in MacIntyre's terms, institutions corrupt practices when they transgress their borders and impose upon them an instrumental rational order and a set of extrinsic goods that imperil the form of life they instantiate and exemplify. Said otherwise, institutions usurp practices when they mistake them for bureaucratic undertakings and treat them as essentially devices for attaining external goods and for exercising arbitrarily held power over others.

In the case of specific practices such as sport, the question that needs to be asked, and, of course, answered with some reasonable assurance, is, What constitutes their institutional domination? When, that is, does their institutional oversight and support turn into something more troubling and sinister? More specifically, when does the application of managerial "expertise" to sporting practices cease to be merely a way to more or less effectively present and promote sports to increasingly larger audiences and become instead a way of defaming them? And when does offering financial enticements to athletes for participating in sports cease to be merely a way to allow them to earn a living at what they do best and turn into a way of prostituting them for the sake of a few paltry external goods? We can put the point in the words of a long-forgotten practitioner of baseball and of a still, alas, well-known critic of sports: when did sporting practices go from being what John Montomery Ward, a disgruntled baseball player of the 1890s, describes as "not simply game[s]" but "business[es],"[30] which plaintively concedes their double standing, to what Howard Cosell describes as mere "entertainment," which boastfully proclaims that sports are nothing more than entertainment extravaganzas, nothing other than "show biz" writ large?

It might be helpful here to begin by laying out a few historical markers. Though the seeds of sport's institutional corruption were sown, as mentioned above, at the turn of the twentieth century, they did not fully develop until the postwar period of the late 1940s and 1950s. This was the period in which sport's steady but relentless submission to prevailing economic, social, and political forces reached its apex, when it became, as Lasch argued, an object of mass consumption.[31] The same entrepreneurial iniatives that had organized our factories and shaped the character of our work were now well on their way to doing the same to our leisure and sporting pursuits. It is not surprising therefore that in this commodious climate investors tripped over one another to acquire new professional sports franchises at huge sums, or that local municipalities built stadiums and granted profitable concession rights to owners at little or no cost, or that athletic stars milked their newly won free agency for all that it was worth (egged on and schooled by their personal certified public accountants, lawyers, and agents), or that athletic equipment companies paid handsome fees to advertisers and the media to hawk their wares, or that the television networks obligingly supplied the massive capital required to support the entire venture.[32]

At both the professional and collegiate levels, then, sport was molded to accommodate the engines of mass production and consumption. The games themselves receded in importance as the preparations required to stage them grew more extensive. Television was a major culprit in this respect; for while it enlarged the audience for sport it lowered its level of understanding.[33] That meant that sports' spectators, many of whom lacked a knowledge of the finer points of the games they watched, had to be placated by all sorts of extrinsic effects. The institutional sponsors of sport happily responded with innovations such as exploding scoreboards, colorful uniforms, synthetic turf and lively balls that sped up the action, fireworks, gate prizes of every conceivable sort, cheap beer, and prime-time scheduling of athletic events. This was also about the time in which the gentleman-owner types of professional sports and the athletic-smart types of collegiate athletic directors were replaced by aggressive entrepreneur types who knew more about business and negotiating contracts than they did about the sports they administered. This new breed of athletic entrepreneurs and managers had, as Baker astutely notes, "no fear of turning sport into a business: [because] they assumed that it already was [one]."[34] They operated under the self-fulfilling premise that spectators were more interested in having a good time than they were in becoming better acquainted with the intricacies of the games they watched. And so they sought, with great vigor and considerable business acumen, to pack as much entertainment as they could into sporting contests in order to make them as palatable as possible to a progressively less sophisticated but ever-growing sporting audience.

What this mass commodification of sport amounts to is the capitulation of the practice side of sport to its business side. This much at least can be discerned from its historical evolution to its contemporary status as an object of mass consumption. But we have still to consider what it is about this capitulation that warrants the claim that it is a corrupting rather than simply a distracting force. We have yet to show, that is, that the present institutional predicament of sport qualifies, in MacIntyre's and Walzer's terms, as a bona fide case of usurpation and domination.

We can shed some light on this issue by noting that the focus on the external goods of sport ordained by its institutional subordination cannot adequately reflect the value of the internal goods they displace. That is because goods such as money are, as Nozick points out, "not a vehicle for nuanced expression."[35] They lack, that is, the capacity to convey the subtleties and complexities of goods that are amenable to measures of quality as opposed to quantity, that cannot be reckoned with in valuational units of magnitude. To the extent that it is the external goods that occupy the attention of sporting participants, what captures their fancy is not in any meaningful respect intrinsic to what they feel, experience, and discern as participants of sporting practices.

Still, although the external goods sponsored by athletic institutions fail to convey the value of the internal goods they replace, and although they typically deflect sport's participants from an awareness and appreciation of such internal goods, this in itself does not make them agents of corruption. In order to establish their corrupting influence one must show not only that they distract or otherwise deter agents from realizing the goods internal to a practice, but that they degrade those goods by subordinating them to external goods. All one may legitimately infer from the coarse character of external goods is that if agents occupy themselves with such goods they may not realize the internal goods of a practice, not that such occupation itself counts as a distortion of the goods specific to a practice.

What does explain the corrupting potential of external goods is, as argued above, the dominance institutions confer upon them. The dominance of external goods is, as we also argued above, a function of their reach, of their intrusion into spheres of action to which they have no intrinsic, substantive connection. I believe that what distinguishes this most recent phase of the institutionalization of sport is the scope of its meddling in the internal affairs of sporting practices. Its previous bureaucratic meddling was confined more or less to the marketing and presentation of sports to a wider public that had little trouble in discerning the difference between the market and organizational forces that made that diffusion possible and the nuances of the games themselves that commanded their critical attention; but its present meddling extends to the production of sporting spectacles themselves and to their presentation to a viewing public more interested in their unfettered consumption than their critical reception. The laws of bureaucratic administration and of the market have managed, therefore, to insert themselves into the very core of sporting practices and have become an integral part of their formative development. This is the sense of Lasch's complaint that contrived managerial qualities such as "prudence, caution, and calculation," qualities that are, he contends, "inimical to the spirit of games," have "come to shape sports as they shape everything else."[36]

It is this active meddling of athletic institutions in the very production of sporting practices and their viewing publics that justifies treating the difference in degree of their involvement in the internal affairs of sport as a qualitative difference in kind. If it is plausible to treat this institutional meddling as a genuine difference in kind, then it is no longer plausible for bureaucratic types to insinuate that in lending their managerial expertise to the marketing of sport they are merely making its presentation to an expanding audience more effective. Claims to efficiency can be considered valid, as Anderson insightfully argues, "only when ends are unchanged by alternate means of provision."[37] What distinguishes the invasive manner of our present institutions is precisely their interference in the qualitative character of the goods and the ends pursued in sport.

This tampering with the kinds of goods and ends pursued in such practices is what corrupts. By molding the rational preferences of practitioners to accommodate those of their bureaucratic organization, institutions are able to countermand the rational preferences that are vital to the sustenance and flourishing of practices. That is because the rational aims and motives proper to practices are bound to reasoned ideals that reflect the logic and goods specific to their conduct and the shared and informed understandings of their practitioners; whereas the rational preferences proper to institutions are bound to the notion of "use," where use refers to the license to subordinate something, be it a practice, a good, or a thing, to ends without regard for their intrinsic value or meaning.[38] The connection of the notion of use here to that of domination specified above is also crucial to the distinction between the rationality of practices and institutions. Both use and domination make possible the incursion of bureaucratic interests into practices, the sort of incursion that attention to the rational detail and goods of practices is meant to forestall.

In the final analysis, then, the dominion that athletic institutions hold over sporting practices reduces to their capacity to shape the rational preferences of practitioners to suit their own particular bureaucratic interests. So when athletes adopt the goals of the organization as their goals in order to advance their athletic careers they are acting in the rational manner prescribed by their institutions. It is no accident, therefore, that athletes chase the very same external goods that institutions chase, nor is it an accident that they consider the pursuit of such institutionally legitimated goods to be in their own best interests as well as those of the sporting practices they engage.

In one sense at least, the present predilection of athletic institutions to enforce their dominance over sporting practices by openly relying on their own bureaucratic and market devices marks an advance of sorts. This advance is the elimination, or at least the diminution, of the exploitation built into its earlier handling of practices in which institutional types tried to disguise their economic interest in sport as an interest in its basic welfare and integrity. The ploy of passing off economic interests of this sort as lofty humane ones was not, of course, confined to athletic and cultural institutions, but, for example, characterized the relation between firms and their employees in liberal capitalist society.[39] By dissembling their financial interest in employees as a paternalistic interest in their well being, firms tried to extract a level of loyalty and trust from them that is not normally accorded to, nor considered appropriate of, market enterprises. The modern corrective to this exploitation of workers by firms is to ensure that both adhere to market norms by, for example, contractually specifying the formal obligations of firms to employees and employees to firms. The same is true of potentially exploitative social relationships like the traditional marriage in which the disadvantaged economic position of wives is remedied by the marriage contract—the effect of which is to treat marriages as one would market transactions.[40] In practices such as sport a similar effect is achieved, as noted above, by slipping economic clauses and incentives into players' contracts, which by putting sporting practices on a par with business transactions openly acknowledges their co-optation by the instrumental logic of the market.

While treating sports explicitly as business enterprises may be less exploitative than trying to do the same by other devious means, its impact on practices such as sport is anything but positive. Though it may reduce, or even perhaps eliminate, the select exploitation of individual athletes, it does so at the cost of savaging the very sporting practices that enlist their commitment and devotion in the first place. That is because the seepage of instrumental qualities such as prudence and calculation into sportive endeavors does not just, as Lasch supposes, suppress the "appropriate abandon" with which players pursue their gratuitous challenges,[41] but destroys the rational underpinnings of that pursuit itself. It destroys them by installing market norms and its train of external goods as the proper ends of sporting practices thereby depriving their practitioners of any reason, let alone a compelling one, to value or engage the particular competitive challenges they present, the select athletic skills they call upon, and the human qualities and virtues they excite. In short, it provides practitioners with no reason not to cheat, and every reason to cheat in order to obtain the external goods they desire.

This encroachment of institutional preferences, goals, and values into the rational center of sport counts as a legitimate case of distortion and corruption because it does more than simply deter practitioners from achieving the standards of excellence and goods specific to sport, but bastardizes the whole point and purpose of its practice. It effectively strips sport of the gratuitous logic that fuels its eccentric pursuit of contrived difficulties, and in so doing, makes its practice pointless save as an instrumental exercise in acquiring external goods. In the effort to minimize this pernicious effect, it won't do to argue that the distortion it engenders resides only in the false estimate of the external goods one can acquire by participating in sport and not in the actual practice of sport itself. As Nozick reminds us, human projects and relations cannot be neatly parceled out like this. So it is, he continues, that "someone who loves money more than he loves a person does not love that person."[42] What goes for persons here also goes for practices like sport as well. But its application to sport in this instance is particularly apropos, since the view of sport that our present institutions cultivate is precisely the view that goods such as money, power, and fame are themselves integral and indispensable elements of sporting pursuits. It is the very view that we, after Suits, have called "radical instrumentalism," which insists that such ends and goods are built into sporting practices, and so can be properly thought of as athletic ends and goods.

Institutions defame practices such as sport, therefore, when they substitute their own ensemble of external goods and instrumental brand of rationality for the goods and logic of practices. By breaching the rational boundaries of sport and the like, they succeed in reducing them to the common coin of contemporary consumerist culture, that is, to matters of money, power, and status. In the specific case of sport, that means "that in the absence of [trying to achieve such external goods] . . . nothing worthwhile—or, indeed, intelligible—can be going on" within it.[43] What is radically instrumentalist, not to mention corrupting and implausible, about this conception and treatment of sport is that it supposes that sport is synonymous with the external ends it subserves. In other words, what we have here is not the simple and relatively harmless view that sport may be used to achieve further purposes (say, money or fame), which presupposes the detachability of sport from the purposes to which it is put, but the more complicated and menacing view that sport is itself an instrumental device for achieving such purposes, which presupposes that sport is neither detachable from, nor different from, the purposes to which it is put. The first view reflects a benign institutional intrusion, which often obtains when external goods are offered as rewards for excellent performance, whereas the second reflects a malignant institutional intrusion, which obtains when practices succumb to the institutional pressures brought to bear on them.

Nowhere are the problematic effects of this institutionally wrought instrumentalization of sport more apparent than in the technical regard it engenders for its rules. Under its sway, rules become little more than technical directives that enable practitioners to acquire the external goods they seek. This technical recasting of the rules ensures that the only demands they make on practitioners are technical, as opposed to moral, ones. D'Agostino formalizes this technical interpretation of the rules for us as follows, "Rp: if x performs action b, then x is subject to penalty p."[44] On this institutionally compatible reading of the rules, all penalty-bearing rules of sporting practices have the form of Rp and none have the form "Rv: action b is prohibited in G."[45] This entails that we are to follow rules only when it is technically feasible to do so, only, that is, when it is the most expeditious way to get the goods we want. Put in cynical rather than formal jargon, we are to break every rule we can get away with, and comply with every rule that we cannot. There is not the slightest inkling here that there might be something morally disagreeable about performing b-like actions, for performing b-like actions is, on this rendering at least, entirely a matter of prudential calculation, entirely, that is, a technical matter. So if one gets caught one can rightly be accused of being insufficiently clever—or, more to the point, stupid—but this is a technical infraction and miscalculation, not a moral one.

One can discern in this instrumental regard for the rules a technical reason not only to break or comply with them but also a technical strategy for ensuring their compliance. It is implicit in this technical interpretation of the rules that the only rational and practically felicitous way to compel compliance with them is to raise the costs of breaking rules, to increase the severity of the penalties dispensed for rule infractions. So one may, if one wishes, appeal to a technical remedy, a technical quid pro quo, to discourage rule-breaking behavior.

This qualification is important because it suggests that just as there is a distinctive instrumental logic that governs the institutional sanction of rule-breaking action in sport—when, of course, it suits its bureaucratic fancies—there is additionally a distinctive instrumental logic that governs its sanction of rule-complying action in sport, again when it suits its fancies. While that suggests that there is a certain perverse consistency in the way institutions sponsor rule-breaking and rule-complying actions in sport, it also suggests that the technical fix it offers to stem "excessive" rule-breaking is doomed to failure. The problem with this particular bureaucratic brand of rule compliance is that it fails to remedy, let alone address, the institutional imperatives that underwrite and legitimate such rule breaking, nor does it do anything to dissuade efforts to undermine any achieved technical quid pro quo by devising clever ways to get around penalty-fortified rules. That is as it must be because the technical measures institutions adopt to stem deliberate rule breaking come out of the same technical logic that excites such disdain for the rules in the first place. That explains why practitioners, who have been fed a steady diet of such calculative logic as a part of their own introduction to, and socialization in, institutionalized sports, typically greet such technical limits on their athletic behavior not so much as deterrents but as challenges to be gotten around, as, that is, invitations to hone and refine their own already ample rule-breaking skills. That also explains why institutions sometimes find themselves in the odd, not to mention precarious, position of trying to discourage certain rule-breaking actions encouraged by their own displacement of the logic and goods internal to sporting practices.

It is worth reiterating that the debased manner in which athletic institutions manage the internal affairs of sporting practices is emblematic of the debased manner in which all of the major institutions of advanced capitalist society handle the social practices entrusted to them. The social pathology that infects sporting practices is a systemic one that infects every social practice that it comes into contact with. So it is that the practice of democratic politics in our culture, which derives it vitality and meaning from the exercise of self-governance directed to the common good, has degenerated into the bureaucratic management of external goods directed to private interests.[46] This is the source of Birnbaum's scornful jab that "much of what passes for politics [today] is force unlimited by constraint, fraud untouched by moral rigor, [and] manipulation devoid of reflection."[47] So it is also that Andy Warhol's cheeky remark that "being good in business is the most fascinating kind of art"[48] aptly captures the commercial ethos of the contemporary art scene, and serves as a credo of sorts for the throngs of artists holed up in the major metropolitan centers of Western culture trying to get profit-conscious galleries to sell their work.[49] The conditions in which many of these artists eke out a living, and their increasing dependence on advertising and public relations to advance their careers, explains the demise of what Suzi Gablick calls the "artistic vocation," of a way of life dedicated to values that are impervious to market norms.[50] Educational practices prove to be no different in this respect, in which, as Menand relates, "Even comfortably middle-class students feel an economic imperative almost unknown to middle-class students of twenty years ago."[51] If educational practices differ at all from the other cultural practices, it is that the titans of private enterprise think them still insufficiently touched by the salubrious "invisible hand" of the market. That explains why they have joined in the clamor for reform, arguing that what ails our schools can be best remedied by operating them, to quote Lewis Lapham, "as if they were a chain of successful motels."[52]

Insofar as it is our institutions that lie behind this scourge of our social practices, and that are responsible for ensuring the dominant grip that money, power, and status hold over them, Lasch is correct in saying that they not only tempt practitioners to take up practices for the wrong reasons, but that they actively "underwrite" and "legitimize" such facile reasons. It is no mystery then why the "uneasy" relation that has always persisted between practices and institutions has taken on a more troublesome and sinister mien. As things presently stand, "practices have to be sustained by institutions, which in the very nature of things [by our present institutional lights at any rate] tend to corrupt the practices they sustain."[53]

The Ideological Distortion

In light of the foregoing discussion, it can be plausibly claimed that the social acids that corrode the living core of our society have to do with the unwarranted incursion of institutional demands on the conduct of practices. That claim, however, brings us back to the question broached at the outset of this chapter, which we are now in a better position to answer: namely, what social interests and influences are swirling about in present society that prevent us from seeing clearly the institutional predicament practices like sport find themselves in? Put in more practical terms, what ideological forces are at bay that discourage or otherwise block us from taking measures necessary to relieve the practices that so enrich our life from their suffocating institutional encumbrances?

The reason we seem to have difficulty grasping the precarious state of our present ensemble of social practices is that we (meaning the citizens, bureaucrats, practitioners, and especially theorists who populate this society) tend to view them, to use Stout's apt metaphor, "with one eye shut."[54] That is, we are inclined to see practices, not to mention virtually everything else that goes on within the boundaries of contemporary society, from the very same institutional perspective that undermines those practices in the first place. What we get for our squint-eyed, half-hearted, exertion is, not surprisingly, a distorted vision of a distorted social reality. That flawed, unfocused discernment, I contend, is not simply the product of a botched conceptual effort at reflection, not the mere result of a cognitive misstep. We have been socialized as members of this social order to view matters in just this institutionalized way. That explains the current rage for "reductionist" sociology and political theory, even among those who explicitly proclaim their disgust for such theory, and that also explains why our theoretical and practical discussions about almost any human endeavor, be it religion, politics, art, or sport, predictably make them all out to be at bottom pursuits tied to the acquisition of external goods in which people are only disposed to act for want of money, status, and power.

Leftist theorists of sport are, I argue, blinded by this same institutional vantage point, and so they are inclined in the same reductionist direction as other forms of social and political theory. This is readily apparent in the two strains of Leftist sport theory that we have critically examined here. The New Left, as we have seen, was hell-bent on reducing sport to labor. Hegemonists responded, as we have also seen, to what they regarded to be the unsatisfactory reductionist manner in which the New Left crudely tried to link sport (considered part of the superstructure of society) to labor (considered its material base) by undercutting the base-superstructure paradigm altogether. What they got for their efforts, which effectively closed any discernible gap between social labor and cultural forms, was the hardly less reductionist view that sport is itself, in the first instance, a material, practical social activity, and not some once-removed, cheap imitation. This shared and radically reduced conception of sport as practical social activity is the source of the Left's contentious claim that even the presumption that cultural forms such as sport might be treated as discrete categories of social life is conceptually, not to mention ideologically, flawed. It is also the source of its equally contentious thesis that society is a seamless whole, that, at the level of social practices at any rate, there are no privileged places within the social totality.

In saying that the Left's reductionist and integrationist treatment of sport betrays the ideological reductionist and integrationist party line of late capitalist society, I am not implying that its treatment of sport is a complete critical failure. Rather, what I am saying is that while its institutionally informed perspective on sport makes it ill-equipped to explain, let alone recognize, the intricacies of its practice, it makes it well equipped to explain the aggressive manner of the institutions that govern it. In at least this latter sense, then, we are indebted to the Left for its probing analysis of how such institutions have made over practices like sport to suit their own narrow interests. These institutions have run roughshod over sport in just the ways that the Left have recounted. They have sought to amalgamate sport under their institutional wings, and in so doing consolidate their power over it, not to separate or insulate sport from unseemly influences. So from this social angle the Left's insistence on lumping sport with all the other spheres of social life, which derives from its treatment of social spheres as simply passive reflections or active reproductions of others, is not off the mark. Indeed, here the Left's exuberance for drawing connections between social spheres and impugning distinctions between them must be counted as a strength rather than a weakness, reflecting as it does a careful sensitivity to the wayward aims of invasive capitalist institutions.

But, to reiterate, in the same measure that the Left's fondness for connections and contempt for distinctions makes it wise to the ways of institutions, it makes it obtuse to the ways of practices like sport by dulling its capacity to grasp their basic point and purpose. So while it is all too aware of how capitalist institutions lord their power over sport, its cynical and hardened institutional outlook gets in the way of its comprehension of sport as a practice and, therefore, clouds its assessment of the kind of damage such institutions are able to inflict upon it. I believe that the cynical and hard edges of the Left's radically contextualized accounts of sport betray the ideological influence of the very advanced capitalist society that it claims to criticize.

The Left, of course, sees the matter differently. It maintains that its refusal to cede any special standing to sporting practices, that its censure on attributing anything to such practices that is not supplied by their dominant institutionalization (save, of course, the influx of social class interests) is the correct view. This is especially the case, it contends, on the ideological front. The Left is convinced that the chief way in which the ideologues of capitalist society delude us about sport is by recourse to idealistic depictions that make it out to be a thing *sui generis*. It is little wonder that in reminding us of the firm institutional ligatures that bind sport to the rest of society, it thinks it is fulfilling its appointed task of critical demystification, of ideology-critique.

However, it is precisely its assertion that in treating sporting practices largely as artifacts of their institutionalization it is rescuing us from the ideological snares of advanced capitalist society that reveals, I argue, that the Left has lost historical touch with that society. Despite all of its rhetoric about the relevance of historical data to critical inquiry, its own critical investigation of sport seems not to have noticed an important ideological shift in the transition from early liberal capitalist society to late bureaucratic capitalist society. That shift precipitated a fundamental alteration in the way in which the capitalist powers ensured their hegemonic position in the social order. What changed, in short, was that they came increasingly, almost exclusively, to rely on the market and on the prerogatives of their basic institutional structures to enforce the terms of their social domination. By letting the market and these institutional structures do their direct bidding for them, two things changed about the character and style of their social rule. First, the new managerial oligarchies that arose to direct and administer the vast apparatus of mass production and consumption no longer had to depend on the more virulent forms of social repression that marked the tight and often violent reign of their entrepreneurial predecessors, forms of repression that consorted with egregious forms of militarism, chauvinism, racism, and sexism.[55] Second, and more important for the present point, these new managerial cadres no longer had to disguise their real interests in managing the economic and important social affairs of capitalist society by dressing them up in high-sounding ethical or aesthetic ideals. That is to say, since their dominance now rested squarely on their ability to turn a handsome profit, they no longer had to pretend that their pursuit of that profit would make the world a better and safer place—a materially richer place perhaps, but by no means a morally superior or qualitatively happier one.

It is the latter point I want to focus on because it suggests, as I insinuate above, a new ideological wrinkle in the manner in which the reigning captains of industry handle cultural practices like sport. In the liberal phase of bourgeois society, capitalists were intent on concealing their undeniable economic interest and involvement in cultural practices by insisting on the latter's basic purity and autonomy; but in the bureaucratic phase, managerial types let it be known that their interest and involvement in such practices was, and is, an economic one. They allayed any initial fears or misgivings that admission might arouse by assuring all concerned that since cultural practices were themselves, after all, largely business affairs that offered attractive careers to those who possessed the relevant talents, there was nothing to fear and everything to gain from their interest and involvement in cultural matters.

David Rockfeller's speech to the National Industrial Conference Board concerning the benefits of corporate involvement in the arts proves instructive in this regard. It captures well the current official institutional view of cultural practices like art and serves as a credo of sorts for this corporate view. As he proclaims in the following excerpt from that speech, which he gave while the chairman of the Chase Manhattan Bank and the vice chairman of the Museum of Modern Art, the following benefits are to be expected from corporate support of the arts: "it can provide a company with extensive publicity and advertising, a brighter public reputation, and an improved corporate image. It can build better customer relations, a readier acceptance of company products, and a superior appraisal of their quality. Promotion of the arts can improve the morale of employees and help attract qualified personnel."[56] Rockfeller could, of course, just as easily been talking about the corporate sponsorship of sport or painting or music. The ready transferability of his words extolling the instrumental values of the arts to other cultural practices is telling. It represents the new ideological posture toward cultural practices, one that is conversant not with the idealist gambit of radical dissociation, which insists on portraying them as something special, but with the gambit of radical association, which insists on portraying them as nothing special—as business ventures and careers open to talent no different in kind from any other.

What is specifically new about this revised ideological posture is, as Adorno rightly asserts, "not that [art] is a commodity, but that today it deliberately admits it is one; that art renounces its own autonomy and proudly takes its place among consumption goods."[57] What was once considered a mark of depravity is today considered a mark of normalcy, of good common sense, or what comes to the same thing, of good business sense. What goes for art goes again for all of our cultural practices, none of which is disposed in the least to feign its indifference to the established order but only its complicity in its dingy daily detail. It is thus obvious that contemporary ideologues have abandoned the kinds of wishful, idealistic thinking practiced by their predecessors, which created abstract, romantic doubles of cultural practices that conveniently eliminated the seamy side of actual ones, and have taken up instead hyper-realistic forms of thinking, which create concrete duplicates of existing institutionalized practices that resemble actual ones in every important respect. Whereas, therefore, liberal ideologues appealed to ideals of practices that were true in themselves (to virtues such as justice and honesty that are an integral part of any social practice rightly understood), but which were falsified by the heady claim that they were already perfectly embodied in actual practices, their modern-day counterparts appeal to institutionally sanctioned modes of action and behavior that are false in themselves (that, for instance, practices are centrally about the pursuit of external goods), that don't have to prostitute themselves in order to confirm their untruth. Whereas the measure of duplicity of the ideology pushed by liberal apologists had to do with the lack of correspondence between its ideological principles (ideals) and their social referents, the measure of duplicity of the ideology pushed by the new apologists has precisely to do with the tight correspondence between its ideological principles (institutionally sanctioned beliefs) and their social referents.

By spurning idealism to concoct their justificatory schemes, the proponents of the new ideology have been able to induce what Adorno aptly calls a "faithless belief in pure existence," or what Marx more colorfully calls "a kind of fiction without fantasy, a religion of the vulgar."[58] What gives this new ideology its potency is precisely its truncated view of the world, its sticking to beliefs, claims, and principles that already inform existing society, and whose very immediacy, therefore, suggests that this is the way things really are. As Adorno avers, the new ideology "hardly says more than that things are the way they are, its own falsity . . . shrinks to the thin axiom that it could not be otherwise than it is."[59] That this "thin axiom" is able nonetheless to occlude the arteries of critical thought is testimony to its own immanent confirmation of prevailing social reality, to its transparent pretense to convey the way things really are today.

Someone might object at this point that it is an act of sheer ideological suicide, not to mention lunacy, to try to prop up a society such as our own by directly and openly invoking the established institutional standards of that society. The only thing to be gained by such a transparent tactic, the argument continues, is to expose the unpleasant social realities and injustices that it is the job of any defender of the status quo to conceal and distort. To make the ideological standards by which a society legitimates its dominance correspond to the existing standards by which it actually executes that dominance is to confuse, rather fatally, the role of the ideologue for the social critic.

But this objection lacks persuasiveness for two related reasons. First of all, what the new ideology lacks in subtlety it more than makes up for in its omnipresence. These two qualities are, of course, bound up with each other, for it is its lack of subtlety that accounts for its omnipresence. It is only by replicating existing society that current ideologues are able to inculcate in its members a "faithless belief" in that society. That "faithless belief" in society is able to pack the ideological wallop that it does because it effectively reifies the status quo. What it installs is a deep-seated belief in the immutability of the present social order, a belief that is recalcitrant to the notion that our institutions might be different from, or perhaps even better than, they presently are. This explains why radical schemes to revamp contemporary society strike us as "terminally wistful," as quixotic, hopeless gestures.[60] Any such scheme is likely to come across as "terminally wistful" and/or quixotic if we are unable "to imagine a full-blown alternative to our society that would be both achievable by acceptable means and clearly better than what we have now."[61]

That resignation is apparent in the message that leftist critics of sport wish to convey about its ideological handling. Such critics eagerly take bourgeois ideologues of sport to task for implying that the intrusion of big business, bureaucracy, and politics into sport is an unfortunate, fortuitous, and somehow avoidable development.[62] In suggesting that it is not, in claiming that such intrusion is inevitable, calculated, and somehow intractable, the Left is lending credence to the very view that I suggested contemporary ideologues of capitalist society typically convey: namely, that things couldn't be different than they presently are. It should be clear by now that this is hardly a salubrious message for critical theorists to be delivering, and it should surprise no one that it is a message that is firmly rooted in the Left's own institutional treatment of sport.

Drawing out the connection between the cynical story the Left tells about sport and its institutional treatment of sport reveals the second reason why bourgeois ideologues who tell pretty much the same story about sport risk little—contrary to our above hypothetical rejoinder—

by their candor. This can best be seen by showing how the sorts of disclosures the Left makes about the shoddy treatment sport receives from its governing institutions lack the critical edge it imputes to those disclosures.

In order to claim, as the Left does, that the institutionalization of sport constrains, and in the process damages, the kinds of agency that can be realized in sport, one must be able to establish that such constraints somehow violate sport. One must show, in other words, that sport is inviolate in some crucial sense, that it possesses a distinctive kind of agency that marks it off from other practices and, if usurped, undermines its basic integrity. But it is precisely this that the Left is unable to establish. It is unable to do so because it treats sporting practices as essentially empty vessels of their institutionalization, as little more than blank tablets whose constitutive structures and substantive elements are filled in by the specific terms of their institutionalization. That means that whatever the process of institutionalization inscribes on the blank tablets of sporting practices literally defines those practices and so cannot be said to violate or undermine them in any meaningful sense. This explains why any critique of sport the Left has tried to launch by its exposure of the institutional roots of sporting practices has proved to be stillborn. This is as it must be since the Left's own institutional rendering of the social constitution of sport forces it to play the role of the cultural relativist on such matters, for all that it is warranted in saying about the institutionalization of practices like sport is that one form of institutionalization is as good or as bad as any other.[63]

When proponents of the new ideology then push what amounts to the same assimilationist line as leftist critics of sport do, they are not being so stupid as to confuse their apologist task for a critical one. They need not fret about disclosing what their undisguised petitioning of the existing institutional standards of society reveal about practices like sport. They would have reason to worry, as I argue above, if and only if certain ways of institutionalizing practices could be said to deform them in some relevant pathological sense. Since these bourgeois apologists treat practices, as their leftist accomplices do, as simulacra of institutions, they are preempted, quite happily in this case, from coming to any such conclusion.

I have been claiming that in treating sport in terms that bespeak its institutionalization, the Left has been blinded by the same institutional vantage point from which the new ideology takes its point of departure. But the Left's blind spot regarding sport as a practice goes well beyond obscurantism. Its wholesale rejection of sport as an au-

tonomous, distinctive sphere of life, and its insistence that good social criticism is always a matter of undoing apparent distinctions between social spheres, never one of respecting or repairing such distinctions, reflects not so much a historical sensitivity to the pulse of
sporting practices as it does an a priori commitment to holistic accounts of social development and transformation. This is the sort of
doctrinaire outlook that does not merely incline one to overlook what
might be different or special about sporting practices, but that fore-
stalls looking in the first place, indeed, that reduces looking to a fundamental irrelevancy. Insofar as what we are discouraged from looking at coincides with what it is that the powers that be don't want us
to see, as I have been claiming throughout, then Hearn's trenchant
reminder that "a social theory that on important points merely reflects
the society it seeks to understand is hardly critical" finds a suitable
target in leftist accounts of sport.[64] So if anyone has confounded the
tasks of apologetics and social criticism it is not contemporary bourgeois ideologues but members of the Left, who in spouting an institutional line on practices like sport wind up legitimating what they
intended to criticize.

We have yet to consider what it is that leftist critics of sport screen
off from our view of modern sporting practices. What is it that the Left
would see if they bothered to take a long, hard look at sport? The answer is something considerably more than the embodiment of institutional imperatives. While it is true that practices like sport have been,
and remain, captive to the systemic directives foisted upon them by
their institutions, it is also true they have not exactly been deaf and
blind to their own internal logic, to the goods and standards that endow them with the specific meaning and sense of purpose they possess. That sporting practices are still responsive to their own internal
logic, that they have not been completely co-opted by institutional
mandates, is, I presume, the chief reason why practitioners and other
folks associated with sports continue to call for their reform. What is
true of sport here is true of many of our other important social practices as well. Despite the inroads institutions have made on all of them,
many of those practices have managed to survive their institutional
ordeal. Their survival confirms that relatively autonomous spheres of
life still really do exist and are not, as the Left would have us believe,
merely figments of our overactive idealist-fed imaginations. So it is, as
Walzer reminds us, that the clergy continue to criticize the military
policies of their host governments, that university officials still shelter
and abet self-professed radicals on their campuses, and that state bureaucrats not only subsidize but regulate the market.[65]

If the Left bothered to take a closer look, they would also see the relatively autonomous cultural traditions that give continuity to our practices and that continue to hold together, however precariously, the loose threads of our modern social orders. These traditions are passed down from one generation to the next through the practices that we take pains to introduce to our young. Parents, as Stout keenly observes, play a large role here, for they invest a considerable amount of their time, effort, and money conscripting their children into an astonishing array of such practices.[66] There is the endless stream of piano and ballet lessons, not to mention soccer and baseball practices. Schools also play a hefty role here, enlisting our kids in band and chorus, science and foreign-language clubs, and, of course, sports.

This conscription of the young into different social endeavors signifies that contemporary society is more so a jumble of disparate cultural traditions than it is a seamless whole. Kids don't grow up speaking just one moral language, and the first language that they learn is not the atomistic, cost-benefit language of the market—though, to be sure, this is one they learn rather early. Instead, they grow up speaking many different moral languages, at least as many as the social practices to which they have been exposed. What they learn from their training for, and socialization into, such practices is to appreciate diverse forms of human excellence and, perhaps most important, to evaluate their own lives from a variety of perspectives. Sports exert an undeniable influence in this respect. Indeed, if cultural critics like Lasch are to be believed, they play an especially important and poignant part in the socialization of youth. Sports, he claims, "resist assimilation more effectively than many other activities, since games learned in youth exert their own demands and inspire loyalty to the game itself, rather than to the programs ideologues seek to impose on them."[67]

It would be a mistake, however, to think that the lessons that sport and ballet teach us are left behind as we enter the adult world. When as adults we try, for the first time or the hundredth time, to muster the perseverance required to excel in sport, or to marshal the wisdom to try a difficult case in court, or to summon the courage to perform a life-threatening surgical procedure, we never start from scratch.[68] Rather, we always build from what we have imbibed in the way of virtues—and vices—from the practices of our youth. That is perhaps why adult life isn't as scary a prospect, nor as drab and as dreary an affair, as it might otherwise be. It is also why we ought to resist being taken in by any view of social reality that obscures those lessons from our vision and that erases the traces of their memory from our consciousness.

What is required, therefore, to grasp the institutional bind that our social practices are presently in, and to see what we are not supposed to see, is to keep both eyes open. That is, we need to keep one eye carefully trained on our practices and the other carefully trained on our institutions. It is only in this manner that we will be able to, as Stout puts it, bring "social practices and institutions, internal and external goods, into a single frame."[69] Once we bring them into a "single frame," I contend, we will not only be able to see clearly for the first time how perilous a threat the stranglehold our institutions currently hold over our practices really is, but we will be able to tap resources that offer some reasonable hope for transforming society from within.

Just how we might get practices and institutions into a single frame, and just what conceptual and cultural resources might be enlisted to transform society from within, are matters I will take up in some detail in the ensuing chapter. For now, I want to make clear that it is not part of my argument that the antidote for our myopic, one-sided, institutional way of looking at and thinking about society is to romanticize practices like sport.[70] That would only dim our awareness and understanding of the perturbational effects of our institutions, not to mention the important lessons that the Left and others have taught us about these same hyperactive institutions. Instead I am arguing that we cease and desist both in romanticizing our practices and in overstating their institutional plight. Once we do, we will realize that what practices like sport teach us is a mix of virtues and vices. Stout, I think, gives a good accounting of that mix in his following remarks:

> [We] learn about vicious owners who show no appreciation for the goods of the sport and who manipulate and humiliate their employees. [We] learn about managers, commissioners, bureaucrats, superstars, agents, markets, racial prejudice, sexist exclusion from a social practice, the intemperance of drug use, corruption by fame, and insanely unjust salaries. Meanwhile, [we] also learn to love the way Don Mattingly swings a bat, to retell stories of moral heroes like Jackie Robinson, and to understand the pleasure that supervenes upon the realization of goals sought for their own sake through long and arduous effort.[71]

What is telling about Stout's remarks is their evenhandedness, that they succumb to neither the false optimism of the social prophet nor the no-less-false pessimism of the hardened cynic. In short, they demonstrate that we don't have to overplay the merits of our practices to counter the omnipresence of their institutions. Rather, all that is required is that we, like Stout, tell the whole story, which nowadays means that we make a concerted effort to disclose what the institutional standing of our practices conceal. Making that effort removes an important impediment to real social change: namely, the stubborn and widespread belief that proposals to alter radically the face of existing society are to be dismissed as the wistful yearning for something that can never be. While it is "mere wistfulness" to strive for a society in which there are only practices and no institutions, and while it is also "mere wistfulness" to strive for a society in which none of our present institutions figure—for that would mean a society in which none of our present practices figure as well—it is not "mere wistfulness" to strive for a society in which institutions cater to and serve, rather than usurp, the goods specific to practices.[72]

In one of his less lucid moments Adorno saw fit to implicate sport directly in the furtherance of capitalist domination. In particular, he argued that the "adaptation of men to social relationships and processes . . . is fed by . . . the effective rearrangement of industry, the mass appeal of sports, [and] the fetishization of consumers' goods. . . . The cement which once ideologies supplied is now furnished by these phenomena, which hold the massive social institutions together, on the one hand, the psychological constitution of human beings on the other."[73] Adorno's claim is right about one thing and wrong about two others. It is right in supposing that sport, in particular mass sport, plays a significant part in holding contemporary society together just as it is. In this sense then, it is complicit in capitalist domination. It is wrong, however, in supposing that the social cement mass sport supplies takes the place of, in the sense that it ends rather than simply replaces and updates, ideology.[74] The sticking element that sport furnishes is itself an ideological one, and one that is predicated on a false, one-sided construal of its basic character. Adorno's claim is wrong in a second sense, then, in directly implicating sport in capitalist domination; for it can play this role only if its institutional side is emphasized at the expense of its practice side.

My point in citing Adorno's claim regarding the status of modern sport is that what is wrong with it, in this last sense at least, is precisely what is wrong with the Left's treatment of sport. Insofar as the Left insists, and persists, in reading the institutional structures of capitalist society back into the constitutive structures of sport, it merely ends up endorsing Adorno-like readings of sport as just another hy-

pertechnical, institutionally top-heavy enterprise.[75] It does so under
the smug cover that in telling its skewed story of the travails of modern sport it is, to quote Howard Cosell's endearing phrase, "telling it
like it is." What the Left has had to say about sport has approximat-
ed the truth about as often as Cosell's self-serving and shrill pronouncements on sport have managed to hit the mark—not a high-
scoring percentage however you figure it.

The Psychological Side of the Distortion

If we ignore the end-of-ideology quip in Adorno's above claim, there
is one other thing that it gets right. That is that the new ideology, just
as the old one, holds together not only the major social institutions
of society but the psychological constitution of the individuals that
comprise it. The psychological constitution of the self and the social
constitution of society are, of course, of the same piece. The psychological makeup of the self derives in significant measure from the social forces that envelop it and that give it its determinate shape. The
current institutional forces that have debased the social practices that
are the wellspring of our public life, and that have given wings to
the new ideology, are once again at work reconstructing a new psyche
to conform to its changed social surroundings. What they have fashioned, and are still in the process of fashioning, I argue, is a cynical
self out of a narcissistic one.

The connection of advanced capitalist society to narcissism is not
hard to discern. A society that installs external goods as the be-all and
end-all of human existence encourages their fetishization. And a society that fetishizes external goods sanctions their pursuit as the proper preoccupation of the individuals that populate it. More precisely,
it sanctions narcissistic forms of self-exploration centered on the pleasures, however fleeting, of acquiring and consuming such goods.

But the narcissism of which we speak is, as Lasch has persuasively argued, a distinctly modern one that first made its appearance in
the twenties and blossomed in the postwar period.[76] It is, therefore,
not to be confused with its classical prototype, the self-assertive youth
depicted in the legend of Narcissus, who, consumed with fantasies
of omnipotence and eternal youth, succumbed to his own reflection.
For the modern narcissist is neither selfish nor self-assured. She is,
by contrast, a psychological type marked by an alarming loss of ego,
not an alarming growth of ego, as she confronts social forces that
make it increasingly difficult to grow up, and increasingly difficult
to discern her own outlines and boundaries—where she precisely

ends and the world begins. She is above all a "minimal" self whose preoccupation with self-preservation and psychic survival is an adaptive response to the collapse of public life,[77] a collapse predicated on the disintegration of the family, the undermining of durable relations, meaningful standards, and consensual values, and the loss of faith in social and political institutions. Faced with this decline of public life, and cynical of political and humanitarian solutions, the narcissist retreats into her shell, living only for the moment, keeping her options open, and avoiding emotional and moral commitments. The modern version of the narcissist is at bottom, therefore, as Lasch sees it, a profoundly antireligious type, not because she abides by any canons of scientific reason, but because she sees herself without a future and so gives little thought to anything beyond the gratification of her immediate needs.[78] While the lure of external goods no doubt fills a hole of sorts in the narcissist's angst-filled life, it is unable to ward off the despair that accompanies and colors her every acquisitive and consumptive impulse.

However, this is a psychological type not apt to endure in perpetuity if only because the social conditions that spawned it are themselves fragile and transitory. Lasch concedes as much, arguing that the limited economic base of capitalism cannot sustain indefinitely the self-indulgences that shaped the culture of narcissism. When it can no longer deliver the necessary economic growth, he argues, society will exact its revenge by demanding our collective discipline and sacrifice, not our narcissistic self-experimentation. Lasch was not alone in thinking that contemporary capitalist society was headed for a major economic decline, nor was he alone in thinking that that decline would spell the demise of the narcissist and the emergence of something more sinister than the cynic. Richard Sennett, for example, mused that sadomasochism would succeed narcissism in economically trying times. Lasch, in turn, feared that a significant downturn in the economy might ignite a wave of draconian authoritarian measures, which would eventuate in an openly regressive system of social controls and a psychology more virulent and violent than that of narcissism.[79]

I do not wish to underplay Sennett's and Lasch's sober fears for the future—in fact for the present that is unfolding before our very eyes—for they reflect the gravity of what is being played out in this shifting constellation of social forces. Indeed, what they portend is the dissolution of the compromise between capital and labor that has kept the peace for the better part of the postwar period: the acceptance of debased work for higher wages and the pleasures of consumption they make possible. I am persuaded, however, that the collapse of this *modus vivendi* points to cynicism as the most likely successor to narcissism. That is because the forces behind this collapse are themselves based on, and contribute to, a widespread disillusionment with economic, political, and cultural institutions. Where once people could put faith in the market to disburse a sufficient, to be sure not an equitable, amount of goods in the hands of most of its economic players, where once people could in good faith entrust the state to remedy inequities that crop up in the market and elsewhere, and where once people could count on cultural practices to explore boldly the outer horizons of conscious experience, today no one takes seriously any of these hopes. Instead, what fills their heads is a deepseated cynicism, a pervasive disbelief in any difference, whether economic, political, or cultural, that might make a difference. The unmistakable resignation that is the signature of this cynicism might very well stave off the sadomasochism that Sennett refers to and the harsh paternalism that Lasch speaks of. This is a weary and paralyzing cynicism that can't be extricated from its present social predicament, but, notwithstanding nagging doubts, can only be reconciled with it. This is a cynicism that will toe the line without the coercive pressures of social controls because it hasn't any other social setting that is better than, and qualitatively different from, its present one.

The transition from the psychology of the narcissist to that of the cynic, which I claim to find in the latest phase of bureaucratic capitalism and its new ideology, is not a sharp, radical one, but a measured, dialectical one. Both the narcissist and the cynic are steeped in the disenchantment of the world and the disintegration of public life that it entails. Further, both are preoccupied with self-preservation, having lost faith in changing the social system that they inhabit. In addition, both are dependent creatures that engage in manipulative and exploitative relations with others in part to compensate for their own ample deficiencies. Finally, both the narcissist and the cynic are well schooled in social reality; they are convinced that their quest to survive is what that reality itself demands of them, at least as defined by the current capitalist regime. Indeed, Sloterdijk's description of the cynical self as a complicated bundle of "strategy and tactics, suspicion and disinhibition, pragmatics and instrumentalism—all . . . in the hands of a political ego that thinks first and foremost about itself, an ego that is inwardly adroit and outwardly armored" comes close to Lasch's description of the narcissistic self.[80]

If there is anything that distinguishes the cynic from the narcissist, it is the lucidity of his cynicism. The cynic is too much a part of this world, too keenly aware of its parsimony and sharp edges, to engage in the escapist, solipsist flights of the narcissist. Moreover, he knows too much to be taken in by the consumptive strategies of the narcissist in his futile bid to deflect his gnawing despair with the immediate pleasures that external goods bring. So the cynic ekes out his survival without trading in the illusions that sustain the narcissist's angst-ridden life, and he does so because the force of circumstances and his instinct for self-preservation tell him the same thing: "that it has to be so."[81]

However gradual the transition from narcissism to cynicism, and however close the connection between them may be, the fact remains that we are presently in the throes of such a transition and that the cynic has taken up residence as the stock figure of contemporary society. It is a stock figure that we are talking about here, for unwavering cynicism typifies the central characterological types on MacIntyre's list (the manager, therapist, and aesthete)[82] as well as those on Sloterdijk's slightly longer and slightly odder list (the unscrupulous entrepreneur, the disillusioned outsider, the jaded systems analyst, and the conscientious objector without ideals).[83] They all share the sense of having been worn down by the sheer "power of things," of living their lives without the customary blinders and yet settling for what life has dealt them. We have here what Goldfarb aptly refers to as a "form of legitimation" rooted in the "disbelief" that things might be different than they presently are.[84] This explains how cynics, whom Sloterdijk describes as "borderline melancholics," are able to contain their depression and keep on doing whatever society expects them to do. It is this steadfast insistence on staying the course, despite their misgivings, that is the hallmark of their cynicism. It should be underscored that cynics are not dupes; they are self-aware, shrewd emotivists, whose psychological apparatus is "sufficiently elastic," as Sloterdijk aptly puts it, to include recurrent doubts about what they do. That they continue to work and fulfill the institutional roles expected of them, therefore, is a sign of neither their naiveté nor their stupidity, but of their unflinching conviction that this is the way it must be in the absence of any clear alternative to the status quo.

What accounts, it must be asked, for the lucidity of the cynic's relation to society? The answer is manifold. To begin with, this lucidity is deeply etched in bureaucratic capitalism itself, which makes no amends for its technically driven disenchantment of the world, and so wastes little time and spares no indignity in replacing the old, grand narratives of legitimation with its own scaled-down, homely one: diligently and artfully pursue almighty capital and the world will be yours. The accompanying new ideology also plays a major part here. Its purposeful reduplication of existing reality takes delight in draining whatever utopian impulses remain in society. The "faithless belief" in present society it inspires is itself, of course, awash in cynicism. And, of course, there are the harsh economic realities that Sennett and Lasch refer to above, which if they don't directly trigger the cynical impulse at least they dash the optimism that suppresses its upsurge.

But the lucidity of the cynic is also a product of so-called enlightenment discourse practices. Here the culpability of the Left's contribution to the spread of cynicism comes to light. To see this, we need to consider Sloterdijk's tantalizing claim that cynicism is a kind of *"enlightened false consciousness."*[85] Sloterdijk doesn't intend his provocative claim to be read either as an oxymoron or as a stillborn effort at ironic expression. Rather, he wishes it to be read as conveying what he takes to be a simple truth: that the modern cynic owes much of his lucid, "faithless belief" in the present to the lessons he has learned from the standard leftist critique of ideology. The old-styled critique has taught the cynic to be alert to all manner of socially false consciousness, to be on the constant lookout for lies that this or that social order is true or just. It has taught him to be leery of everything that smacks of the traditional language games of truth, justice, and beauty. It has taught him to deconstruct knowledge as power and to despise the "love of wisdom." Above all, it has taught him to think historically.

But the problem with all of this is that it has taught its lessons, in one sense at any rate, too well. The cynic is not merely disillusioned with theory but altogether distrustful and sick of it. And while he now knows how to think historically, he has long since doubted that he lives in a meaningful history.[86] Faced with this daunting prospect, the Left is at a loss about what to do, about how to get enlightenment going again. So it reverts back, unsurprisingly, to what it knows best: coaching the cynic in the ways of skepticism, teaching him to see the institutional imperatives that strap our social practices rather than the virtues and internal goods that still uplift them, all the while that it encourages, despite significant evidence to the contrary that it itself has amassed, a positive, ennobling view of select features of the life of select subcultures like the working class. But since the effects of consciousness raising are both contagious and irreversible, the cynic is swayed little by this talk of the emancipatory credentials of this or that subculture. While he may wish naively to indulge himself in such historical, class-based narratives, he is too enlightened to do so.

The long and short of it is that the cynic is no longer moved—toward enlightenment that is—by the standard critique of ideology. That is because its enlightened discourse practices kill off any sustainable belief that tomorrow might bring a brighter day at the same time that they bar the cynic from seeing the falseness of his own consciousness: that there is nothing in the current social landscape that is capable of making a difference. What the traditional leftist critique of ideology has wrought, therefore, is not a new, vibrant emancipatory narrative, but a new nightmare for critical theory. The old nightmare of critical theory, it will be recalled, was the unreflective dupe, who cheerfully accepted the unjust and stilted social conditions that framed and severely limited his life. The new nightmare for critical theory, hatched, as I argue above, by critical theorists themselves, is the cynic, the reflective, enlightened agent who sees through the inequities and stilted conditions of prevailing social arrangements but nonetheless accepts them as the limit conditions of his own existence.

What we have in the example of the cynic, then, is what amounts to an arrested case of human agency, one that is stuck somewhere in the dialectic of freedom between engulfment and detachment. This is not the way the dialectic of freedom is supposed to work, not at least according to Marx's gloss on it, nor according to G. A. Cohen's penetrating interpretation of that gloss.[87] Cohen characterizes engulfment as the immersion of an agent in a particular social setting. It is because the agent is so steeped in her milieu, so attached to it, that she lacks the freedom to realize herself as an autonomous being. By contrast, Cohen characterizes detachment as the disengagement of an agent from a particular social setting in which she was once fully immersed, and as the realization of a certain freedom that comes from that detachment. But, interestingly enough, the freedom gained by detachment is not a freedom from constraint as such. Indeed, not only is the agent's disengagement from her social situation compatible with the experience of it as constraining, it is what makes that experience of social constraint possible in the first place. A subject can feel constrained by something if and only if she is aware of herself as somehow separate from it. This is precisely the freedom of constraint that an engulfed subject lacks. Insofar as an engulfed subject is not aware of herself as separate from the social context in which she resides, she will be unable to experience that context as a limiting one, as one that constrains her desires and actions in one way or another. She is unable to experience her surroundings as impinging on her precisely because those surroundings quite literally envelop her whole being. So, for example, the young child who is completely engulfed by her parents' world does not feel in the least constrained by that world since she is unable to conceive herself apart from it.[88]

Engulfment in some context or situation means, therefore, that one is unable to conceive of oneself as independent from it. This inability to see oneself apart from some particular setting, Cohen argues further, explains why engulfment cannot "survive a lucid recognition of the nature of one's relation to the engulfing agency."[89] Once the relation becomes perspicacious, once one grasps in what sense one is attached to it, its spell is broken. One is then free in this detached state to experience one's situation as more or less constraining, or, of course, as not constraining at all.

But it is here that the fully integrated cynic proves himself to be something of an exception, for he evinces a "detached negativity" that is for all intents and purposes bereft of hope. His lack of hope has as much to do with his inability to see how he might extricate himself from existing social reality as it does with the constraint exacted by that reality. In other words, the cynic is both a detached being, since he clearly recognizes the otherness of what drags him down, and an engulfed being, since he cannot fathom how he might survive and function outside of that which oppresses him.[90] Here his lucidity is not a guarantee of his safe passage from what engulfs him but a formidable obstacle to any such passage. Indeed, in this instance it is his lucidity that gets him mired between engulfment and detachment; he must suffer both the indignity of what absorbs his being that comes with his engulfment and the weight of what constrains his being that comes with his detachment. It is in this complicated, muddling sense that the dialectical course of the cynic qualifies as a regressive one, or, to cite Lowenthal's more famous and telling phrase, as a case of "psychoanalysis in reverse."

Conclusion

It is clear from our sketch of the new array of social, psychological, and ideological forces that make up the core of advanced capitalist society that the established enlightenment discourse practices of leftist sport theorists no longer work. They no longer work because the standards by which they critically appraise sporting practices and their larger social context reflect the very standards of the practices and society they purport to criticize. So critical theorists of sport seem to have painted themselves into a corner from which they cannot escape, not easily at any rate; it is no longer apparent, in their terms at least, how to pursue enlightenment these days. They leave us, therefore, with some haunting questions about how to get enlightenment going again, and about where in the present social landscape one might find a viable standpoint to criticize existing society and its practices, questions for which there are no obvious answers.

But if there are no obvious answers about how to break this critical impasse, there are at least some indications about how we might proceed in this regard. In particular, there are, as I see it, two ways to go, both of which require that we take leave of traditional leftist practices of justification and emancipation. The first, which comes out of our above discussion, is that we reverse the order of primacy by which we typically view the social world, and by which the Left insists that we view it, so that social practices rather than their institutions become our critical and practical focal point. This can be done without taking our eyes off of what our institutions are up to, and would allow us to derive a significant part of our critical vocabulary from the internal logic and ethos of the practice of sport itself. Since the vision of the social world this practice-view provides persists in deep tension with the vision of the social world the institutional-view provides, we will be able to vouch for the critical veracity of the standards we glean from it: that they don't reflect but rather contest the standards by which society judges itself.

The second way to proceed is not as apparent, not at least from our discussion so far. It requires that we retrace the path by which leftist theorists of sport arrived at the standards of criticism that guided, and ultimately undermined, their critique of sport. The point of retracing this path is that it opens up an unlikely, heretofore untapped source of conceptual tools and argumentative resources with which to resuscitate the enlightenment prospects of a critical theory of sport. That source, which the Left summarily dismissed and skipped over in favor of a privileged treatment of subcultural lifestyles and beliefs, is the liberal tradition itself, to be specific, a certain political variant of that tradition and a certain mainstay of that political variant: what Michael Walzer calls the liberal art of separation—which is essentially a device for carving up the social world in ways that protect particular spheres of life from outside interference. I will argue in the ensuing chapter that when the liberal art of separation is combined with the practice-standpoint of sport, so that the target of liberal divisions becomes social practices like sport rather than individuals and their rival conceptions of the good, we will be able to reconstruct a conceptually and practically more powerful critical theory of sport.

NOTES

1. Robert Bellah, *Habits of the Heart* (New York: Harper and Row, 1986); Richard Bernstein, "Dewey, Democracy: The Task Ahead," in *Post-Analytic Philosophy*, ed. John Rajchman and Cornel West (New York: Columbia University Press, 1985); John Dewey, *The Later Works, 1925–1953, Vol. 5* (Carbondale: Southern Illinois University Press, 1984; Jürgen Habermas, *The Theory of Communicative Action, Vols. 1 and 2* (Boston: Beacon Press, 1984–87); Alaisdair MacIntyre, *After Virtue* (Notre Dame, Ind.: University of Notre Dame Press, 1984); Gilbert Meilander, "Individuals in Community: An Augustinian Vision," *The Cresset* (November 1985): 5–10; Richard Rorty, *Contingency, Irony, and Solidarity* (Cambridge: Cambridge University Press, 1989); Jeffrey Stout, *Ethics After Babel* (Boston: Beacon Press, 1988); Michael Walzer, *Spheres of Justice* (New York: Basic Books, 1983).

2. As quoted in Stout's *Ethics After Babel*, p. 284.

3. Habermas, *The Theory of Communicative Action, Vol. 2*, pp. 322–25.

4. It is because sport still speaks, however muted, the language of virtues that Postman considers the analogy of politics to sport to be much preferable to Reagan's analogy of politics to show business. See Neil Postman, *Amusing Ourselves to Death* (New York: Penquin Books, 1985), pp. 125–26.

5. MacIntyre, *After Virtue*, p. 187. MacIntyre's rendering of a social practice conforms in the main to the implicit notion of sport as a practice I have employed, with the help of Searle and Taylor, in my criticisms of leftist sport theory. It differs, therefore, from the Left's understanding of social practices not only in cleanly separating off the structures and elements responsible for the accomplishment of sport as a social action from those responsible for its institutionalization, but in marking off instrumental activities whose point is to secure our material well-being from social practices whose point is to extend our conception and achievement of excellence in its various forms.

6. Ibid., p. 188.

7. Ibid., pp. 189–90.

8. Ibid., p. 188.

9. It is because the relation of external goods to practices is a contingent one that such goods do not figure in MacIntyre's conception of practices.

10. MacIntyre, *After Virtue*, p. 190.

11. Ibid., p. 191.

12. Stout, *Ethics After Babel*, p. 272.

13. MacIntyre, *After Virtue*, p. 193.

14. Ibid., p. 274.

15. MacIntyre uses the example of a chess player who is a grand master. Ibid., p. 274.

16. As quoted in Ron Smith's *Sports and Freedom* (New York: Oxford University Press, 1988), p. 214.

17. MacIntyre, *After Virtue*, p. 193.

18. External goods, therefore, have the properties of "exclusivity" (they can be limited to those who achieve or purchase them) and "rivalry" (the

more a particular agent holds or consumes them the less there is for everybody else to hold or consume). On this point, see Elizabeth Anderson's excellent essay, "The Ethical Limitations of the Market," *Economics and Philosophy* 6 (1990): 183.

19. MacIntyre, *After Virtue*, pp. 23–35, 74–86.

20. Anderson, "The Ethical Limitations of the Market," p. 183.

21. MacIntyre, *After Virtue*, p. 25.

22. Christopher Lasch, *The Culture of Narcissism* (New York: Warner Books, 1979), p. 197.

23. On the above points, see William J. Baker, *Sports in the Western World* (Totowa, N.J.: Rowman and Littlefield, 1982), pp. 125–26, 147–48.

24. On the changing terms of professional players' contracts, see John Wilson's insightful essay, "Efficiency and Power in Professional Baseball Players' Contracts," *Sociology of Sport Journal* 8 (December 1991): 326–40.

25. J. Feinman, "Critical Approaches to Contract Law," *UCLA Law Review* 30 (1983): 836. I owe this point and source to Wilson's "Efficiency and Power in Professional Baseball Players' Contracts."

26. Stout, *Ethics After Babel*, p. 274.

27. Walzer, *Spheres of Justice*, p. 95.

28. Ibid., p. 96.

29. Ibid., p. 19.

30. Baker, *Sports in the Western World*, p. 148

31. Lasch, *The Culture of Narcissism*, p. 211.

32. Baker discusses these points at length. See his *Sports in the Western World*, pp. 304–29.

33. Lasch, *The Culture of Narcissism*, p. 25.

34. Baker, *Sports in the Western World*, p. 311.

35. Robert Nozick, *The Examined Life* (New York: Simon and Schuster, 1989), p. 177.

36. Lasch, *The Culture of Narcissism*, p. 217.

37. Anderson, "The Ethical Limitations of the Market," p. 203. Stout thus misspeaks somewhat when he muses how the market and bureaucracies provide the material conditions necessary for social practices to flourish but not the necessary moral conditions for practitioners to realize their internal goods. *Ethics After Babel*, p. 289. While it is true that capitalism has managed to bankroll an impressive, and no doubt an unprecedented, array of social practices, it is the way that it capitalizes such practices, insinuating itself in their very production, that compromises their moral integrity. Contra Stout, then, capitalism's failings in this regard are both material and moral.

38. On the notion of use and its connection to the market see Anderson, "The Ethical Limitations of the Market," pp. 180–81.

39. On this point see Anderson, "The Ethical Limitations of the Market," pp. 190–91.

40. Ibid., p. 190.

41. Lasch, *The Culture of Narcissism*, p. 217.

42. Nozick, *The Examined Life*, p. 177.

43. Bernard Suits, *The Grasshopper: Games, Life, and Utopia* (Toronto: University of Toronto Press, 1978), p. 147.

44. Fred D'Agostino, "The Ethos of Games," in *Philosophic Inquiry in Sport,* ed. William J. Morgan and Klaus V. Meier (Champaign, Ill.: Human Kinetics, 1988), p. 65.

45. Ibid.

46. Stout, *Ethics After Babel*, p. 291.

47. Norman Birnbaum, *The Radical Renewal* (New York: Pantheon, 1988), p. 29.

48. Quoted in Suzi Gablick, *Has Modernism Failed?* (New York: Thames and Hudson, 1985), p. 56.

49. Gablick estimated that in the mid-1980s anywhere from thirty thousand to ninety thousand artists resided in New York alone.

50. Gablick, *Has Modernism Failed?*, p. 58.

51. Louis Menand, "What Is the University For?" *Harper's* 283 (December 1991): 48.

52. As Lapham makes clear, operating schools as if they were successful motels comprises "impos[ing] uniform rules of procedure; cut[ting] costs; meet[ing] the customers' demand for better service; teach[ing] the kitchen staff to speak English; insist[ing] that the desk clerks know how to work the imported technology." "Achievement Test," *Harper's* 283 (July 1991): 10.

53. Christopher Lasch, "The Communitarian Critique of Liberalism," *Soundings* 69 (Spring 1986): 69.

54. Stout, *Ethics After Babel*, p. 288.

55. I had occasion to comment on this point in my previous discussion of the historical shift in the administration of sport. See p. 140 above.

56. As quoted in Gablick's *Has Modernism Failed?*, p. 67.

57. Theodor Adorno, *Dialectic of Enlightenment* (New York: Herder and Herder, 1972), p. 157.

58. Adorno's remark was quoted in Habermas's *The Structural Transformation of the Public Sphere* (Cambridge, Mass.: MIT Press, 1989), p. 216; Karl Marx, *Theories of Surplus Value, Volume 3* (Moscow: Progress Publishers, 1971), p. 453.

59. Theodor Adorno, *Aspects of Sociology* (Boston: Beacon Press, 1972), 202.

60. The phrase comes from Richard Rorty's essay "The Priority of Democracy to Philosophy," reprinted in volume 1 of his *Objectivity, Relativism, and Truth* (Cambridge: Cambridge University Press, 1991), p. 194.

61. Stout, *Ethics After Babel*, p. 229.

62. John Hargreaves, "Sport, Culture, and Ideology," in *Sport, Culture, and Ideology,* ed. Jennifer Hargreaves (London: Routledge and Kegan Paul, 1982), p. 34.

63. While the Left's institutional reading of sport consigns it to play the role of the cultural relativist with respect to its practice, it doesn't do so with respect to the use that social classes and groups make of sport. On the latter point, see Chapter 2, pp. 73–78.

64. Francis Hearn, "Toward a Critical Theory of Play," *Telos* 30 (1976–77): 146.

65. Michael Walzer, "Liberalism and the Art of Separation," *Political Theory* 12 (August 1984): 319.

66. Stout, *Ethics After Babel*, pp. 270–71.

67. Lasch, *The Culture of Narcissism*, p. 205.

68. I owe this point to Stout, *Ethics After Babel*, p. 271.

69. Ibid., p. 280.

70. It is part of my argument, however, that though it would be wrong from a conceptual standpoint to romanticize sport, it would not necessarily be wrong from an ideological standpoint to do so. That is because what distinguishes a conceptually errant account of some thing or action from an ideologically suspect one is that the former concerns only the epistemic properties of our beliefs while the latter concerns both the epistemic and, mainly, the functional properties of our beliefs. So what makes a particular belief an ideological one is a matter not of its cognitive standing alone, whether or not it accurately corresponds or refers to some thing or action, but how it functions in a given social setting. That means that a belief that is discursively true may nonetheless turn out to be ideologically false if, for example, it deflects our attention from some important feature of social reality. That also means that a belief that is discursively false may turn out to be ideologically unproblematic if it draws our attention to some feature of social reality that might otherwise go undetected. Thus, what beliefs are ideologically false ones will vary according to the particular historical context. That explains why a set of beliefs in one historical context may support repressive social structures (as the belief in the inviolability of practices no doubt did in liberal capitalist society), and in another historical context may undercut repressive social structures (as the belief in the inviolability of practices in bureaucratic capitalist society may well do today). For an excellent discussion of the delicate interplay between the epistemic and functional properties of ideological beliefs, see Raymond Geuss's *The Idea of a Critical Theory* (Cambridge: Cambridge University Press, 1981), pp. 12–44.

71. Stout, *Ethics After Babel*, p. 276.

72. See Stout's further discussion of this point. Ibid., p. 289.

73. Theodor Adorno, "Society," *Salmagundi* (Fall 1969/Winter 1970): 152. Adorno makes the same point in his essay on "Ideology" in *Aspects of Sociology*, p. 201.

74. Martin Jay has rightly criticized Adorno on this very point for smuggling a fascist model of domination into his account of the new ideology. See his "The Frankfurt School's Critique of Karl Manheim and the Sociology of Knowledge," *Social Research* 39 (Summer 1972): 85–86. What distinguishes the fascist model is that it depends on outright force and intimidation to coerce compliance with its decrees, rather than some spurious set of rational beliefs, some ideology, to legitimate such compliance. So while the fascist model garners support for the status quo by coercion rather than legitimation (the former, of course, makes the latter superfluous), the ideological model garners support for the status quo by seeking its legitimation. Adorno's treatment of the Nazi's reign of terror typifies the heavy-handed fascist approach

to social stability. He refers to Nazism in this regard as a "manipulative contrivance, a mere instrument of power, which actually no one, not even those who used it themselves, ever believed or expected to be taken seriously. With a sly wink they point to their power: try using your reason against that, and you will see where you will end up; in many cases the absurdity of the theses seems specifically designed to test how much you can get people to swallow, as long as they sense the threat behind the phrases or the promise that some part of the booty will fall to them." Quoted in his "Ideology" essay, *Aspects of Sociology*, p. 190. Though Adorno understood well that Nazi domination was impervious to rational critique because it contained no rational elements (discursive beliefs) that could be criticized, he erred grievously in making the same claim of the new ideology of late capitalism. While it is true enough that the transparent demeanor of the new ideology makes any appeal to exotic epistemological justificatory beliefs superfluous, it does not make any appeal to false rational beliefs superfluous. Indeed, what it is that distinguishes the new ideology from the old one is that it confuses practices for their corresponding institutions, which means that much of what it has to say about practices like sport is simply false.

75. Adorno had a lot to say about sport that was quite perceptive and on the mark. For a positive account of his general treatment of sport see my "Adorno on Sport: The Case of the Fractured Dialectic," *Theory and Society* 17 (1988): 813–38.

76. Christopher Lasch, "Politics and Social Theory," *Salmagundi* 46 (Fall 1979): 194.

77. The appellation "minimal self" is the one Lasch uses in his later book that bears the same name, *The Minimal Self* (New York: Norton, 1984).

78. Lasch, *The Culture of Narcissism*, p. 42.

79. Lasch cites Sennett's claim, and raises his own claim in his essay, "Politics and Social Theory," p. 201.

80. Peter Sloterdijk, *The Critique of Cynical Reason* (Minneapolis: University of Minnesota Press, 1987), p. xxix. For the relevant similarities between the narcissistic and cynical self, see Lasch's *The Culture of Narcissism*, pp. 85, 100–101, 106; and Sloterdijk's, *The Critique of Cynical Reason*, pp. xxix, 4–6.

81. Sloterdijk, *The Critique of Cynical Reason*, p. 5.

82. MacIntyre, *After Virtue*, pp. 27–31.

83. Sloterdijk, *Critique of Cynical Reason*, p. 4. My ensuing discussion of cynicism and the cynical self is heavily indebted to Sloterdijk's book, particularly chapter 1. I should also make clear that that discussion is limited to the first of Sloterdijk's three conceptions of cynicism. For a useful summary of those three conceptions see pp. 217–18 of his *Critique*.

84. Jeffrey C. Goldfarb, *The Cynical Society* (Chicago: University of Chicago Press, 1991), p. 1.

85. Sloterdijk, *Critique of Cynical Reason*, p. 5.

86. Ibid., p. xxvii.

87. G. A. Cohen, *History, Labour, and Freedom* (Oxford: Clarendon Press, 1988), pp. 187–90.

88. The example, as well as the accompanying line of argument, comes from Cohen, *History, Labour, and Freedom,* pp. 187–88.

89. Ibid., p. 188.

90. It won't do here to rejoin that the cynic's getting bogged down between engulfment and detachment is itself an indication that his relation to his social context is not a perspicacious one. The force of this rejoinder is that it rightly discerns that the perspicacity of the cynic is not a full-blown one; for while the cynic is wise to the ways of institutions he is not so with respect to practices. But the rejoinder fails because the lucidity required to break the spell of engulfment is not the more penetrating one of seeing the salient differences between practices and institutions, but the more superficial one of seeing that the self is not one with its social setting. On this latter score, there can be no doubt that the cynic is indeed perspicacious.

2   THE RECONSTRUCTED THEORY

FOUR

The Path to a Critical Theory of Sport: Transcendent or Immanent?

In this chapter I lay the groundwork for a new critical theory of sport. My intent in doing so is to break the impasse that has thus far stymied the Left's efforts to come to grips adequately with contemporary sport. The revamped critical theory of sport I offer to accomplish this aim, to get the critical process going again, takes its point of departure from sport conceived as a social practice, and from a critically extended use of the liberal device of walling off social spheres to protect them from unsavory outside influences.

My two-pronged proposal to rebuild critical sport theory is rather unorthodox. It may not win any immediate converts among my leftist counterparts. That is because leftist critics of sport put little stock in analyses that privilege sport or any other social practice, and they put even less stock in appeals to liberal social theory no matter how qualified. Thus, my proposal may be greeted by the Left, notwithstanding my injection of democratic socialist elements into its liberal plank, as disingenuous.

I maintain, however, that only if critical theory is reworked in some such fashion will it have anything to say to us about sport and society that is worth hearing, that has any real critical bite. I will argue that if we go over the same ground that the Left itself went over in its unsuccessful bid to come up with standards of criticism adequate to the institutional and ideological predicament of practices like sport, then we will be led back to the practice-standpoint of sport and to the liberal device of separation as the legitimate starting points of our project to get critical sport theory back on its feet.

An Overview of the Critical Project

What makes a critical theory of sport, or of society generally, critical is that it is not content merely to understand or to explicate sport and its social surroundings, but that it seeks to bring about its practical transformation. The way that critical theory tries to impel such sweeping social transformation is by attacking the beliefs, values, and forms of consciousness that prompt social agents to accede to social arrangements that are not, and were not designed to be, in their best interests nor in those of the practices that they take up. So critical theory doesn't just give agents information about how it would be rational to act *if* they had certain interests, rather it purports to tell them what their true and rational interests are.[1] It does so by appealing to standards of rational acceptability, or to what Geuss simply calls "epistemic principles." Epistemic principles are second-order beliefs about what kinds of first-order beliefs it is acceptable or unacceptable, valid or invalid, for agents to hold.[2] It is these second-order normative beliefs that critical theorists dabble in and try to modify, refine, and legitimate so that they can reasonably assure the rest of us what our true and rational interests are in this or that practice or in this or that social arrangement.

It is no exaggeration to say that the worth of a critical theory of sport is directly proportional to the worth of the standards of rational acceptability that guide it. It is on the basis of the conceptual and normative evidence that such standards supply, that critical theorists sort out true from false conceptions of sport, and acceptable from unacceptable ways of valuing it. Everything hangs on whether they are indeed able to establish the legitimacy of the normative standards that anchor their investigations of sport. Absent such a justification, no one would have reason to take anything they say about sport seriously. So while critical theorists claim to be able to tell the rest of us what our true interests are in sport and larger society, they pay a hefty price for their temerity in the justificatory burden they automatically shoulder in assuming the role of the critic. Unless they are able to shoulder that burden, to back up the criticisms they venture, they risk the rightful scorn of those they seek to enlighten.

Viewed in this light, my argument that leftist enlightenment discourse practices no longer work with regard to sport or society, that they are conceptually and ideologically bankrupt, can be construed as a direct attack on the reflective adequacy of their epistemic beliefs. What I am claiming is that the standards of appraisal that derive from these epistemic beliefs have lost their critical edge, that they can no longer be counted on to deliver the cognitive and normative firepower necessary to accomplish the practical transformation of sport. It is apparent, therefore, that any attempt to refashion a new, truly critical theory of sport must start with an entirely different set of evaluative standards. Though that task is a daunting one, for the theorist must be able to come up with normative principles that are not implicated in our status-quo conceptions and treatments of sport but that somehow connect up with, and are relevant to, them, it is made less daunting by the fact that there are basically only two ways critical theorists can go. The first way is by taking a transcendent approach, by seeking an external, ahistorical, and asocial standpoint from which to criticize existing sporting practices and institutions. The obvious risk with this approach is finding a way to make such principles hook up with the real world. The second way is by taking an immanent approach, by seeking an internal, ethnocentric standpoint from which to criticize existing sporting practices and institutions. The obvious risk with this approach is that such principles might turn out to be uncritical ones, that they might already be co-opted because of their close proximity to our dominant scheme of beliefs.

What I propose to do in the following analysis is to search for a new set of critical standards by exploring both of these paths. Since these paths are the only ones open to theorists of a critical bent, I will of necessity be covering terrain previously covered, as I mention above, by leftist sport theorists. But that is, I argue, more so an advantage than a hindrance, for it will expedite my own search by allowing me to follow up on promising leads the Left made in its attempt to ground its critique of sport, and to concentrate on other promising leads that it ill-advisedly overlooked or simply dismissed out of hand. In the end, then, this exploration should help secure the foundations needed to rebuild a solid critical theory of sport.

The Transcendent Route

As I indicate above, one way that critical theorists try to come up with suitable epistemic principles is by seeking a transcendent warrant for them. The idea here is that critical theory must aspire to be objective if it is to be critical, and that in order to be objective it must detach itself from local historical and social vantage points that limit its vision. There is, of course, a range of objective standpoints one may occupy in this way. One view or standpoint is more objective than another the further removed it is from the particular views of the agents that inhabit a culture, and from the traditions that define that culture at any given time. The objective view that critical theorists of a transcendent drift seek is usually a radically detached one. They wish to view the world from, to use Nagel's telling phrase, "nowhere within it,"[3] to attain what amounts to a God's-eye view of it. They believe that in order to establish the legitimacy of critical theory one must make it universal so that one can give a noncircular, perspectiveless, impartial account of the world, one that is recognizable to, and binding on, all rational persons who view it from the same objective standpoint. On this reading, the key to ensuring that the principles critical theory deploys are indeed critical ones is to struggle, as Dworkin says, "against *all* the impulses that drag us back into our own culture."[4] It is only by resisting such parochial impulses that we can reasonably expect to be able to cast a reflection back on our own culture that reveals it for what it really is, rather than what it fancies itself to be.

This way of understanding the critical project makes the critic out to be a veritable cultural outsider, forced to flee the actual world so as not to be swept into the vortex of its tainted beliefs and crude visions. It seems that the critic has little choice but to set up shop from some point beyond the real world, well beyond the reach of the ideological winds that circulate there, in order to divine new, unspoiled epistemic principles with which to judge and evaluate our received social beliefs.

There are, however, two ways to view this process of radical detachment. The first fancies the critic as a kind of cultural anthropologist, or better, philosophical sleuth, who steps back from the real world to *discover* what is natural in it.[5] In this view, criticism is a matter of discovering the natural bases of the social world, of detecting the natural kinds that lurk behind its social kinds, whether these be natural rights or natural forms of social practices. So understood, the job of the critic is to direct all relevant inquiry about the social world back to these discovered natural premises, to these natural starting points, which is supposed to accomplish their critical resolution. The second way to view this process of radical detachment is as a form of invention.[6] Here the critic is cast as a philosophical scrivener rather than an intrepid explorer, whose task is to concoct a whole new batch of epistemic principles. Since these principles must be invented rather than merely discovered, new methodologies and designs must also be contrived to smooth the construction of these principles. This is the inspiration behind Rawls's "veil of ignorance," which is specially designed to block from our view our own particular interests, holdings, and positions in the world, and of Habermas's universalization principle of discourse ethics, which commands us to assert only those values and interests that can in principle be agreed upon by *all* rational parties, and of Ackerman's regulated liberal dialogue, which disavows all claims made on behalf of particular interests.[7] However these constructive schemes may differ, they are all designed to arm the critic with a carefully contrived set of standards with which to wage war against our everyday social institutions and practices.

What are the merits of such a transcendent gambit, however conceived, for critical sport theory? Is there anything to be said for it as a way of reviving the emancipatory prospects of critical sport theory? If we listen to leftist sport theorists, the answer is an emphatic no. They offer three telling criticisms to back up their negative response, which I will treat in the following order: (1) that there are no vantage points beyond the existing world that provide a privileged view of sport or of any other social practice; (2) that assuming an abstract, objective posture toward sport is no safeguard that that posture is a critical one; (3) that taking a detached perspective on sport encourages a Platonistic account of sport that is largely irrelevant to its social conduct.[8]

The first way that the Left tries to derail a transcendent approach to critical sport theory is by dismissing it as an intellectual pipedream, as an elaborate and cruel theoretical hoax. It is an elaborate hoax because it trades in the wild-eyed notion that there is a natural set of premises, or an ideal set of invented premises, that can be petitioned to settle whatever disputes or crises arise in the conduct of practices like sport. It is a cruel hoax because it inspires the false hope that our social problems in sport and elsewhere can be resolved once and for all by simply referring them back to these natural or contrived premises. The problem is that there are no such sure-fire premises and, consequently, no such magic-bullet answers.[9] The reason why is a relatively straightforward one: our socialization does indeed go all the way down, permeating all our practices and institutional enterprises, to include all of our justificatory practices. There is no way therefore to escape being tarred by the brush of that socialization. Even when we succeed in reflectively putting into question some segment of the social world, some practice or feature of a practice, we invariably take some other part of that world for granted. This was the point of Gadamer's pithy claim that we are always *mehr Sein als Bewusstsein* (more being than consciousness). So we cannot be observers of the social world in which we live without at the same time being participants, and, *a fortiori,* we cannot get a critical perspective on that world without drawing upon some part of it as a resource.

The second way that the Left tries to discredit a transcendent approach to critical sport theory is by arguing that a radically detached view of sport is not synonymous with a critical view of sport. What is being attacked here is the premise that decontextualizing one's account of sport is what makes for a critical treatment of sport. Perhaps the best way to grasp this criticism is to consider an example of such a decontextualized account of sport. Searle's description of American football from the viewpoint of an uninformed, cultural outsider comes quickly to mind precisely because of the level of abstraction it, per necessity, employs. To such a detached observer, Searle contends, football appears to instantiate the "law of periodical clustering," in which "at statistically regular intervals organisms in like-colored shirts cluster together in a roughly circular fashion (the huddle). Furthermore, at equally regular intervals, circular clustering is followed by linear clustering (the teams line up for the play), and linear clustering is followed by . . . linear interpenetration."[10]

I take some liberty in using Searle's description of football as an example of a transcendent account of sport, for it derives not from a point of view nowhere but from a point of view somewhere—albeit somewhere outside of our own culture. But I don't regard this concession to be a fatal one. We have already shown that the notion that there really is a privileged point of view from nowhere is a mere intellectual pretense; no one has ever occupied such a vantage point because no such vantage point exists. So it would have been something of a surprise if Searle's description had turned out, after all, to be a perfectly disembodied one. That it falls short in this respect, however, doesn't change the fact that Searle's description still qualifies as a transcendent one; for the somewhere that it does originate from is at some considerable remove from our particular, cultural-bound, understandings of football. So it seems fair to ask, with the Left, whether we can load such detached descriptions of sport with critical meaning.

We might begin to answer this question by noticing that everything that Searle's detached observer says about football is true. Football is indeed a game that involves various kinds of circular and linear clustering reenacted in some sort of patterned sequence. But before we make too much of this, we should also observe that while Searle's description contains no false discursive beliefs it is, for all that, hardly explanatory of football. It offers those who observe the game from its lofty perch nary a clue as to what all this "periodical clustering" is about. It fails, in other words, to capture the point or the purpose of the game. Its inability to convey what football is about seems to be foreordained, rather than forestalled, by the detached perspective it takes on the game.

What are we to make of this evident shortcoming of the detached perspective? Two salient points, I think. First, the more abstract the account of sport, the greater the level of generality it aspires to, the less substance it possesses. This seems to follow as a matter of course, for the more comprehensive our purview becomes the less we are able to say about what it is we are looking at. The less content our descriptions carry and convey the less we are able to offer in the way of criticism. This suggests that stepping back from practices like sport, dissociating ourselves from all of their cultural particulars, is less a way of getting a critical handle on them than it is a way of consigning ourselves to a superficial understanding of them. Although we are unlikely to misspeak from this elevated standpoint, to say anything manifestly false, we are just as unlikely to say anything that cuts to the heart of the matter—critical or otherwise.

The second salient point about such abstract renderings of sport builds on the first. It requires that we take a closer look at just what content the transcendentally disposed critic forsakes in order to secure his elevated position, and, conversely, what little he then has to go on when he formulates his criticisms from afar. To begin with, when the critic severs all concrete attachments to sport he severs all those attachments that account for its "natural stability," what Habermas refers to as its "unshakeable facticity" that derives from its "embeddedness in naively habituated concrete forms of life."[11] If our critic were content to let matters rest here, of course, he would have heard no complaint from the Left. Shaking up the "unshakeable facticity" of practices like sport is the avowed purpose of the critic, who is, after all, a gadfly by trade, and distancing oneself from the facticity of practices is how the critic manages to pull off such criticism. The problem is that our farsighted critic is not about to let matters rest here; for what he is after is a maximally detached view of sport. So he holds in abeyance not only those attachments that have to do with its "unshakeable facticity," but those attachments that have to do with its rational standing as a practice, that make up its basic intelligibility. What he deprives himself of thereby is *any* foothold in our sporting practices, institutional or otherwise. It is this act of principled forbearance that puts him in the lurch, in what amounts to a critical void. Having eliminated all embodied epistemic beliefs in his pursuit of the ultimate objective standpoint, he has nowhere else to turn, nowhere else to negotiate, to divine new epistemic beliefs to take their place. In short, he has run out of the very epistemic principles he needs in order to get his own critique of sport off the ground, which explains why the descriptions he turns out are not only threadbare but critically suspect as well. Faced with this foreboding prospect, the critic can stand pat, or, more often, pursue one of two avenues.[12] He can either resort to conventional standards of appraisal—disguised, to be sure, as newly discovered or invented ones—or he can embrace what amounts to nihilistic ones. Neither avenue, unfortunately, gets him out of the critical bind he has created for himself.

I can explain what I mean above by returning to Searle's description of football. With nothing to go on but an understanding of football as a curious interplay of circular and linear clustering and interpenetration, the detached critic may well conclude that all forms of clustering and interpenetration are equally privileged and meaningful, that no one way of clustering or interpenetration is any better than another.[13] This suggests that the critic should honor everyone's manner of clustering and interpenetrating, and that no one should be disparaged for however they choose to execute these movements. But this puts the critic in the odd position of endorsing the conventional beliefs and values of practitioners just as they understand those beliefs and values from their own respective personal standpoints. In other words, the critic becomes an apologist, vindicating from nowhere all the beliefs and values that people hold from somewhere—indeed from somewhere deep within their own culture's dominant scheme of beliefs.

But our critic could have just as easily taken a nihilist line here instead of the conventionalist line he takes above. With nothing to go on, once again, but an understanding of football as an interplay of clustering and interpenetration, the critic may well conclude that all forms of clustering and interpenetration are equally worthless and unmeaningful, that one form of clustering and interpenetration is as devoid of value and meaning as another. The critic may come to this conclusion because from his distant perspective not just football but everything appears to be without rhyme or reason, that, to use Nagel's words, "nothing is objectively right or wrong because objectively nothing matters."[14] So now the critic becomes a nihilist, neither disposed from his position nowhere to validate nor to invalidate the particular beliefs and values that people cling to from somewhere.

Neither the conventionalist nor the nihilist predispositions of our hypothetical transcendent critic, as I insinuate above, bode well for critical theory. Indeed, a critic who perfunctorily endorses and/or rejects everything under the sun is no critic. But there is a further complication here, one that suggests that the problem with the view from nowhere is not merely that it gets us nowhere, critically speaking, but that it can be downright dangerous. The complication stems from the leveling manner of the detached critic, of his refusal to acknowledge any difference, be it of a positive or a negative nature, that might make a difference. The abstract, de-differentiating demeanor of our detached critic bears all the traces of a kind of thinking that Habermas calls "abstraction by essentialization."[15] It is the sort of willful leveling abstract manner that Foucault sometimes drifts into with respect to power, that Freud occasionally slips into with respect to sex, and that Beamish at times lapses into with respect to sport. Most notoriously—and herein lies the danger I speak of above—it is the abstract device that Heidegger used to concoct his outrageous and egregious claim that from the lofty standpoint of the history of Being the forcible resettlement of select East Germans during the war was equivalent to the wanton slaughter of millions of Jews at the hands of the Nazis.[16] It is when detachment is used as a pretext to blur important distinctions between kinds of actions and determinate historical events, as Heidegger and others with something to hide have used it, that it becomes not only an ally to some of the worst sort of handwringing imaginable, but a dangerous demagogic tool as well.

There is, however, yet a third line that our detached critic may take, what might be termed a vulgar Platonic line. Here Searlean descriptions will not do because they are threadbare. What the critic requires instead is something a bit more substantive, and this he accomplishes by smuggling concrete descriptions into his own descriptions of sport. The ruse succeeds because these concrete descriptions are then redescribed in more abstract terms to give them the proper transcendent flavoring. The point of the redescription exercise is to enable the critic to manufacture idealized clones of actual sporting practices minus their messy social complications.[17] This can be done in a variety of ways. For example, the redescription may take its point of departure from the rules of sport and redefine them in such a way that a sport qualifies as a sport if and only if none of its rules are violated.[18] More likely, the redescription may take its point of departure from play and redefine sport in such a way that a sport qualifies as a sport if and only if it is taken up in a playful manner, that is, as an end in itself. Both redescriptions require that we view sport in a socially dissociated manner, undeterred and unaffected by the swirl of social interests and sentiments that mark its actual practice.

The problem with this disembodied version of the critic is all too obvious. There seems no manageable way of connecting his idealized abstract ideals with the real world in which sport and everything else must make their way. While it would be nice if sports were pursued in such a way that rule violations were a rarity, and if practitioners took up sports as ends in themselves, the fact remains that real sporting practices seldom, if ever, occur in the absence of some rule infraction or other, and that real sporting practices seldom, if ever, are treated as intrinsic ends. Though these are lamentable social developments, they must be squarely faced by the would-be critic. However, this is what the critic armed with his idealized redescriptions seems unable to do, which explains why the gap between his abstract ideals and motives and those of the practitioners whose sensibilities he wishes to arouse and transform is too great to close. Even though this transcendent critic, as opposed to his counterparts above, is able to spin out ennobling ideals that are worthy of emulation, it is their practical fecklessness in this case that proves to be their undoing.

To sum up, I regard the Left's indictment of a transcendent route to critical sport theory to be convincing, and so I will abandon it in favor of an immanent one that takes its point of departure from our existing cultural practices and traditions. But before I turn my attention to the latter, it bears reminding that our rejection of transcendent critical theory was not because its search for universal standards of criticism proved to be too difficult, but rather too easy.[19] Turning our backs on the culture in which we live out our lives as the particular beings that we are obscures the knotty social predicaments that make social criticism an important, indeed an indispensable, task. That is why looking for principles that apply to everyone in general and no one in particular is a less complicated venture than it might at first appear, and makes criticism more so an intellectual problematic than a social one, and the critic more so an incidental figure than a vital one. The more arduous but meaningful route to take, as I shall argue in the ensuing pages, is to turn toward the thicket of practices and cultural traditions that make up our world, and to probe that thicket carefully for compelling and recognizable epistemic principles that can be marshalled to reconstruct a new critical theory of sport.

The Immanent Route

The second approach to critical sport theory, and the approach favored by leftist sport theorists, as I indicated above, is an immanent one that eschews the God's-eye perspective of its transcendent counterpart, and with it the idea that there are tradition-independent, neutral standards of rational acceptability. The hallmark of an immanent critique of sport is that it concentrates its search for epistemic principles on the local social arrangements and traditions that frame sporting practices. It begins with these enthnocentric starting points per necessity; these are literally the only conceptual materials it has at its disposal, and, fortunately, the only ones it needs, to get its critique of sport off the ground. They are not to be thought of, therefore, as particular prejudices that have to be gotten around somehow, but as the conceptual resources that make it possible to subject practices like sport to social criticism. So understood, the job of the critic is to make explicit the normative standards we already implicitly use in the course of our sporting lives, and then to bring those standards to bear on the actual conduct of those lives.

There is, however, one glaring problem with this prescription for doing critical sport theory. It isn't critical in the least. While invoking the normative standards that are actually embodied in society may be a fail-safe way to come up with recognizable principles of theory and practical conduct, it hardly is a way, fail-safe or otherwise, to come up with critical principles. If anything, it merely seems a not-so-clever procedure for endorsing the status quo whatever that might happen to be at any given moment. It doesn't help matters at all to dress it up in the formal garb of a philosophic theory of truth, a theory, and a prominent contemporary one at that, that usually goes by the name of "warranted assertability," and that holds that beliefs that conform to our prevailing cultural norms are warranted, true beliefs. However we may choose to pitch this putative match between our beliefs and those of larger society, it always boils down to saying something such as "*we* are in a privileged position simply by being *us* . . . that truth can only be characterized as the outcome of doing more of what we are doing now."[20] If anyone still has doubts that this is an incredible thing for a critical theorist to say—that accepting on face value what society regards to be a justification as a real justification is a reputable way to conduct critical inquiry—then consider the result if *we*, perhaps out of cowardice, or sheer stupidity, or fear, were to let the fascists that still populate our ranks have their way, if we were to permit their loathsome beliefs to become *the* standard beliefs of our culture. In that case, we would be warranted on this view of right assertability and justification to say, as Sartre once said, that "fascism would be the truth of man." It would be the "truth of man" because according to this ethnocentric version of critical theory there is no way to gauge the truth, to justify the beliefs that we hold, save by making them mesh with the reigning beliefs of larger society.[21]

But this obviously won't do. There are far too many beliefs embedded in our culture that are shallow, unreasonable, vague, inconsistent, and even mean-spirited. Unless the critic is able to distance his inquiry from these sorts of cultural beliefs he won't have anything to say that is really critical. But this raises the whole question of whether there is any way to steer critical theory in an ethnocentric direction without selling out its critical convictions. The answer is yes, and requires that we distinguish a vulgar sort of ethnocentrism, as exemplified above, from a reflective one. What distinguishes these two variants is that the former appeals to the prima facie, taken-for-granted, precritical conventions of a culture that are internalized as its dominant beliefs, whereas the latter appeals to the deep, reflectively secured, critical norms of a culture (such as the present belief in equality and fairness) that form a background repository of beliefs that can be tapped to criticize its dominant beliefs. Because this second version of ethnocentrism requires the critic to stand back from particular social relations of dominance and authority, and from the dominant set of beliefs of his culture, it can function in a genuinely critical manner. And because it doesn't require him to retreat to some imagined point beyond the culture he occupies, it can function in a genuinely immanent manner.

The task of the immanent critic so conceived is not an easy one. She must be able to appropriate the principled and settled convictions of our cultural practices and traditions without falling prey to their less principled and more expedient dominant beliefs and institutional set-ups. This she does by a process of critical interpretation in which those beliefs are carefully scoured for normative standards that can stand up to reflective scrutiny, that are supported by better rather than worse reasons. The *modus operandi* of the immanent critic, therefore, is interpretation as opposed to discovery or invention.[22] What the immanent critic is after are conceptual resources that already exist, that don't need to be either discovered or invented. These resources are to be found in the key canonical texts and historical precedents that make up a larger tradition of argument and interpretation. The traditions from which we draw such resources are thus best characterized as "historically extended," "socially embodied arguments."[23] The job of the immanent critic here is not, as Putnam avers, "to mechanically apply [the] cultural norms [that are extracted from such traditions], as if they were a computer program and we were the computer, but to interpret them, to criticize them, to bring them and the ideals that inform them into reflective equilibrium."[24] Once the critic has these standards in hand, she can then deploy them against the conventional norms we use to assess our conduct, looking for inconsistencies, contradictions, and argumentative gaps, and against our actual forms of life, evaluating whether they measure up to the reasoned ideals brought to bear on them.

I should point out, if only to confirm the ethnocentric bases of immanent critique, that the very distinction I draw between vulgar and reflective ethnocentrism, and the distinction the latter draws between majoritarian conceptions of the truth (which equate truth with what most of our cultural peers believe) and reflectively warranted conceptions of truth (which equate truth with beliefs backed up by good reasons), are themselves culturally conditioned and rooted distinctions. The belief in what Habermas calls "the unforced force of the better argument," the belief that epistemic principles require rational warrants, is one of the most deeply held and revered beliefs of the discourse practices of liberal and socialist modernity, which depend exclusively on their own conceptual resources to derive the normative principles they require.[25] The very impetus to question and criticize our dominant beliefs, therefore, is a culturally based impulse, not a transcendentally contrived one.

It might be rejoined that this professed self-reliance, this exclusive appeal to culture's internal justificatory devices, this privileging of interpretation over discovery and invention, trades on a "fantastic conceit" of its own, one that easily rivals the transcendent critic's conceit that there are knockdown philosophical arguments that can solve once and for all our most important social problems. The conceit of the immanent critic, it might be alleged, is that she thinks that all the principles of criticism that one ever needs to know to engage in criticism are known, that all the normative standards that ever need to be discovered and/or invented to conduct critical inquiry have already been discovered and/or invented, and need only be interpretively applied.

This is indeed a "fantastic conceit," but it is not one harbored by the immanent critic who rightly understands what the immanence of her critical stance entails. For the immanent critic's reliance on the conceptual resources of her own culture, and on critical interpretation as the best way to gain access to those resources, is a historically qualified, fallibilistic, and contingent one. It says only that as matters presently stand we have all the conceptual tools we need to get the critical process going, and that no new ones need be contrived for this purpose. It acknowledges that the better reasons that serve as the warrants for the critical standards the immanent critic uses, not to mention the interpretive process itself from which such reasons and warrants are culled, are as historically contingent as the worse reasons she rejects as warrants for such standards. It realizes, therefore, that if those better reasons are themselves put into question, the immanent critic has no noncircular argumentative recourse. She must concede that this is where her spade is turned, that she has run out of reasons because her justificatory resources can be stretched no farther. But as Putnam astutely observes, "recognizing that there are certain places where one's spade is turned; recognizing . . . that there are places where explanations run out, isn't saying that any particular place is *permanently* fated to be 'bedrock,' or that any particular belief is forever immune from criticism. This is where my spade is turned *now*. This is where my justifications and explanations stop *now*."[26]

Thus, new critical standards will need to be discovered and/or invented as cultural traditions themselves change and develop. The immanent critic doesn't deny this; on the contrary, it is a pivotal supposition of her own social criticism. What she denies rather is that the critical theorist plays any special role in divining such new standards. It is culture itself that does the lion's share of this work, which means that the primary role of the immanent critic will remain an interpretive one, that is, one of looking, retrieving, glossing, sorting, and checking what culture has thrown her way in the effort to locate something reasonable and substantive to stake her criticisms to. And the regress of her interpretations, along with all the concomitant conceptual activity it excites, will cease only when cultural development and innovation itself ceases.

As I suggest above, I find this immanent approach to critical sport theory to be thoroughly persuasive, on both its conceptual and historical merits—indeed it seems especially suited to dealing with beleaguered practices like sport. As far as I can see, it has no obvious theoretical and practical shortcomings as its transcendent opposite does. But I am speaking in generalities here when I should be speaking in particulars, for immanent critique, even of the reflective variety, comes in many different shapes and sizes. Some are rather clearly plagued by serious problems that it would be wise to avoid. I have singled out the sort of reflective ethnography practiced by leftist sport theorists as one such problematic example. But instead of steering clear of the difficulties that beset their immanent critique of sport, I want to engage them directly and to use my criticisms of them as a springboard to reconstruct an unproblematic—or less problematic—immanent critical theory of sport.

First it is important to reiterate just what kind of immanent critique leftist sport theorists practiced, and in what sense it qualifies as a form of reflective ethnography. Having roundly rejected any transcendent approach to the social criticism of sport, the Left had to find some way to make good on its historicist pretensions without compromising its critical ones, some way, in other words, to avoid the vulgar ethnocentrist trap. It did so in the accustomed immanent manner by flaying existing cultural practices and traditions in search of appropriate critical landmarks to lash its critique of sport to. But the Left took to its task with a meat cleaver rather than a scalpel. Not surprisingly, its cultural incisions were often indelicate and indiscriminate. In one of its most sweeping and important swipes, for instance, it excised most of our current crop of sporting practices and the entire liberal tradition because of their apparent complicity in capitalist hegemony. What emerged unscathed from its probing cuts, however, were certain disenfranchised social groups such as the working class and women. They were spared, the Left argued, not because they somehow escaped the stain of capitalist repression—on the contrary they were stained by that repression more severely than most—but because their various sponsored oppositional movements provided a stock of beliefs and values that could be effectively played off against capitalism's stock of dominant beliefs and values. The Left thus took it upon itself to become their partisan, though not uncritical, spokesperson, using their epistemic beliefs as its critical weapons to undercut the dominance of bourgeois sporting practices and institutions. It conceived its critical mission, therefore, as the self-clarification and self-edification of the aims and struggles of oppositional social groups as these bear on the conduct of sport.

I have three criticisms to make of this class-based, subcultural approach to critical sport theory: (1) it discounts the critical import of sport conceived as a social practice; (2) it requires subordinate social groups to carry a normative burden that they cannot bear; (3) it dismisses out of hand the potentially critical resources of the liberal tradition. I have already expounded at some length on the first two criticisms, so I will not belabor them here except to summarize their main point. It is the third criticism that I want to elaborate, particularly because it sets the stage for my own reconstruction of critical sport theory.

With regard to the first criticism, we need only recount that the Left mistook the structures responsible for the contemporary institutional standing of sports for the structures responsible for their standing as discrete social practices. As a consequence, it failed to take into account the distinctive rationality, goods, virtues, forms of socialization, and traditions particular to sporting practices. What is significant about that explanatory gaff for our present purposes is that in effectively snubbing this practice-side of sport, the members of the Left missed an important critical opportunity to deploy a compelling alternative conception and image of sport against its dominant capitalist conception and image. That missed opportunity, as we shall soon see, will come back to haunt them.

My second criticism takes issue with the Left's contention that the partisan championing of the oppositional sporting movements of subordinate social groups is the linchpin of any reputable social criticism of sport. While some members of the Left, as I have previously noted, have been less judicious and scrupulous in their partisan identification with such groups than others,[27] all have seen fit to ground their critique of sport in the epistemic beliefs of such groups. It is this linkage of partisan identification with social criticism that I object to. What is problematic about it is not that the members of subordinate groups are the social dupes that some on the Left have made them out to be; on the contrary, if there is anything to be said in favor of this linkage it is that it exposes this false presumption of ineptitude for the intellectual conceit that it is. Rather, the problem is that it rests on the no less false presumption that the accepted standards of a subculture can define the principles of rational acceptability, of normative rightness. This presumption proves to be false for the same reason that the presumption that the dominant standards of our culture can define such principles proved to be false: neither set of standards can define reason because they both presuppose their own reasonableness.[28] Deriving canons of criticism from the aims of subordinate social groups is mere question-begging, and, therefore, no confirmation that one has made it around the vulgar ethnocentrist bend. What we need here is some critical warrant, some independent test, to establish that the beliefs of subordinate groups do indeed provide reasonable normative guides for responsible social criticism and practical action. Rallying behind the socially accepted beliefs of some favored social group supplies no such warrant. In supposing that it does, the Left confuses criticism for partisanship, objectivity for solidarity, which explains its penchant for social-class apologetics.

In claiming that the Left cannot be both the partisan and the critical spokesperson for oppositional social groups and their movements, that its partisan predilections cannot be reconciled with its critical ones, I am not claiming that the Left should abandon its partisan advocacy of repressed groups from a moral standpoint. On the contrary, I believe that we have a firm moral obligation to listen, and listen attentively, to the plight of those less well off than we, to their suffer-

ings, struggles, hopes, and aspirations. But this is a moral pronouncement, not a conceptual one; an ethical plea, not a methodological stricture.[29] It is important not to confuse the two since our interest in im-
proving the lot of the disenfranchised in sport and elsewhere may
well require us to discount its own diagnosis of how this unseemly
fate befell it and its own hunches about how to better itself. That
doesn't eliminate or diminish, however, our moral responsibility to
hear them out, and to do so compassionately, openly, and resolutely,
whether they see fit to offer diagnoses or remedies as to what ails
them and larger society.

If I am correct that the Left cannot secure the critical canons it needs
by deriving them from the epistemic beliefs of groups such as the
working class, then its own immanent slant on the social criticism of
sport is jeopardized. If, as it argues, sporting practices are merely simulacra of their institutions, and if, as I argue, working-class involvement in sport offers no reliable guides to its practical transformation,
then there is nowhere else to turn in the present social landscape to
sponsor an immanent critique of sport. In short, it appears that all
the cracks in the social order have been sealed, that society has succeeded in making itself a seamless whole. That, of course, doesn't
make the practice of immanent critique simply more difficult to pull
off, it makes it quite impossible. It suggests that Adorno's suspicion
that "there is not a crevice in the cliff of the established order into
which the [theorist] might hook a fingernail"[30] was essentially correct.
So the Left seems to have steered us once again into a kind of conceptual and historical cul de sac, one more suited to Adorno's obdu-
rate images of cliffs and broken fingernails than to revolutionary images of sweeping social transformation.

The Left, however, was not unaware that its immanent critique of
sport was in some trouble. While it may not have been attuned to its
conceptual problems, it was to its historical problems. Its own definitive studies of working-class involvement in sport revealed that such
groups were not exactly teeming with revolutionary fervor, that they
were more complacent than they were insurgent. That explains the
Left's resorting to what amounts to a transcendent gambit to rescue
its theory of sport from the discouraging historical data. I am referring to its tactic of filling the mouths of its anointed groups with a
revolutionary prose they seldom, if ever, spoke. Tired, no doubt, of
the reactionary rhetoric typically served up by such groups, the Left
took to scripting their words and actions for them, to attributing slogans and deeds to them that made them appear less tentative and
contented and more angry and strident than they evidently were.

What the Left was trying valiantly to do in this backhanded way was to suffuse the cultural traditions of the working class with an alien socialist vocabulary that would validate its assault upon the dominant cultural traditions of capitalism as, potentially at any rate, a revolutionary one. In other words, it tried to engineer an immanent critique of capitalist sport by making out its working-class adherents to be native speakers of socialism.

Aside from the deception, there is nothing particularly wrong with this sort of tradition-hopping. In fact, it's a good way to get some perspective on the culture in which we live and the traditions that we actually cling to. It gives us some idea of what sort of social beings we might have become and what sorts of social practices we might have contrived had we been subject to different cultural influences and different forms of socialization. This sort of information is useful because of its contrastive value; it just might spark a new way of thinking about or doing something that has always been done the same old and tired way, or forge new vistas by breaking encrusted conventions. The same might be said of the Left's effort to infuse our cultural views of sport with socialist panache.

But tradition-hopping turns out to be a profitable critical enterprise only if it is done the right way, that is, only if it makes some meaningful connection to the lives we are currently living and the traditions that presently inform those lives. The problem with the Left's injection of socialism into our cultural understanding of sport is that it doesn't make that connection, that it is largely a disconnected attempt to keep its critique of sport alive. It falls prey, then, to the same problem that skewered our Platonic transcendent critic who was unable to bridge the gap between his idealized conceptions of sport and its actual, embodied forms. The point is not, therefore, that the Left is being inconsistent when it reaches out to the disparate tradition of socialism to try to salvage its critical theory of sport, which it manifestly is,[31] but that it is being ineffectual when it does so. The shame is that in failing to find something in our present conceptions and notions about sport to fasten its socialist vocabulary to, the Left missed a golden opportunity to, as Walzer aptly puts it, "describe socialism in socially validated and comprehensible terms."[32]

This brings me to my main and last criticism of the Left's immanent approach to critical sport theory: its contemptuous repudiation of the liberal tradition. The Left's disdain for liberal theory is as legendary as it is unsparing. It issues from the Left's conviction, largely unexamined and certainly unchallenged within its tight circles, that liberalism has played a major part in the triumph of capitalism and in the spread of bourgeois forms of sport throughout the world. It has done so, the Left argues, by spinning out individualistic conceptions of sport that succeeded only in giving theoretical voice and credence to such archetypal bourgeois fetishes as maximizing individual choice, promoting rational self-interest, and opening up opportunities for involvement in sport. While liberals are also fond of talking about such things as rights, justice, pluralism, and the separation of social spheres and powers, these are merely a cover, the complaint continues, to promote their own asocial, atomistic conceptions of sport and to obscure important questions about social power and control that weigh heavily on practices like sport, and that limit the freedom of its participants in ways they scarcely imagine. It is no accident either, the Left finally insists, that such talk conveniently obscures capitalism's own complicity in the degradation of sport.

It is fairly clear, then, why leftist sport theorists never considered hitching their socialist agenda for sport to liberal themes, never tried to find a soft spot within liberalism to root their own socialist package of reforms. Liberal theory was for them a big part of the problem, not the key to its resolution; that is, it was part of the vulgar ethnocentric refuse of capitalist society that had first to be discarded if the Left ever expected to make good on its promise to deliver a genuinely critical account of sport.

I am not persuaded, however, that the Left was correct to finger liberal theory as one of the principal culprits behind the spread and dominance of bourgeois conceptions of sport. I don't deny that liberalism must share part of the blame for capitalist hegemony in sport and elsewhere.[33] Rather, I take issue with the Left's misguided attempt to levy this charge against the entire liberal tradition as if it were some monolithic, unitary, conflict-free, and fully settled body of thought. The problem is that it has never been anything of the kind, neither in its inception nor in its present developed state. Herzog's rendering of the liberal tradition as a "family of disagreements," and MacIntyre's as a "conflict in continuity," are much closer to the mark.[34]

However, it is not only that the Left misreads the conflict-riven character of liberal theory in a way that makes its indictment of liberalism vague: just what branch of liberal theory and just what liberal doctrines does it mean to dispute?[35] It is that it misreads it in a way that seriously damages its central charge that liberalism has acted, and continues to act, in cahoots with capitalism. The Left's forced unitary reading conflates two strains of liberal thought that have been at odds with one another from the very beginning, and that ought to be clearly distinguished. The one strain, variously referred to as bourgeois or economic liberalism, takes its point of departure from the inviolate, presocial individual, and is an ardent defender of the market as the preeminent sphere in which human agency is exercised and of property rights as the main safeguard of our liberty. By contrast, the other strain of liberal theory, most commonly referred to as political liberalism, takes its point of departure from the social individual and from its repertoire of social and political practices, and is an ardent defender of rights (conceived not as trump cards individuals play to protect their autonomy but as social guarantees of democratic voice and deliberation), pluralism, a suitably chastened state, and a clear separation of spheres of life.[36] If there is anything at all to be said for the Left's stinging accusation that liberalism has been a pawn of capitalist interests, then it is to be said only of its economic and not its political arm. Political liberalism has been a continual thorn in the flesh of capitalism, admonishing strongly against a slavish addiction to property rights, working strenuously to protect political and cultural forms of life from the long arms of the market, and arguing tirelessly for the democratic reform and control of the workplace.

That the Left has carelessly, or perhaps worse, unknowingly, run together these two contending currents of liberal thought is good enough reason, I contend, to reject its monolithic rendering of liberalism as well as the presumptive denunciation of its critical credentials that that rendering falsely entails. It is also good enough reason to reopen at least the political side of liberalism for exploration by would-be critical theorists in search of the normative standards they require to subject the likes of sport to social criticism.

C. Wright Mills was one of the first to recognize the possible worth of such an exploration, but he chose to append a cautionary note to his admittedly tentative endorsement of liberalism. He wrote:

> Liberalism, as a set of ideals, is still viable, and even compelling to Western man. That is one reason why it has become a common denominator of American political rhetoric; but there is another reason. The ideals of liberalism have been divorced from any realities of modern social structure that might serve as the means of their realization. . . . The detachment of liberalism from the facts of a going society make it an excellent mask for those who do not, cannot, or will not do what would have to be done to realize its ideals. . . . if the moral force of liberalism is still stimulating, its sociological content is weak.[37]

If we read Mills's observations as a commentary on the contemporary standing of political liberalism, then I think they capture the special but precarious salience of its principles for a critical theory of society and sport. I think Mills exaggerates the degree of detachment of its ideals from "going society," its principle of democratic accountability (which roughly stated says that everyone should have a say in decisions that directly affect their lives), for example, still enlivens much of the political debate of that society; yet it can scarcely be denied that the major social structures of capitalist society are driven by market imperatives rather than liberal political ones. This disengagement of liberal principles from the daily details of life might well, as Mills seems to think, be used as a mask to cover up rather than expose what ails the prevailing practices of society. In his favor, it must be said that the standards of a tradition can always be interpreted in an apologetic or a critical manner. But how they are to be interpreted is never a matter of idiosyncratic choice nor idle speculation; rather it is an empirical matter requiring a careful historical call. That is why I am persuaded that such principles are uniquely poised today—but not, to be sure, in perpetuity—to exercise a critical rather than an apologetic role. If what imperils practices like sport nowadays is that they have become hostage to institutions that are themselves preoccupied with, not to mention fueled by, market imperatives, then I think we have good warrant to place our critical faith in liberal devices such as boundary-mapping to stem the tide of such intrusive economic influences. It is for this reason that, while mindful of Mills's caveat, I second Dewey's call for liberalism to become radical, which even Dewey seemed implicitly to recognize requires that it play up its political side. He wrote:

> Liberalism must now become radical, meaning by "radical" perception of the necessity of thorough-going changes in the setup of institutions and corresponding activity to bring the changes to pass. For the gulf between what the actual situation makes possible and the actual state itself is so great that it cannot be bridged by piecemeal processes undertaken *ad hoc*. . . . The liberals of more than a century ago were denounced in their time as subversive radicals, and only when the new economic order was established did they become apologists for the *status quo,* or else content with social patchwork. If radicalism be defined as perception of the need for radical change, then today any liberalism which is not also radicalism is irrelevant and doomed.[38]

This completes my criticisms of the Left's social-class slant on critical sport theory as well as my larger sketch of the transcendent and immanent ways of doing social criticism. I have shown that there are two sites within the social terrain of advanced capitalist society from which one might successfully launch an immanent critique of its dominant forms of sport. They are, as I have intimated throughout, sport conceived as a social practice and political liberalism conceived as a device for insulating practices like sport from outside interference. It is upon these two pillars that I will reconstruct a critical theory of sport, one that makes the practice of sport the focal point of a liberal scheme of demarcation.

NOTES

1. Raymond Geuss, *The Idea of a Critical Theory* (Cambridge: Cambridge University Press, 1981), p. 58.

2. Ibid., p. 61.

3. Thomas Nagel, *The View from Nowhere* (New York: Oxford University Press, 1986).

4. Ronald Dworkin, "To Each His Own," *New York Review of Books*, April 14, 1983, p. 6. The emphasis on "all" in the text is mine.

5. On this point see Michael Walzer, *Interpretation and Social Criticism* (Cambridge, Mass.: Harvard University Press, 1987), pp. 4–6.

6. Ibid., pp. 8–13.

7. John Rawls, *A Theory of Justice* (Cambridge, Mass.: Harvard University Press, 1971); Jürgen Habermas, *Moral Consciousness and Communicative Action* (Cambridge, Mass.: MIT Press, 1990); Bruce Ackerman, *Social Justice in the Liberal State* (New Haven: Yale University Press, 1980). I should mention that Rawls's later work revises the conception of the veil of ignorance in a way that does not completely accord with the view of criticism as invention I discuss above. In his more recent essays, Rawls presents the veil of ignorance as a way of screening off our particular interests so that we can tap into the deep and settled convictions that undergird our liberal political tradition. Viewed thus, the veil of ignorance is less a way to escape the world than it is a way to get in touch with the more reflective and critical principles of that world. See especially Rawls's "Justice as Fairness: Political not Metaphysical," *Philosophy and Public Affairs* 14 (Summer 1985): 223–51. For an excellent critical discussion of all three of the above constructive designs see Michael Walzer, "A Critique of Philosophical Conversation," in *Hermeneutics and Critical Theory in Ethics and Politics*, ed. Michael Kelley (Cambridge, Mass.: MIT Press, 1990), pp. 182–96.

8. While all three criticisms are implicit in the writings of leftist sport theorists, only the first has been enunciated by them in any appreciable detail.

9. Walzer dismisses the search for the definitive, knockdown argument as a philosophical conceit, specifically as a piece of "philosophical impetuosity." See his "'Spheres of Justice': An Exchange," *New York Review of Books*, July 21, 1983, p. 43.

10. John Searle, *Speech Acts* (Cambridge: Cambridge University Press, 1969), p. 52.

11. Habermas, *Moral Consciousness and Communicative Action*, p. 177.

12. He actually has a third option that we will examine in due course.

13. Walzer develops a similar criticism of Nagel's impartial conception of equality. See his "The View from Somewhere," *The New Republic*, February 17, 1992, p. 30.

14. Nagel, *The View from Nowhere*, p. 141.

15. See his essay "Work and Weltanschauung: The Heidegger Controversy from a German Perspective," in *The New Conservatism*, ed. Shierry Weber Nicholsen (Cambridge, Mass.: MIT Press, 1989), p. 163.

16. Ibid.

17. This was also, as was discussed in the previous chapter, a favorite ploy of early bourgeois apologists of sport.

18. On this Platonist version of sport, see D'Agostino's "The Ethos of Games," in *Philosophic Inquiry in Sport*, ed. William J. Morgan and Klaus V. Meier (Champaign, Ill.: Human Kinetics, 1988), pp. 64–65.

19. For further discussion of this point see Walzer, *Interpretation and Social Criticism*, chapter 1.

20. Richard Rorty, *Consequences of Pragmatism* (Minneapolis: University of Minnesota Press, 1982), p. 173.

21. I lifted Sartre's remark from Rorty's provocative discussion of it in *Consequences of Pragmatism*, p. xlii. For an interesting analysis of Sartre's claim and Rorty's interpretation of it, see Jeffrey Stout, *Ethics After Babel* (Boston: Beacon Press, 1988), pp. 255–60.

22. On the critical role that interpretation plays in social criticism, see Walzer's analysis in his book *Interpretation and Social Criticism*, pp. 19–32. In my ensuing discussion, I also make use of ideas gleaned from Walzer's "'Spheres of Justice': An Exchange," pp. 43–46.

23. Alaisdair MacIntyre, *After Virtue* (Notre Dame, Ind.: University of Notre Dame Press, 1984), p. 222.

24. Hilary Putnam, "Why Reason Can't Be Naturalized," in *After Philosophy: End or Transformation?* ed. Kenneth Baynes et al. (Cambridge, Mass.: MIT Press, 1987), p. 233.

25. On this point see Habermas's essay "The New Obscurity: The Crisis of the Welfare State and the Exhaustion of Utopian Energies," in *The New Conservatism*, ed. Nicholsen, pp. 48–49.

26. Hilary Putnam, *The Many Faces of Realism* (LaSalle, Ill.: Open Court, 1987), p. 85.

27. The range of partisanship varies here from Fraser's less-than-cautious view that with respect to justification there is no "philosophically interesting" difference between an uncritical and a critical theory of society but only the political difference of the latter's identification with oppositional subordinate groups—which seems to say that all such identifications are, *ipso facto*, justified ones—to Gruneau's more circumspect view that only certain forms of partisan class identification can be justified. Nancy Fraser, *Unruly*

Practices (Minneapolis: University of Minnesota Press, 1989), pp. 113–14; Richard Gruneau, *Popular Cultures and Political Practices* (Toronto: Garamond Press, 1988), pp. 26–27.

28. For more on this see Putnam, "Why Reason Can't Be Naturalized," pp. 228–32.

29. I briefly discuss this point in Chapter 2, p. 125 n. 130. See also Rorty, *Consequences of Pragmatism*, p. 202.

30. Theodor Adorno, *Minima Moralia* (London: Verso, 1985), p. 211.

31. If only to underscore the inconsistency of the Left in resorting to such tradition-swapping, it should be said that the only way to make such wholesale transitions work is to adopt the Cartesian device of radical doubt: to put everything we believe into question simultaneously. For an interesting discussion of this point see Alaisdair MacIntyre's essay "Epistemological Crises, Dramatic Narrative and the Philosophy of Science," *Monist* 60 (October 1977): 465–66.

32. Walzer, *Interpretation and Social Criticism*, p. 57.

33. Bowles and Gintis, for example, argue that in the last two centuries there have been four major accommodations struck between capitalist economic imperatives and liberal principles. See their *Democracy and Capitalism* (New York: Basic Books, 1986), pp. 41–56.

34. Don Herzog, "Up Toward Liberalism," *Dissent* (Summer 1989): 358; MacIntyre, *After Virtue*, p. 222.

35. There is something disingenuous about the Left's unitary reading of liberal theory. When the Left is attacked by loose-lipped detractors for promulgating Stalinist conceptions of state socialism, or by more sober-minded but no less false critics for becoming Weberians (bureaucrats and managers) when forming into movements seeking power, or for entertaining Nietzschean fantasies about the revolutionary prowess of working-class factions (Lenin's "ideal revolutionary" and Lukács's "ideal proletarian," which come across as modern versions of the *Übermensch*) when historical conditions augur for a far less optimistic assessment, members of the Left correctly point out the relevant differences that separate them from such mindless, knee-jerk socialists, and are quick to tick off Gramsci, Habermas, and Williams, and in sport studies, Gruneau, as counterexamples to dissociate themselves yet further from the horrors perpetrated in socialism's name. Yet when confronted with the same shoddy characterizations of liberal thought and with knee-jerk liberal types, the Left slips into the same dismissive posture as some of its most misinformed and outrageous critics. Liberal theory deserves at very least the same sort of consideration that leftist theorists accord their own theories when falsely caricatured. I owe the above Weberian and Nietzschean characterizations (caricatures) of Marxism to MacIntyre, *After Virtue*, pp. 261–62.

36. For an excellent discussion of the civic, communitarian import of rights such as freedom of speech and assembly, see Cass R. Sunstein, "Rightalk," *The New Republic*, September 2, 1991, pp. 33–36. The literature on liberalism, on its different forms, scope, and relation to other political theories, is immense. For starters, I would recommend Bowles and Gintis's wide-ranging

and helpful discussion of political liberalism in their book *Democracy and Capitalism.* I would also recommend R. Bruce Douglass's excellent anthology *Liberalism and the Good* (New York: Routledge, 1990). Finally, for a discussion of the differences between economic and political liberalism similar to my own, I would recommend Chantal Mouffe's "Rawls: Political Philosophy without Politics," in *Universalism vs. Communitarianism,* ed. David Rasmussen (Cambridge, Mass.: MIT Press, 1990), pp. 217–35.

37. C. Wright Mills, "Liberal Values in the Modern World," in *Power, Politics, and People,* ed. Irving Louis Horowitz (New York: Oxford University Press, 1963), p. 189.

38. John Dewey, *Liberalism and Social Action,* reprinted in *The Philosophy of John Dewey,* ed. John J. McDermott (New York: G. P. Putnam, 1973), pp. 647–48.

FIVE

A Reconstructed Critical Theory of Sport: Social Criticism with a Liberal Twist

My reconstruction of a new critical theory of sport must be preceded with further discussion of the liberal art of separation itself, in particular, its purpose and the mechanics of its operation. My discussion will concede and incorporate an important socialist criticism made of its use by bourgeois and political liberals.

The Liberal Art of Separation

I suggested at the outset of the last chapter that there is a perfectly good liberal remedy for the institutional fix that plagues sport and our current slate of practices. That remedy consists of what Walzer calls the liberal art of separation, which tries to situate practices in the right social context so that they might prosper and even flourish.[1] It is a device that is familiar to most of us who have grown up in the liberal democratic cultures of the West, and who have become accustomed to debates about the separation of state and church, about how to make sure that the affairs of statecraft don't meddle in those of soulcraft and vice versa. It is especially well known to those of us who labor in academia and who are keenly aware of how vital academic freedom from political and religious intrusion is to the teaching and research enterprises we carry on. It has become almost second nature for us to think that freedom and equality are best served when our standing in one sphere cannot be jeopardized by our standing in another.

But I want to cast this familiar liberal stratagem in a slightly less

familiar critical light. I believe that its partiality for carefully differentiated and buffered spheres of life, for protecting the relative autonomy and constitutional integrity of the different realms in which
we pursue our life projects, offers no mere reformist solution to the
institutional quandary of practices like sport, but a radical solution.
The solution it offers is a radical one because the existing tensions
that rack our athletic institutions and sporting practices have themselves become radical. As the tensions escalate, the liberal method of
defusing them by cordoning off sporting practices grows progressively more radical. What it would take to shield sporting practices in this
fashion is a complete revamping of our reigning network of institutions, a wholesale reconfiguring of their relation to practices in order
to ensure that the internal imperatives of practices prevail over the
external, systemic imperatives of their institutions. It is the institutional drift of bureaucratic capitalist society itself, therefore, that has
turned the liberal art of separation into a radical one, one that if allowed to ply its craft would dramatically change the face of contemporary society, and change it, I argue, for the better.

The Left, not surprisingly, cleaves to a contrary view. It does not
regard the liberal practice of putting up walls to protect favored social practices as a radical remedy, much less a practical one. Indeed,
the whole notion of separating spheres is anathema for the Left and
curtly dismissed by it as a bogus exercise. That is because it runs
against the grain of one of its most cherished and deeply held convictions about society: that it always works and is ruled as a whole.
Capitalist society proves to be no different in this respect, the Left
stoutly maintains, for it too is ruled as a whole, and that whole is governed by clear economic mandates. So it is mere pretense to think that
the economic forces that drive capitalist society can be stemmed by
building a wall around the market, or that religious, political, intellectual, and sporting practices can be protected from each other and
the menacing arms of the market by building walls around each of
them. All of this barricading of practices behind walls, which seems
a social blueprint more suited to a feudalistic world order than an
advanced democratic one, would be laughable, the Left continues, if
it weren't for the ideological overtones. For what this liberal pretense
lacks in the way of practical felicity, it more than makes up for in the
way of ideological felicity. So while it is clear that erecting flimsy partitions will not be able to hold back the tide of market forces that fuel
the whole capitalist enterprise, it may well be able to disguise the
manner in which such market forces tether religious, intellectual, and
sporting endeavors to the pursuit of the dollar.

I do not dismiss this complaint out of hand. All too often liberal partitions have not held, and the economic imperatives of the market have spilled over into our religious, political, intellectual, and sporting lives, savaging each in the process. Indeed, this is precisely the institutional dilemma that I earlier argued bedevils all of our important social practices. But the reason why such liberal partitions have turned out to be as porous as they are is, I contend, not hard to figure out, nor especially difficult to correct. The problem is that liberals habitually privatize the lines they use to carve up the social world, a habit whose dubious legacy is apparent in the uneven and uncomfortable cleavage one often finds in liberal democratic social orders between the private and public realms of life. Liberal theorists typically appeal to individuals, and to the rights that are said to accrue to them naturally, as the measure (literally the ruler) for the lines they draw. The autonomy of social practices is the intermediate but not the end point of liberal divisions.[2] That end point rather is reserved for the autonomy of individuals. And so it is their autonomy, as opposed to that of the social practices they take up, that liberals target when they build their walls.

One can see this disposition to privatize straightaway in bourgeois liberalism, which, as we noted above, makes the inviolate and inalienable rights of the individual economic actor the centerpiece of its private-public distinction. The market, it argues, is preeminently a private venue, which means that economic actors are to be left alone to act on their own preferences free from outside political and social pressures.[3] By contrast, the state, it argues, is a public venue, which means that individuals should be allowed to express their own political choices, and additionally, should be held democratically accountable to those who are affected by their decisions. While political liberalism tried to bridge the gap between our private and public lives introduced by economic liberalism by treating both the economy and the state as public venues in which the principles of liberty and democratic sovereignty mutually apply, it nonetheless retained a privatistic bent in its consideration of cultural practices. It considered artistic, intellectual, religious, and sportive endeavors to be principally matters of individual conviction and private perfection. So it treated the freedoms that undergird these pursuits as rights, which entitled the individuals who held them to engage in these practices in any way they fancied. Academic freedom came to be thought of, therefore, as the freedom to study or to pursue any line of inquiry one desired, and so as having nothing essentially to do with the social settings (universities, scholarly societies) in which such freedom is exercised.[4] Similarly, freedom in sport came to be thought of as the freedom to participate in sport in any way one pleased, and so as having nothing essentially to with the social settings, goods, and standards that define its practice. Likewise for the rest of our cultural practices, which were all treated, as I indicate above, according to the dictates of individual temperament. In matters cultural, therefore, political liberals ended up drawing a nebulous line of their own between our private and public lives, one that in giving such wide scope to individual preferences short-changed the cultural practices that comprise a goodly part of our public life.

I am not inveighing against liberalism for its vigilance in looking after our private lives. On the contrary, I think we all are heavily indebted to liberal types for keeping a sharp eye on Big Brother; for safeguarding our right to profess unorthodox religious beliefs; for protecting our right to entertain and utter unpopular thoughts and ideas; and for defending our right to control our own bodies. Rather, my criticism of liberal theory is that in ignoring the public venues and social settings in which these cherished rights and freedoms get played out, it has failed to keep apace of the dangers that threaten social practices like sport as well as the communitarian core of our public lives. If liberalism is to correct this oversight, then it must acquire a more comprehensive and complex understanding of our social life than it has thus far. It must, that is, set its sights beyond the protection of our privacy, as important as that is, and realize that in order to preserve and nurture the endangered ways of living embodied in our social practices it will have to socialize its art of separation; it will have to make the protection of practices from their institutions, rather than individuals from intrusive corporate and state bureaucracies, its *main* point of departure.[5] Unless liberals are prepared to go public with their differentiating wand, I fear that the private walls with which they have managed to encircle individuals will continue to prove ineffectual in staving off the impressive economic forces arrayed against practices like sport.

Where I part company with the Left's complaint against liberal divisions, however, is its contention that such divisions are irredeemable, that they cannot be fortified in a way that would make them resistant to market incursions. This wholesale rejection of the liberal art of separation reflects what I earlier termed the Left's doctrinaire reliance on holistic theories of society,[6] in this case the notion that society is always ruled as a whole, which derives from its key thesis of "radical interdependence": the idea that spheres of life are either "passive reflections" or "active reproductions" of others. The problem with this doctrine of "radical interdependence" is its ahistorical drift, its treatment of the historical tendency of advanced bureaucratic capitalist societies to function in a radically interdependent fashion, that is, to let market forces prevail wherever they might, as an exemplification of an iron-clad law of social reality. So instead of treating this integrationist tendency for the historically conditioned and contextualized one that it is, the Left pronounced it an a priori, decontextualized principle of social conduct. In doing so it not only overestimated the extent to which institutions hold practices in bondage, and obviated the need to look for signs of independence or relative autonomy in existing practices, as I argued in Chapter 3,[7] it also discounted practical measures like the liberal art of separation that might keep the market from overspilling its boundaries. Had the Left been sensitive to the historical dynamic responsible for the dominant position market forces enjoy in bureaucratic capitalist societies, I argue, it would have realized that one promising way to contain intrusive institutions is to keep them out of social settings in which they don't belong, in other words, to barricade practices behind carefully constructed, heavily fortified partitions that institutions can't penetrate. If there is anything bogus here, it is not the claim that liberal divisions might be refurbished in order to make them effective deterrents to runaway bourgeois institutions, but the spurning of that liberal device altogether in favor of some yet to be discovered or invented revolutionary measure culled from the epistemic beliefs of this or that subculture. Indeed, what is so hard to abide by in the Left's censure of liberal separation is that it leaves practices like sport in the lurch. While it probes for a better, truly radical solution to their predicament by taking up the causes of such subcultures, it leaves sport and the rest of our practices at the mercy of institutions bent on their destruction.

Instead of rejecting liberal divisions outright, however, I propose that we incorporate them within the corpus of socialism itself, that we, as Walzer aptly puts it, "enlist liberal artfulness in the service of socialism."[8] That is what my argument to socialize the liberal art of separation comes to in the final analysis. This follows from the fact that socializing the lines we draw not only requires that such lines mark off practices, as opposed to individuals, so that they are each accorded a slot within which they can flourish free of outside interference, but that we wrest control of such practices from bureaucratic types and turn them over to the practice-communities to which they rightfully belong. Thus, when Walzer argues that a "consistent liberalism . . . passes over into democratic socialism," he knows of what he speaks.[9] But what we end up with is a decidedly liberal sort of socialism, a socialism that calls not for the abolition of the market or the state, but only for their proper location and their carefully delimited sphere of influence. It does not exhort us, therefore, to dis-

pense with the entire old social order so as to make room for a completely new social order, but urges us to alter radically the existing
divisions within society in order to make them more effective and
democratic blocks to market encroachments. This is a socialism of
putting things in their proper place so that the lopsided market orientation of capitalism might be turned on its head. It is the sort of
socialism that Habermas champions in the following passage:

> What constitutes the idea of socialism, for me, is the possibility
> of overcoming the onesidedness of the capitalist process of ra-
> tionalization. . . . Onesidedness, that is, in the sense of the rise to
> dominance of cognitive-instrumental aspects. . . . With the over-
> coming of that system, these aspects would be shifted to their
> proper place. . . . In socialism, too, one would have to live with
> an economic system which operates exactly like a partial system,
> a system which is separated out from the political context.[10]

It is important to remember that this socialized version of the liberal art of separation, with its talk of placement, displacement, con-
finement, and limitation, is intended to break the dominance of institutions and their train of external goods over practices and their
train of internal goods. Though this requires that the monopoly institutions' hold over such external goods be scuttled, this is only the
intermediate aim, not the terminus, of its employment. It is only the
intermediate aim because while dismantling such monopolies will
preclude institutional types from controlling and exploiting such external goods, thereby guaranteeing their wider, more equitable distribution, it will not of its own accord be able to break the dominant
grip such external goods have over practices. For that we need to ensure that the convertibility of external goods is properly delimited,
that they cannot be fitted to things or goods internal to practices to
which they have no intrinsic connection. Drawing lines is especially
suited to this task in a way that monopoly breaking is not. This is
because it is specifically designed to prevent the external goods sponsored by institutions, or for that matter any set of external goods sponsored by any outside social agency, from attaining or maintaining
dominance by truncating their sphere of influence and circulation.[11]

If undoing the dominance athletic institutions hold over sporting
practices is a matter of limiting the convertibility of the external goods
they trade in, then the question becomes How do we draw the lines
of our social map to ensure this result, to ensure that our sporting
practices will be protected from their incursion? In a word, how do
we get the lines right in a way that does justice both to the sporting
practices we partake of and to the individuals who take them up? My

answer is twofold: first, by appealing to the internal logic of sporting practices themselves, and second, by tapping our critically backed shared conceptions of the social goods that we regard to be intrinsic to such sporting practices. The first appeal requires an immanent consideration of the character of sporting practices, the second an immanent consideration of their practice-communities.

The Logic of Sport and Its Social Demarcation

As I noted above, the liberal practice of drawing lines is founded on the notion that social practices and the specific goods they deal in fare better in certain social contexts than others. The difficulty lies in fitting practices to the right social contexts to ensure the realization of their particular goods. What we need to get the right fit is to locate internal principles of differentiation, that is, principles that derive from the structural and historical core of practices themselves. While practices may not have essences that demarcate natural, preordained boundaries, they do have what Walzer calls "characteristic normative structures" that demarcate limits of appropriate behavior and social spaces conducive to the goods internal to them.[12] It is, for example, intrinsic to our notion of political practices that their offices should be held by the politically astute and qualified rather than the financially astute and endowed, and it is intrinsic to our notion of medical practices that curing the sick ranks above making money off of the sick. So it seems at least plausible to connect the lines we draw around practices to the characteristic normative structures that derive from their internal logic. When we do we get a segmented social world, a social map of sorts, that looks and functions very much like the kind of social world Pascal and Marx, respectively, describe below:

> Tyranny is the wish to obtain by one means what can only be had by another. We owe different duties to different qualities: love is the proper response to charm, fear to strength, and belief to learning.

> Let us assume man to be man, and his relation to the world to be a human one. Then love can only be exchanged for love, trust for trust, etc. If you wish to enjoy art you must be an artistically cultivated person; if you wish to influence other people, you must be a person who really has a stimulating and encouraging effect upon others.[13]

Pascal's and Marx's claims that personal attributes, social acts, and goods are appropriate to certain social spheres and not to others, and that tyranny ensues when the connections between these actions and spheres are violated, illustrates well the way such liberal divisions are supposed to work and what their ostensible purpose is. It also illustrates the first way we suggested above to fix the boundaries of sporting practices to protect them from institutional encroachment. They too possess characteristic normative structures that can be read from their internal logic. By specifying what that logic is and what it comprises and entails we can begin penciling in the borders of sport on our social map.

What our manifold sporting practices share in common, as we observed in our previous criticisms of the Left, is that they are all contrived pursuits that seek to overcome unnecessary obstacles. While sport shares this delight in gratuitous difficulties with games, differing perhaps only in the physical sorts of challenges it poses, that is not problematic for our purposes. Although the extension of games is broader than sports, which simply means that not all games are sports, the relevant point here is that all sports are games. That is the relevant point because it means that the gratuitous logic that runs through our sporting practices runs through all, and not just some, of them. That also means that by tapping the gratuitous logic inscribed in our sporting practices, we can demarcate their proper sphere of action without making much ado about their physical dimensions.[14]

What is crucial to the proper demarcation of sport, however, is to notice how its gratuitous logic is bound up with its constitutive rules, which make up the most basic layer of its complex social constitution. As Suits and others have argued, such rules always prohibit the simplest, easiest, most direct ways to achieve the goal of the game in favor of more complex, more difficult, more indirect ways to achieve it.[15] The means allowed by the rules in the pursuit of sportive goals must always fall short of "ultimate utilities," which is to say that the permissible means to their attainment must always be narrower in scope than the possible means to their attainment. Put differently, the specific ends of sporting practices (crossing the finish line first, putting the ball into the hole) are considered unimportant in themselves, and so they are considered worth pursuing only if they include a quite definite specification of the way such ends may be attained (crossing the finish line first by, among other things, running around the track rather than across it, putting the ball into the hole using the fewest number of strokes).[16] In each case, of course, the specification makes the end more difficult to attain in order to make it more challenging, which is, after all, the main point of sportive endeavors.

Becoming clear about the distinctive way that constitutive rules function in sport allows us to get a better fix on its gratuitous rational demeanor, which, in turn, allows us to understand better what distinguishes its practice from other human undertakings. Aside from a game, the arbitrary imposition of unnecessary obstacles to the attainment of an end is considered an irrational thing to do, whereas in a game it is considered a perfectly rational thing to do.[17] So conflating the constitutive rules and gratuitous rationality of sporting practices with the constitutive rules and instrumental rationality of everyday social activities only serves to render both absurd. It is a salient fact about everyday life activities that their goals are valued and found sufficiently challenging in themselves, such that the arbitrary introduction of obstacles to their accomplishment would be regarded as a queer, unintelligible thing to do. It is no less a salient fact about sporting practices that their goals are found compelling only when they are made more difficult to accomplish, such that any refusal to abide by the proscriptions on means that make them difficult to attain would be regarded as a queer, unintelligible thing to do.

So it seems that petitioning the constitutive rules of sporting practices is a good way to get a handle on their distinctive rational character and so a good way to demarcate their proper sphere of operation and influence. Indeed, we already have a clear sense that sporting practices need to be cordoned off from instrumental ones that hew to an alien technical logic, and from institutions that are oblivious or otherwise indifferent to this difference. But I may have spoken too soon, for it seems that even drawing this line embroils us in a controversy in at least two senses. That this tentative start to mark sport off from other human endeavors can itself be challenged no doubt confirms what I said earlier, that lifting criteria of demarcation from the founding rules and logic of sport is bound to be controversial if only because neither those rules nor their accompanying logic are algorithms that can be mechanically plotted to yield the thick divisions we seek. But reiterating that such criteria must be carefully coaxed out of those rules and that logic by a delicate process of critical interpretation won't resolve the objections to the line we have inserted between technical pursuits and sportive ones. To accomplish that we must clearly spell out the objections and answer them, not merely to rescue what I regard to be a legitimate separation, but to specify in greater detail what it stands for and requires.

The first objection is that our principle of demarcation is too thick, that its separation of sporting practices from other practices is too severe and excludes and settles too much that should be left up for grabs. It is too thick, the objection continues, because it makes the constitutive rules of sport out to be essences, and so, sport out to be a natural kind rather than a social kind. Our demarcation effort went awry then because we aimed too high, because we tried to capture what is common to *all* sporting practices, to define their universal core, which amounts to a thinly veiled attempt to come up with something knockdown and conclusive like an essence rather than something less knockdown and conclusive like an immanent principle of distinction.

The force of this objection, however, is not just that it requires us to concede that sport is a social kind rather than a natural kind, its rules conventions rather than essences, but to concede that it is foolhardy to even try to read criteria of rationality and demarcation from social practices like sport. It is foolhardy to do so, it is argued, because sport and the like are contingent social productions through and through. They are not to be thought of on the model of "alternative geometries," which differ from one another because they were designed to be different, because they have different axiomatic structures.[18] Sporting practices possess no axiomatic structures; they were not designed to be different. Accordingly, there is no reason to forcibly separate them from other practices, no reason why they cannot be combined with other practices, no reason why we shouldn't let the chips fall where they might with respect to their relations with other practices without forcing them to conform to some theoretical grid. If it is rejoined that practices like sport are, after all, framed by "institutional norms," it is retorted that this only confirms what people like Foucault and Rorty have been trying to tell us all along: that so-called "rational" ways of ordering and conceiving practices like sport are inseparable from power, that the backups of our institutional divisions are not criteria of rationality but bureaucrats, politicians, and policemen.[19] To think otherwise, to see axioms where there are only contingent constellations of power, is, in this view, to confuse our "paper" conceptions of rationality and the clever social maps they yield for the real, contingent, structureless things that populate our social world.

Considered in this unflattering light, which mixes Foucaultian themes of contingency and power with such standard leftist fare as the doctrine of "radical interdependence," the whole business of deriving criteria of rationality and demarcation from the rules of sporting practices is a shady one. The logic of separation it preaches, it is objected, is not a logic of emancipation but a logic of, in Derrida's words, apartheid.[20] That is because its effort to size up practices like sport by measuring them against antecedently existing criteria (rules) is merely a power play designed to block alternative conceptions and treatments of their practice. It is an exclusionary tactic meant to hypostatize some preexisting or existing set of sporting practices in order to make it more difficult to reform them or to replace them with a new set of practices.[21] It is, in short, a device whose basic point is to enshrine the status quo as the best of all possible worlds, not to change it in some meaningful, substantive way.

Before I try to answer this objection, however, I want to consider the second objection to our effort to come up with demarcation criteria by probing the rules and internal logic of sport. The objection here is the opposite one, that our principle of demarcation is too thin. The separation between sport and the technical activities it gives rise to is criticized for being too elastic and open-ended to be of any real help in sorting out the complicated social and political controversies that beset the world of sport. Indeed, the only action-guiding principle it can muster, it is alleged, is the hollow one that one ought to obey certain rules of sport. It is alleged further that the only alternative model of sport it offers is a sterile, formalist one. In reducing sport to the formal set of rules that define its present practice, this model seems not even to have taken account of the fact that sport possesses an ethos, a social context that plays a large part in shaping its practice, let alone a determinate set of goods or virtues. Far from furnishing a safe haven for sporting practices to operate free of extraneous influences, then, this formalist division between sportive and instrumental pursuits is adjudged too vapid and imprecise to be of any critical or practical use.

Let's take a closer look at both of these objections, neither of which I find persuasive. The first objection alleges that I illicitly transpose the constitutive rules of sporting practices into essences and thereby preempt their much-needed reform. This criticism is mistaken on a number of counts. To begin with, my interest in the constitutive rules of sport is only to get at its underlying gratuitous logic. It is that logic itself, and not the rules per se, that guides my separation of sportive pursuits from technical ones. As far as the rules themselves go, I second the notion that they are entirely social constructions, and that in this respect at least there is nothing natural or magical about them. Indeed, it is the social rootedness of these rules that explains the resonance that certain sports have with certain historical periods and social contexts. This was the basis of my earlier argument that medieval sports such as jousting have an undeniable connection to the social relations of feudalism and that modern sports such as American football have an undeniable connection to the social relations of capitalism.[22] That feudal lords, nobles, and peasants were very much enamored with jousting, and that modern-day professionals and middle- and lower-class folks are very much enamored with football, cannot be explained unless their respective constitutive rules are social kinds that stand in some definite relation to the respective social orders in which they resonate. There can be no serious question about this, just as there can be no serious question that such rules are subject to the ebb and flow of the social conventions that underwrite their vitality and that fix their intelligible relation to their social setting. That accounts for why shifts in those social relations more often than not result in shifts in the constitutive rules of those sports.

But my argument cuts deeper than this. I also hold that the logic that undergirds and informs the constitutive rules of sport is a social logic as opposed to a natural logic, and that its social fabric qualifies it further as a contingent logic. While this may seem to be a concession to the first objection raised above, it is not. Although I concur with its contention that both the rules and founding logic of sport are social artifacts, I take issue with its implied central premise that a socially contingent property of a sporting practice cannot stand as a universal, transcultural property of a sporting practice, that, to fit it to our present case, since the gratuitous logic of sport is a socially grounded, contingent logic it cannot claim to be a universal, transcultural logic. I dispute here the supposition that identifying a logic common to all sporting practices, a universal core that purports to capture their intrinsic makeup and their characteristic normative structures, is tantamount to identifying an essence of sporting practices. I deny this supposition because it falsely equates contingency with the absence of universal properties, because it wrongly supposes that the opposite of contingency is universality. The fact is however, as McCarthy astutely points out, that the opposite of contingency is necessity, not universality.[23] This suggests the alternative possibility—the one to which I subscribe—that the gratuitous logic of sport is a contingent universal condition of its practice.

To say, as I do, that the gratuitous logic of sport is a contingent universal condition of its practice is to say that when such practices cease, when they no longer resonate in any social order or are no longer found sufficiently worthy to be included as a part of any cultural tradition, then the logic that founds and sustains them will cease as well. As long as these practices survive in some discernible form, however, the intelligibility of deliberately forsaking more efficient in favor of less efficient means to realize certain goals will endure and will continue to enliven some part of our action in the world. What is important about the concrete universal status of that logic, then, is not that it guarantees that sport will continue to play an important role in our lives, not that it ensures that sport is a lock to persist in perpetuity, which its contingent status precludes it from doing; but rather, that it establishes that while the rationality of sport is immanent to its social practice it is not immanent to the social systems and institutional networks in which it is situated. That is, it upholds the claim that the logic of sport is continuous with its social practice without making it an instrumental handmaiden of any social order, whether that social order be feudalism or capitalism.

It is the irreducibility of that logic, therefore, that makes the relation between sport and society the complicated and tangled affair that it is. It disconnects sporting practices from whatever obvious links they might have to society and to the rest of our lives and molds them into novel, distinctive undertakings. It was with this point in mind that I earlier hedged my claim that sports stand in certain definite relations to their surrounding social settings. Though it is right to say that jousting intimates a certain military posture toward life that is reminiscent of the kind of social anarchy that once reigned in feudalistic society, and equally right to say that football intimates a certain regimented and aggressive stance toward life that currently reigns in advanced capitalist societies, it is quite wrong to say in either case that jousting is "irreducibly" a feudalistic practice or football an "irreducibly" bourgeois one.[24]

When we prick the rational core of a practice like sport, we find not something natural, pure, inviolate, or necessary—not an essence—but something social, impure, and contingent. The mistake comes in supposing that what one finds within the heart of sport that is impure and contingent is what implicates it in larger society. This is the mistake the first objection commits, for it harbors the plainly reductionist belief that the social properties that constitute a practice like sport are cut out of the same cloth as the social properties that define a social system like capitalism. It is this reductionist reading of the logical core of sport that our rendering of it as a contingent universal is meant to foil. It is able to do so because its logical core is indeed a universal one that speaks a transcultural language, one that resists ready translation into the language of capitalism or of that of any other large-scale social system.

Still, it is important not to lose sight of the fact that the universal language it speaks is a social language and not an artificial one, that it doesn't converse in Esperanto but in rich culturally inflected tones. That is important because it means that what it has to say to us is always said in a socially mediated way, in a socially accented voice that conveys something about the context of our present lives without being reducible to that context. The social accent with which it currently speaks is a decidedly modern one that in giving voice to the distinctive forms of life opened up by the autonomization of sporting practices reflects the differentiation and complexity of modern life itself. The rational language of sport is a modern, secular one, then, not in the sense, as Hans Kamphausen writes, "that an originally religious phenomenon becomes worldly," but rather in the sense, as he continues, "that an athletic game (*sportliches Spiel*), originally laden with religious significance, concentrated itself upon its own . . . elements."[25] So while the rational language of sport drives a wedge between it and the systemic imperatives of society, it nonetheless manages to tell us something about the modernness of modern life that is not, and cannot be, conveyed by those imperatives. That is another reason why, I maintain, it still resonates so with us moderns, and why the normative guidance it provides is relevant to the contemporary situation in which sport finds itself.

Skimming off criteria of demarcation from the logical core of sport is not, then, a matter of lining up an unadulterated essence with a principle of right conduct, not a matter of locating the one true interpretation of sport and then deriving normative standards from it, but of carefully transcribing its language in a way that conveys its intrinsic character and its proper sphere of action and influence. The nonreductionist, contextual criteria that it supplies should not, however, be interpreted in a strict isomorphic way, in a way that insists on a one-to-one correspondence between the rational complexion of a practice and the judgments that can be made about it. This view would have us believe, for instance, that political judgments and evaluations are restricted exclusively to the sphere of politics, aesthetic ones to the sphere of art, economic ones to the sphere of the market, and sportive ones to the sphere of sport. By contrast, my reading of the gratuitous rationality of sport allows for a certain mixing of rational and normative judgments within a single sphere, which means that sport is not only capable of, but in certain cases requires, political, aesthetic, and economic comment. This is allowed from the contextual thread of my interpretation; what is clearly disallowed by that same thread, however, is the simple reduction of sport to any one or combination of these exoteric judgments.

We have already said enough to deflate another salient premise of the first objection, the claim that if practices like sport have structures at all they are institutionally embodied ones that yield criteria of power, not criteria of rational demarcation. This is just another rehash of the facile doctrine of radical interdependence, which by illicitly mapping the institutional structures of sport onto its practice-structures obliterates any difference between them. Once we grasp what is errant about this conflation of the institutional structures with the practice-structures of sport, it becomes plainly evident that one can very well invoke the latter without encumbering the former, and that doing so doesn't implicate one in some sort of power scam. The criteria that the social logic of sport supplies are rational ones that set the intelligible limits of sportive conduct. Fastening on to those criteria and their normative derivatives is not a matter of hypostatizing the rules of sport so as to block its reform or wholesale transformation; in fact, it has nothing at all to do, as I indicate above, with tinkering with its rules. Rather, it has to do with locating the rational seat of our sporting practices in order to safeguard their integrity. It should be clear from my earlier analysis of the institutional plight of sport that safeguarding its integrity is going to require a great deal of reform, if not extensive reconstruction, of its current institutional setups, hardly the stuff out of which Foucaultian genealogies of power are spun.

Finally, we have already said enough to refute what has to rank as the silliest premise of the first objection: the notion that sport is a radically contingent practice, which reduces to the claim that it is an amorphous, structureless practice. The argument here is that it is just wrongheaded to think about a contingent practice like sport in terms of criteria or structures, or to try to pigeonhole it into some category on the basis of such criteria or structures. Rather, since sport comes in no preconstructed, prepackaged shape, it is up to us to impart some shape to it, to imprint it with some defining, if tentative, marks. The best way to do this, we are told, is to do a bit of experimentation, to view sport through a kind of kaleidoscope. By peering at it from a number of different perspectives, and by weaving and reweaving the various descriptions of it that are revealed by these multiple perspectives, we will be able to settle on a conception of sport that is to our specific liking. The settled-on conception is not, of course, the one that best encapsulates what sport is all about; to view the matter this way is self-defeating because it smuggles criteria and structures back into the picture. Rather, it is the one that most people can agree on, the one, in other words, that is able to attract the most adherents.

There is a grain of truth to this view: practices like sport can't be likened to alternative geometries; they don't possess axiomatic structures. But it is a rather large leap from this premise to the conclusion that sport is a radically contingent, structureless practice. What it lacks in the way of axiomatic structures, it doesn't lack in the way of rational structures that mark it off from other practices. While sport and the like may not have been designed to be irreconcilable in the sense of radically incommensurable with other social endeavors, they were designed to be different in ways that make irreconcilable demands on those who take them up: such that, if one devotes oneself to their curious, means-limiting logic, one preempts oneself from achieving a number of other ends that cannot be pursued in this limited fashion.[26] So adducing criteria from the gratuitous logic of sport, and holding its practice accountable to such criteria, is not so much a matter of illicitly judging it by antecedently existing criteria as it is a way of honoring Rorty's altogether reasonable stricture that we give up "attempts to ground some element of our practices on something external to these practices."[27] Honoring that stricture, I maintain, doesn't require us to forsake assessing practices like sport by stacking them up against immanent criteria, but only to forsake doing so by stacking them up against exoteric criteria.

It is not just that this sort of free association doesn't follow from the stricture that practices must be grounded from the inside-out, that it is a non sequitur, but that the perspectivism it prescribes is tantamount to what Hilary Putnam calls "mental suicide."[28] It is tantamount to such because in urging that we simply drop all criteria in our dealings with practices like sport, it is exhorting us, in unmistakable terms, to eliminate the normative dimension from our critical inquiries, literally to stop trying to justify what we do. There is a related complication here as well. The perspectivism it advocates forces us to play the role of the cultural outsider, to ignore, in effect, not just the rational core of practices like sport but the historical traditions that frame their practice and that endow them with special meanings. It does so because it erroneously supposes that the multiple traditions that inform and enliven our sporting practices provide a multiple number of perspectives from which to view and treat them, rather than, as MacIntyre correctly argues, a "multiplicity of antagonistic commitments."[29] This is the source of its contentious claim that it can blithely disregard the historical claims such traditions make on the goods that our practices trade in, and can treat and dispose of these goods in any way it pleases. What feeds this perspectivist view of traditions is precisely its disengagement of their normative elements, the very elements that prompt people to commit themselves to one tradition rather than another. What is problematic about this perspectivist disengagement is that the normlessness it espouses mirrors, as MacIntyre further observes, the *anomie* that Durkheim attributed to the pathological breakdown of community in modern society, to the loss of membership in the traditions of one's culture.[30] What Durkheim didn't foresee, however, was the possibility that at some point down the road of history, anomie would be seen as an achievement of sorts, as a form of liberation from the social relations of traditions, rather than as the pathological condition that it is. So what Durkheim diagnosed as a pathological condition is now depicted, as MacIntyre laments, as a new "mask of philosophical pretension."[31] If my argument is cogent to this point, however, this is one philosophical pretension that we ought to resist with all our might: presuming, of course, that it is the welfare of sport, and not its demise, that is our foremost concern.

So it appears that our effort to extract criteria of demarcation from the internal logic of sports is a tenable one, and that the boundaries between sportive and instrumental endeavors that they produce are not too thick as to be useless in instigating their much-needed reform. But that leaves the second objection, that our rational criteria of demarcation are too thin and the boundaries they produce too weak to be able to stave off the institutional pressures brought to bear on them. Unlike the first objection, this objection doesn't mistake our appeal to the internal logic of sport as a covert attempt to hypostatize its constitutive rules, but rather argues that the appeal to that logic only requires that some subset of its founding rules be strictly adhered to. That requirement is much too formalistic, much too nondescript, it is argued, to be able to offset the dominance athletic institutions hold over sporting practices. Indeed, it is even too threadbare to be of normative assistance in settling less radical, but still momentous, controversies in the world of sport: whether, for instance, the introduction of certain sophisticated technological equipment into sport (aluminum bats, fiberglass poles, steel golf shafts) compromises its basic character, or whether certain styles of play (the minimalism of power tennis that largely reduces the game to "scorching" serves) excessively detract from its artistry, or whether imbibing certain substances (steroids, amphetamines, and the like) to enhance performance violates its integrity. On these and more radical matters then, simply insisting that certain rules be observed is insisting on precious little, certainly too little to extricate sports from their present institutional burdens.

I am, however, persuaded that my internal demarcation of sport is sufficiently robust to ward off intrusive institutional forces and to provide normative guidance in settling some of the most pressing questions that it currently faces. My strategy here will be to show that appealing to the logic of sport encompasses more than an appeal to its central predilection to forsake the easiest path to the attainment of its goal, and requires a good deal more than simple compliance with some subset of its rules. I will try to establish, in short, that the supposed formalism of my demarcation of sport is not that at all, that it requires, not just allows, recognition that sport possesses and is in part governed by an ethos, and that that ethos is itself parasitic on its internal logic.

However, saying that appeal to the internal logic of sport provides the necessary critical footing to protect sport from unwholesome outside influences and to assist normatively in resolving controversial aspects of its practice is not saying that it provides a knockdown, determinate answer to every question that is directed its way. I concede, therefore, that such appeal will not always prove to be decisive, that it will not always settle the issue all at once, and once and for all. I concede as much because it is neither crucial nor damaging to the argument I am making here. That argument only requires showing that the invocation of the logic of sport is an effective way to deter its wholesale co-optation by institutional forces and an effective way to sort out which conceptions and treatments of it are conducive to its practice and which are not; it does not require "holding the silly claim that there are [or will be] no indeterminate cases at all."[32]

I also want to claim that maintaining a certain indeterminate posture in one's critical deliberations about sport and the like is, methodologically and critically speaking, a good thing, instead of merely not a bad thing. For example, because I base my separation of sport from other pursuits on its logical demeanor, a demeanor shared by all forms of sport to a greater or lesser degree, I have refused to identify or endorse, much to the consternation of my critics, a particular level or kind of sport as *the* paradigm of an emancipatory sport. However, I regard that refusal to be salutary because I cannot see any critical advantage to be gained by singling out such an emancipatory paradigm of sport.

Perhaps the best way to understand my reluctance here is to first note how easy it is to come up with such a model of sport. If one wants to locate a level or kind of sport that has been least tainted by the corrosion of contemporary capitalist society one need look no further than the class of noninstitutionalized sports, or what some theorists call "folk" sports and others call recreational sports, or simply preinstitutionalized sports. The model I identify here, of course, is pretty much the same one that Rigauer and Gruneau earlier identified in their analyses of sport.[33] The ease, however, with which all of us were able to come up with a model of an emancipated sport, or at very least an uncorrupted one, should have alerted us to the problem of doing critical theory in this fashion. The problem is that championing such models of sport provides us with little leverage to criticize our dominant menu of sports, which explains, no doubt, why Rigauer saw fit to recant his own rosy assessment of the emancipatory pedigree of recreational sports and lump them under the same social dynamic that governs institutionalized sports.[34]

The problem of trying for too much determinacy in one's critical treatment of sport actually comprises three separate, albeit related, problems. The first is that taking up the cudgels of folk sports cuts the critic out of a large part of the action. It does so because it forces her to operate at the margins of the world of sport, playing up elements of sport that are hardly given any play at all in the sports that command the most attention in prevailing society, and writing off most, if not all, of these sports as incorrigible. And while launching one's criticisms from the margin may be an effective stopgap measure to keep alive alternative forms of life in danger of immediate extinction, our current regime of sports is not, at least not yet, I argue, in such dire straits as to require critical treatment of this once-removed sort. Second, championing the cause of folk sports entangles the critic in the kind of wistful utopianism we spoke of in Chapter 3. The kind and scope of deinstitutionalization that would be required to transform folk sports into the dominant paradigm of sport is simply unimaginable by our present lights—indeed the means by which such a far-reaching deinstitutionalization of sport might be carried out literally boggles the mind, and it ignores the important point that practices like sport require institutional props to sustain them—all the more they aspire after a privileged place in our social lives. Third, and finally, deinstitutionalizing our current ensemble of sporting practices would eliminate some of our most cherished sporting practices, which hardly seems an antidote for relieving already beleaguered practices from forces that threaten to tear them apart.

One final point about the indeterminacy of my rational demarcation of sport is in order before I tackle the objection that it is insufficiently robust to be critical. That is simply to reiterate that my theory is a two-pronged one, and that part of the slack of what is left unspecified by the first part, which tries to fix the intelligible limits of sport by petitioning its internal logic, is meant to be taken up by its second part, which tries to flesh out that logic by petitioning the critically informed and shared conceptions of practice-communities themselves. So certain specifics of my demarcation of sport have been deferred to a consideration of the interpretive role played by its practice-communities, which accounts for some of the indeterminacy of my theory to this point and about which I will have considerably more to say in due course.

Now to the main objection that my demarcation of sport to this point lacks critical teeth because it is too thin. It is considered too thin, it will be remembered, because abiding by its separation of sportive endeavors from technical ones is said only to require that certain rules of sport be complied with. I don't, of course, dispute that honoring the gratuitous logic of sport mandates that at least some of its rules be followed, but only that its mandate begins and ends with such rule observance. In particular, I argue that one may well obey all the rules of a sportive game and still not be engaged in a game.

Perhaps it is best to begin with an example to illustrate my point. I have in mind a trifler at games, a well-heeled game-type, who obliges most, if not all, of the rules of the games he participates in yet fails to be a player of any of these games.[35] A game-trifler adheres to the rules of games but not in order to realize the ends of these games. A trifler is not interested in pursuing the goals of games, only in indulging his own privately crafted goals. He may be interested, for example, in reenacting some long-forgotten pagan rite in the context of a game, or in realizing some idiosyncratic delight in certain movements required by the game, or in trying to cram as much random behavior as he can in the rule-regulated environment of a game. Whatever his adventitious reason, however, it is apparent that in spite of his observance of its rules he is not actually playing a game, but only making gamelike moves.

Specifying what it is that makes the trifler a quasi–game player rather than a real one will help us begin to unpack what it is that makes action in a game rational as opposed to irrational action; it will help us to discern, in other words, what the logical structure of sportive games requires in the way of intelligible action on the part of its players. To begin with the obvious point, it is not the trifler's failure to abide by the rules of the game that disqualifies him as a player of that game, since as our above example makes plain he is abiding by most of those rules. Nor is it the trifler's failure to realize the goal of the game that accounts for his quasi–game player status, since most players of games fail to realize the goals of the games they play (that is to say, most players lose the games they play) and yet remain bona fide game players. What gives away our trifler as a quasi-player is not his failure to achieve the goal of the game but his lack of interest in doing so, his indifference to its achievement. It is this air of indifference with respect to the achievement of such goals that qualifies what he does as gamelike, but not as a game.

What is significant about the trifler's regard for the rules of games and his disregard for its ends is that it shows that the logic of sport-ive games cannot be reduced to mere compliance with its rules. It shows, that is, that something more is required of practitioners of sport than simple adherence to its rules. What that something more might be is specified by Searle's claim that acting in accordance with the rules of a game necessitates that one follow them in a way that makes clear the aim of that game.[36] Although what Searle means by his specification "making clear the aim of the game" is itself some-what unclear, I interpret him to be saying not merely that one must be cognizant of the aim of the game whose rules one is following, but that one must find that aim compelling in some important sense. To find the aim of a game compelling in this requisite sense means to find the form of life in which it is embedded and which it exempli-fies as compelling, as worthy of one's commitment and devotion. In other words, I read Searle's specification of what acting in accordance with rules entails to be a specification of what might be termed the ethos of a game, of a set of social conventions that, while they are not themselves a part of the formal rules of the game, play a joint role in its social constitution, and so, a joint role in determining its ratio-nal complexion.

My justification for reading Searle's rider in this strong sense is rather simple: this is the only way to mark off quasi-players of games like triflers from genuine players of games. If we read Searle's rider in the weak sense that players are only required to be aware of the ends of the games they play, then triflers, at least those who are not so caught up with their own idiosyncratic aims as to be oblivious to the aims of the games they partake of, implausibly turn out to be real players of games. This is implausible precisely because triflers lack the zeal required to see a game through to its end that makes one a real player of games. What distinguishes triflers and kindred quasi-player types from real players of games, then, is that the latter are bound to the ethos of games, to the ways of life they stand for, in a way that the former are not. In the final analysis, therefore, it is this disregard for the ethos of games that disqualifies triflers as game play-ers, and the games in which they participate as real games, notwith-standing their conformance to the rules and their awareness of the ends of such games.

By the ethos of the game I mean those attitudes, commitments, val-ues, goods, and virtues that are necessary to sustain the ways of life embodied in sporting practices. In its most basic sense, the ethos fur-nishes a compelling reason to make the gratuitous difficulties of such practices the central point of one's engagement in them. More specifically, it supplies a reason to take seriously and pursue diligently the standards of excellence that infuse the aim of the game, a reason to try to win in whatever way the game demands. But the interest in winning that it sanctions is not an interest in those goods one might attain as a result of winning—not, that is, an interest in its external goods (money, status, and power)—but an interest in its internal goods that are realized in the course of trying to achieve its standards of excellence. The ethos speaks to the good of the kind of life embodied in sports and the special regard for and commitment to its particular qualities of action. It speaks as well to virtues such as justice and honesty whose exercise is crucial to the integrity of sporting practices.

I am not the first, however, to have claimed that sports possess an ethos that plays a key role in their social constitution and rational makeup. That distinction belongs to Fred D'Agostino, whose important essay, entitled appropriately enough "The Ethos of Games," showed how the supplementation of formalistic theories of games (which define games exclusively by reference to their formal rules) with an account of their ethos rescues them from otherwise irreparable defects.[37] But my interest in D'Agostino's essay is not that he beat everyone to the punch in recognizing that games have an ethos, but that his rendering differs from my own in two chief respects. This interests me because by explicating what those differences consist of I will be able to clarify further what my own account of the ethos of sports adds to their rational demarcation.

The first, and less important, difference is that D'Agostino's conception of the ethos of a game covers only those social conventions that influence how the rules of a game are applied in concrete circumstances, whereas mine covers the whole gamut of conventions that inform the way of life intrinsic to a game—the rules, mores, goods, and commitments that sustain and enliven its practice. The second, and more important, difference is that D'Agostino's conception of the ethos of a game takes its point of departure from the normal, institutionalized context of a game, from interests that players of a game share with game officials, team owners, and spectators in making it more exciting to watch, and so more profitable to put on, by ignoring certain rule violations in certain situations;[38] mine, on the other hand, takes its point of departure from the logic of its practice inscribed in its rules. Although it would be tempting to cast this latter difference as one between an ethos that sanctions rule breaking and one that sanctifies rule following, it would be wrong to do so. It is true that D'Agostino's ethos is distinguished by its license to override the rules of a game in certain institutionally approved and expedient ways, and it is equally true that the ethos of which I speak is distinguished in part by its normative commitment to a core set of rules that define and make clear the aim of a game. Yet, there is nothing stated or implied in the latter commitment that demands perfect adherence to every rule of a game. On the contrary, my version of the ethos would countenance the violation of rules that determine what players may do in a game (to include certain of its constitutive rules) and who may be players and under what sorts of conditions (to include regulative and what Meier calls auxiliary rules)[39] if the violations in question were in the best interests of its practice.

What distinguishes our accounts on this score is the legitimation given such licentious discretion on the part of the ethos. For D'Agostino it is the interests of the institutional forces that presently frame our sporting practices that authorize our compliance or noncompliance with the rules; for me it is the distinctive rationality and the array of goods and virtues that define sporting practices that authorize said compliance or noncompliance. It is for this reason that I dispute D'Agostino's claim that rule-driven theories of the sort I subscribe to are unable to explain why a game official or player might violate a rule in the interest of promoting some larger good.[40] My counter is that such theories can perfectly well explain rule violations of this sort provided that it is the good of the game and the ethos that supports that good, and not its supporting institution, that is the rationale for such violations.

One other explanatory distinction between D'Agostino's and my renderings of the ethos of a game should be noted here: D'Agostino's ethos artfully explains why habitualized players and spectators of institutionalized games would regard a game in which no deliberate rule infractions occurred as a "strange" game. It explains the queerness of such a game precisely because from its institutional vantage point it makes little sense for players not to break certain rules when it is in their self-interest to do so. At the same time, what D'Agostino's ethos leaves unexplained is why, from the vantage point of the ethos of the practice itself, systematic rule violations of this sort are regarded as abnormal, indeed irrational, occurrences. To less-habitualized players and spectators—to, that is, connoisseurs of games that delight in their intrinsic pleasures—calculated efforts to nullify the kinds of restrictions on means imposed by the rules of games come off as bizarre, altogether confused games. This is because such wholesale rule violations are properly seen to operate at cross-purposes to what is, after all, the point of game-practices: to overcome the gratuitous difficulties they pose. It is this basic fact about the rationality of sportive games that D'Agostino's ethos is at a loss to explain precisely because its vantage point is fixed on the institution side rather than the practice side of such games.

With this specification of the ethos of sporting practices as our backdrop, we can now spell out more fully what constitutes the rational core of those practices and what demarcation criteria can be extracted from their rational core. This is, of course, the reason we undertook this extended excursus of their internal logic in the first place. To begin with the first point, it is apparent that that rational core is much thicker and more robust than first supposed. It encompasses both the gratuitous logic embedded in its basic rules and the ethos embedded in the particular kinds of life it instantiates. So understood, the logic of sport enjoins us to forsake the easiest resolution of its contrived challenges, to delight in the gratuitous difficulties posed by these challenges, and to make the good of the particular way of life it exemplifies the central focus of one's motives, intentions, and actions. It enjoins us further to give other practitioners of sport their proper due, to take whatever risks are necessary to excel in its practice, to try to remedy shortcomings pointed out to us by other practitioners and game authorities, and to commit ourselves to the achievement of its internal goods, resisting, to the extent necessary, the allure of its external goods. In other words, the logic of sport binds us to formal criteria of inefficiency with respect to the means we are allowed to use to attain its ends, and normative criteria of virtuous action with respect to the just, honest, and temperate ways we are to conduct ourselves in its practice.

It is an especially important feature of the thick rational complexion of sport that one cannot be rational in the formal sense of limiting oneself to nonultimate means without at the same time being rational in the normative sense of limiting oneself to virtuous means, and vice versa. As was evident in our example of the trifler, one may well forsake the most expeditious way to achieve the goal of a game and fail to play that game because one is uncommitted and unmoved by the way of life it embodies, and conversely, one can make the good of the form of life embodied in a game one's own good and fail to play the game because one refuses to accept the formal restrictions on means it requires. What is incongruous about failing to abide by either the formal or the normative elements of the internal logic of sport is, of course, that one can hardly make the good of the game the good of one's own life without accepting the peculiar limits on means the game calls for. To make the good of the game one's own good is the best and most compelling reason one can have to accept such limits on one's actions. Today it is regarded as a commonplace that one can satisfy the rational demands of sporting practices by merely complying, in a loose and technical manner at that, with their formal rules in lieu of any normative commitment to the good of the kind of life their practice embodies. However, this does not count against our robust conception of the internal logic of these practices. That commonplace is itself suspect, reflecting as it does one of the more onerous conceits of the contemporary capitalist age in which sport and all other social practices must presently make their way. It deserves our reproach, as I shall argue, because it is an altogether false conceit.

It follows that if indeed the internal logic of sport is a thick and robust logic, then the criteria of demarcation that can be teased out of that logic to ensure that its practice is situated in the right context will also be thick and robust ones. I argue that this is in fact the case. The boundary supplied by the specification of the logic of sport is in fact a substantive one. Although it is not so narrowly conceived as to yield one right conception of sport and one right way to engage in it, this boundary does stake out a limit that, if transgressed, imperils its rational standing as a practice. The boundary is elastic but definitive, one that stipulates that at least one reason for taking up sport *must* be to meet the gratuitous difficulties it poses. Put differently, one can have no reason for engaging the unnecessary obstacles presented in sport that is not also a reason for trying to overcome those obstacles in whatever way the game demands.[41]

The normative force of this dividing line is unmistakable. It forbids the conception, treatment, and engagement of sport in any way that undermines its gratuitous manner and that threatens the goods that attach to the standards of excellence that define its practice. That is, it enjoins against treating the superfluous challenges it presents and the form of life in which they are rooted as if those challenges and that life were somehow incidental to its practice and, as being incidental, capable of usurpation by instrumental ends without pathological effect. So while this boundary marking countenances other reasons for engaging in sport in addition to those that have directly to do with the logic of its practice, it does so only if those other reasons don't impede or otherwise interfere with the point and purpose of its practice. That is to say, while one may with impunity use sport to achieve other ends or to secure goods external to it, one may not with impunity use sport merely as a means, as an instrumental tool, to achieve such ends or secure such goods. To conceive or treat sport as a mere means to the attainment of external ends and goods vitiates its rational core; in effect it denies one any reason to take up its gratuitous challenges or to commit oneself to the good of the form of life it instantiates, and every reason to circumvent such difficulties and to skirt such a commitment. It is, therefore, intrinsic to our notion of sport, to our understanding of its basic logic, that it has a gratuitous quality about it and a normative stake in the forms of life that embody that quality which cannot be abrogated without destroying what it is and what it stands for. This is the source, I contend, of our intuitive, indeed visceral, disdain of cheating. This disdain survives the institutionally driven "normalization" of sport, in spite of our *de facto* acceptance, tolerance, and even expectation that such cheating goes on as a matter of course, which, of course, is the product of that institutionalized "normalization" of sport.

That the demarcation of sport suggested by the specification of its internal logic is a sufficiently robust one is, I contend, borne out by its exclusion of a dominant athletic type of contemporary sport from the ranks of its devotees. I am referring here to the "organization" athlete discussed in some detail in Chapter 3 whose calculated rational demeanor and preoccupation with external goods bears the telltale signs of her internalization of an institutional slant on sport. This dominant type is distinguished by her technical regard for the rules and her instrumental orientation toward the game and its particular ends and goods. It is her technical and instrumental outlook on sport that interests me presently, for that outlook puts her and, of course, the athletic type she represents, on a par with Suits's hypothetical quasi-player Smith.[42] Smith is a curious fellow who finds himself in the thick of a 200 meter race that he has no interest in being in, but no way of getting out of. He finds himself in this predicament by virtue of a series of remarkable coincidences that put him at the starting line of the race at the very moment he learns that someone has planted a time bomb in the grandstand at the finish line, a bomb that he is keen on defusing. At the very instant that he realizes that the only way to get to the bomb in time is by running around the track, it seems the infield is secured by a rather high chain-link fence, the starting gun goes off, and he proceeds to dash madly toward the finish line.

Suits dreamt up this admittedly bizarre example, of course, in order to pose the sticky question whether Smith, who has obeyed all the relevant rules and pursued the end of the game—in this case with particular gusto—is playing a game. Before I consider Suits's answer, I want to draw out more carefully the parallels between Smith and our dominant athletic type. In order to do this I must first point out two relevant differences that distinguish our institutionally bred athlete from Smith. First, our dominant type's technical regard for the rules, which counsels her to break and follow rules according to her strategic self-interests, habitually inclines her to break a lot of rules. In this respect, our dominant type is more akin to another prominent game-type, the cheat, than she is to Smith. Like the cheat, she has a zeal to win that often overrides her adherence to the rules. Since dominant athletic types who ape cheaters are clearly not playing a game, I ignore this side of our dominant athlete and turn to her rule-complying side. But in doing so we notice yet another difference between our dominant type and Smith: Smith's observance of the rules as well as his efforts to reach the finish line first were entirely unwitting, whereas our dominant type's observance of the rules and efforts to achieve the goal of the game were, and are, entirely witting. Indeed, they could hardly be construed otherwise given their strategic character. It may seem that this difference establishes a link between our dominant type and the trifler since triflers also wittingly abide by rules. But that link is clearly suspect because while triflers wittingly observe rules they are conspicuously indifferent to the goals of the games they take up, and our dominant type is anything but indifferent to the goals of the games she takes up. So it seems that the parallel between our dominant type and Smith is not perfect. But parallels of this sort seldom are, nor, fortunately for us, need they be to work. The present one is close enough, I argue, to make Suits's answer to the question whether Smith is playing a game telling and relevant to our answer to the question whether our dominant athletic type is playing a game.

Suits's answer is as forceful as it is clear. Smith is not playing a game, Suits argues, because none of the reasons why Smith accepts the rules of the footrace include a reason to run that race, to be part of a competition whose point is to test one's running mettle. Our answer to our less fanciful dominant athletic type is similarly forceful and clear. She is not playing a game, we argue, because none of the reasons why she is engaged in the game include a reason to play it, to involve herself in any meaningful fashion with its intrinsic challenges. What she lacks in particular is a reason, a thick and substantive reason, to take up its contrived difficulties and to devote herself to the standards of excellence and goods that define its practice. It is this failure to live up to the rational imperatives of sportive games then, to meet the rational constraints that they impose on us, that disqualifies our dominant athletic type, not to mention other game types such as the trifler and the cheat, as a genuine game player. What all of these quasi-players share in common is that their various reasons for getting involved in sport have nothing essentially to do with the form of life it embodies and everything to do with the advancement of interests, private and otherwise, that are incidental to its practice. We know this to be the case because we know that all of these game types would at a moment's notice break the rules of the games they play, and/or sell short its goods and excellences, and/or seek another venue to get what they want, if circumstances permitted such. They would readily do so because there is nothing about the kinds of life sport gives expression to and the kinds of excellence it aspires to that is the least bit compelling to them.

It is this contempt for the logical integrity of sport, therefore, this willingness to subordinate it to ends and goods that have no substantive connection to its practice, that turns our dominant athletic type and her quasi-player cohorts into radical instrumentalists rather than mere instrumentalists.[43] Mere instrumentalists, who engage in sport both because they find the kind of life it instantiates compelling and what they can acquire through their engagement in it in the way of external goods attractive, don't conflate the rational demands of the game with those of the external goods and ends they seek. That explains why they are unwilling to forsake the game for such ends and goods, and why they remain alert to the fact that the external ends and goods they seek are different and detachable from the ends and goods of the games they play. Radical instrumentalists, by contrast, conflate the rational demands of the game with the external ends and goods they seek. Indeed, for them the intelligibility of the game rests precisely on its connection with such ends and goods, such that, if the game were no longer found to be instrumental to the attainment of these ends and goods it would no longer be found to be an intelligible undertaking. This, I contend, is the case with all our above quasi-player types for whom sportive games have little meaning save as devices for the achievement of external ends and goods. That explains why none of these athletic types feel the least compunction in breaking their rules and in snubbing their normative mandates, which ought to give anyone, except, I suppose, the most jaded among us, reasonable pause in calling them real players of games, and the endeavors in which they participate real games.

My foregoing discussion should lay to rest the objection that circumscribing practices like sport on the basis of their internal logics gives rise to divisions that are either too thick or too thin to be of any critical import or practical use. If I have managed to quell the skeptic's doubts on this matter, then I consider my above defense of this demarcation scheme a qualified success. But before I take up an analysis of the second part of that scheme, the part played by sportive practice-communities, I want to say something more about the logical dividing line that we have already drawn between sport and other human pursuits. In the course of defending that line from the above objections, we have specified additional rational constraints that must be placed on its practice and given a clearer, less tentative, account of what sort of social context is required to ensure its flourishing.

Our initial and provisional account of the logic of sport suggested that it be insulated from instrumental pursuits that subscribe to an alien technical logic, a logic of means rather than ends that equates rationality with the efficacious use of means to attain whatever ends we happen to hold. That account also suggested that insofar as our present institutions adopt the very same technical logic in disposing of their bureaucratic tasks, they too need to be cordoned off from the social context of our sporting practices. While it was further implied that sport should also be insulated from market forces that follow their own brand of instrumental reason, it is now explicitly clear that it should be so insulated, and on grounds that are related, but not identical, to the market's instrumental logic. I am thinking specifically of the notions of freedom and value that define and enliven action within the market. What is problematic about these notions is evident once they are examined.

The kind of freedom that the market prides itself on is, as Friedman and Anderson among others have argued,[44] a freedom to use and dispose of things and activities in any way that one sees fit. This economic ideal of freedom is closely bound up with the mode of valuation particular to the market, which sanctions the freedom of individuals to subordinate things and activities to serve their own prized ends without regard for the intrinsic value of these things or activities. So the freedom the market offers is a freedom to value things and activities in the absence of constraints associated with other modes of valuation.[45] But this reveals yet a third relevant feature of the market, one that in releasing agents from the constraints on use required by noneconomic modes of valuation reduces their preferences for things and activities to matters of mere taste that belie rational deliberation. If the wants and desires of individuals are, as the market regards them, self-validating ones, then one preference cannot be regarded as any better or worse than another preference, provided one has the wherewithal to pay for whatever preferences one expresses.

It is obvious that sport cannot prosper in any social setting in which market forces are given full reign. The rational constraints that bind practitioners of sport narrow considerably their legitimate "use" of sport, and the kinds of preferences deemed suitable to its practice are rational ones that are rooted in reasoned ideals as opposed to subjective preferences of taste. It follows further that sport cannot flourish if it is regularly subjected to market-driven institutional pressures. That is yet another reason to bar institutions from insinuating themselves into the operation of these practices.

It should be noted, however, that the insulation of sport from the market I argue for here is one that urges its separation from the market not, as it were, its divorce from the market. That means that while market forces are to be denied any direct say in the internal affairs and conduct of its practice, they need not be altogether banished from the realm of sport. There are at least two grounds for giving them some limited scope here. The first has to do with the provision of sport to the larger public, that is, to its distribution and dissemination to that public. It may reasonably be argued in this regard that if the market does a better job of ensuring such provision, that if it more efficiently makes sport available to the general populace than other comparable agencies—say, the state or certain voluntary, nonprofit organizations—then it is legitimate to entrust that function to the market. However, two constraints apply, one empirical, the other normative. The market is to be conferred this limited role only if it can be empirically demonstrated that it provides such access more efficiently than other agencies, and only if its more efficient provision does not alter unduly the ends, goods, and rational demeanor of sport. The second ground for giving the market some scope here concerns the rights of the practitioners themselves, specifically their right to earn a reasonable living from their athletic prowess. That right, however, is subject to the same normative check cited above, and so can be superseded when it compromises the integrity of sport. It is, of course, dangerous to allot even this limited scope to the market given its well-known propensity to overstep its bounds. The trick here, as elsewhere, is to give the market its due while confining its sphere of influence to goods it can dispose of unproblematically.

As I have argued throughout this and the previous chapters, for some time now practices like sport have had to lead a duplicitous life, straining to meet the imperatives of their own internal logics while continuously barraged by the systemic imperatives of capitalist institutions they can scarcely ignore. It is apparent that if sport and the like are to be liberated from this bondage, then the institutions that preside over them will not only have to be screened off from their internal workings but reconstructed so that they cater to, rather than deter, the kinds of life and goods they embody. That means institutions will have to be reconfigured in ways that make them more responsive to, and supportive of, social practices. If that is to happen they will have to come under the rational jurisdiction of practice-communities, under the control of practitioners who derive their authority to rule not from the wealth they may possess nor the bureaucratic power to manipulate others they may wield, but from their critically informed and shared understandings of practices themselves. It is to an analysis of the role such practice-communities play in the demarcation and oversight of sport that I now turn.

Practice-Communities as Deliberative Bodies

Before I sketch the deliberative part played by practice-communities in fixing the limits of sporting practices and in setting the terms of their institutional reform, I will discuss the character and composition of such communities. It is best to begin in this regard by pointing out that community is an internal good of sporting practices. As an internal good, it must be achieved rather than bestowed, and, therefore, can only be procured by directly involving oneself in the practice of sport. Further, as a good that can only be had by engaging in its practice, the sense of community specific to practices like sport should be distinguished from the one that is specific to what liberals like Rawls call "voluntary associations," that is, groupings founded on individual choice and held together by contractual obligations. It can be so distinguished in at least three senses.

First of all, the attachment of an athlete to a particular practice-community is not the product of anything so willful or determinate as a voluntary decision, nor is the social bond expressed in that attachment reducible to anything so willful and calculated as a contractual agreement. It is not the simple product of such willful agreements because the roots of such communities are deep social ones that literally shape the characters and, as we shall see, the identities of the individuals that comprise them. One is quite literally socialized into such groups, and in the case of sport that socialization typically begins in early childhood. So it seems that one more so enacts than chooses one's attachment to practice-communities,[46] which suggests that the kind of choice exercised here is less a choice to belong to this or that community as it is a choice to either affirm and deepen, or to dilute and truncate, or to negate and curtail a pre-existing attachment. To be sure, we often grow weary of such communities and depart them for others more conducive to our current interests.[47] Athletes are certainly no different in this respect, and frequently sign on with different teams and leagues when it suits them, and when, of course, they are legally permitted to do so. But many of these choices also count as reenactments of loyalties, identities, and aims formed much earlier, for it is other sporting communities, after all, that most athletes seek to join when they tire of the ones of which they are presently a part. Moreover, the attachment of an athlete to a specific practice-community is not something that can be contractually mandated or even agreed to. It is rather something that must be realized, experienced, and lived out. Contracts cannot take the place of, or secure, what can only be secured by one's direct participation in a practice, by the realization of shared experiences intensified by the heat of competition that either bind practitioners to each other and their craft or sunder them from such. So while one may well be able to obtain the services of an athlete by offering her a lucrative contract replete with performance clauses that detail her obligations to the team, one can never obtain the attachment of an athlete to a team in this manner.

The second important difference between a sportive practice-community and a voluntary association is that the ends and aims of sportive-communities are shared ends and aims rather than merely commensurate ones. It is a mark of voluntary associations that individuals enter into them with their own specific aims in mind and can associate with other individuals only insofar as their aims are already compatible with those of others, or can be made so compatible. By contrast, it is the mark of practice-communities, as I state above, that the aims of their members are not just compatible but shared, that they espouse and adhere to the same ends thereby obviating any need to make them compatible. It is a further mark of voluntary associations that the individuals who make them up come with their identities fully intact as well, that they enter into associations as fully individuated, secured selves. By contrast, the identity of members of practice-communities is constituted in part by their membership in such communities. For members of such communities, as Sandel writes, "community describes not just what they *have* as fellow [practitioners] but also what they *are*."[48]

The third, and last, significant difference between sport fraternities and voluntary associations is that the former are not bothered by the free-rider problem that besets the latter. The free-rider problem refers to the reception of benefits by members of an association who for whatever reason no longer actively or directly contribute to the production of these benefits. This is an ongoing and seemingly intractable problem of voluntary associations precisely because there is no intrinsic connection between the goods they produce and those who receive them. There is no such connection because the goods associations deal in are for the most part external goods, goods that by definition can be obtained without being a direct party to their production. And so it is with most associations in which membership in the group, rather than active contribution to its activities, determines who the recipients of such goods shall be. By contrast, since the community specific to practices like sport is an internal good of its practice, and since the primary goods they deal in are internal goods as well, only those who participate in the practice can obtain these goods. There can be no free-rider problem in practice-communities, therefore, because the producers and recipients of their primary goods are one and the same.

It is evident, then, that to be a member of a sporting community is to be a part of a distinctive fraternity, one distinguished by its special social bonds and commitments. If membership in such a community stands for anything, it stands for a shared dedication to the good of the kind of life embodied in sport, and the standards of excellence, values, and virtues that are an integral part of that life. We can reasonably expect that the members of such a community will bring to the game a mutual appreciation of its intrinsic worth as well as a common repertoire of rational preferences, aspirations, and values regarding its proper conduct. It is this shared interest in and regard for the good of the game that brings them together in the first place, and that provides the social glue that keeps them together.

One final word about the composition of such practice-communities is required before we can consider their deliberative contribution to the demarcation of sport. The primary agents of practice-communities are, and must be, the practitioners themselves. In the case of sport, of course, that means the athletes. But as is true of all practice-communities, there are a number of secondary agents who play a vital role in sustaining the vitality of sporting communities. I am thinking here principally of coaches, game officials, spectators, journalists, researchers, critics, and scholars, all of whom have some tangible stake in the preservation of the forms of life instantiated in sport. Since the chief criterion of membership in a sporting community in this second-order sense is fidelity to the goods internal to its practice, which, of course, presupposes more than a passing knowledge and appreciation of the intricacies of its practice, and which means further that even certain athletic administrators, managers, and agents would qualify as members, it is always difficult to get a precise empirical handle on just who belongs and doesn't belong. It is difficult, no doubt, but certainly not impossible. The first impulse of a member of such a community is not to rattle off a cost-benefit analysis of a proposed reform measure, but to thoughtfully reflect on its likely effect on the good of the game. This is a salient sign of membership, I contend, even if it is a somewhat imprecise one.

Having given some idea of the character and makeup of sporting communities, I now want to put these communities to work in refining the lines of our social map so that a proper social context might be found for sport to ensure its flourishing. Specifically, I want to tap the shared and thick understandings of sporting practices such communities possess in order to fine-tune the discriminations between sport and other human endeavors already introduced by our appeal to their internal logics. The only rational way to decide among equally deep and intelligible conceptions and treatments of sport—among, that is, conceptions and treatments that are compatible with its logical core—is to appeal to such communities. Further, it is only by petitioning practice-communities that, as I argue above, we can socialize the boundaries of our social map. I propose that all substantive policy matters regarding the conduct and reform of sport be turned over to practice-communities. This is the only way to prevent athletic institutions and their bureaucratic brethren from meddling in the internal affairs of sport, and to keep them in check while they carry out their legitimate tasks of underwriting the financial burden incurred by its practice and of overseeing the distribution of its external goods.

My resorting to the considered judgments of practice-communities is meant to answer the problem that any critical discourse of this sort must squarely face: what Lyotard encapsulates into two propositions as "the impossibility of avoiding conflicts (the impossibility of indifference)" and "the absence of a universal genre of discourse to regulate them (or . . . the inevitable partiality of the judge)."[49] My solution is to opt for the "partiality of the judge[s]," the partiality of not just any judges but only those who are bona fide members of the practice-communities of sport, for these are its most competent and sympathetic judges. What I offer here as an answer is, in keeping with the liberal-socialist line I advocate in the previous chapter, partly socialist and partly liberal. It is socialist insofar as it turns over the substantive operation and control of sport to the democratic will of its practice-communities. It is liberal insofar as it denies the state a central say in its conduct, relegating the state's role essentially to that of a court of last appeal, one that kicks in if and only if practice-communities are unwilling or unable to regulate sport in the required manner. The only difference between my account of the state and a prototypical liberal one is that my reason for limiting its role is not because it affords insufficient protection of the rights of liberal citizens, but because it affords insufficient protection of the social practices that liberal citizens are fond of engaging in.

I wish to begin by spelling out just what sort of deliberative role I envisage for the practice-communities of sport. The relevant question here is, How are we to conceive of their deliberative function? Lyotard once again supplies some helpful clues as to an answer, this time by way of a pivotal distinction he draws between two types of judicial dispute, which he labels *differend* and *litige,* respectively. A *differend*, Lyotard tells us, is a dispute in which one of the aggrieved parties, the plaintiff, becomes a victim because he is deprived of the means of making his case. He is so deprived because the dispute is mediated "in the idiom of [the other party] while the wrong [he has] suffered . . . is not signified in that idiom."[50] A *litige,* by contrast, is a litigation in which both parties agree on how to phrase the issues that led to the dispute as well as the means for resolving them. In this instance, the idiom is sufficiently inclusive to allow both the plaintiff and the defendant to state their cases and resolve the dispute to their mutual satisfaction. Viewed from this Lyotardian vantage point, I argue that the deliberative process of practice-communities be viewed as an attempt to turn all *differends* into litigations, to, in effect, replace *differends* with litigations. The point of substituting litigations for *differends* is to make the unforced force of the better argument prevail over the coercive force of political power and social domination. This notion of litigation is important in understanding and assessing the contribution practice-communities make to the demarcation of sport in two relevant senses.

First of all, it suggests that we think of practice-communities as judicial bodies, that is, as critical tribunals that supply a forum for settling rival interpretations regarding the proper character of sporting practices and knotty disputes concerning their appropriate conduct. As critical tribunals, they are to adjudicate rival beliefs and values by weighing the merits of each on its rational merits alone. The aim of this process of argumentation is to reach a rational consensus about contending norms and values, a consensus in which only those beliefs that have the strongest rational warrants gain our assent. So beliefs and claims are accepted because we have good rational grounds for accepting them, not merely because they are shared. Indeed, on this judicial model consensus is built by finding the strongest rational warrants we can for the beliefs we put up for reflective inspection.

The notion that sporting practice-communities are best thought of as critical tribunals rules out a number of alternative conceptions of their deliberative purpose. It rules out, for instance, the view that the deliberative intent of such bodies is to provide some mechanism for reaching a *modus vivendi* regarding the rival claims they are forced to entertain. It rules out such a conception because the aim of a *modus vivendi* is to achieve not a rational consensus but a carefully calculated compromise in which reason giving is replaced by shrewd bargaining.[51] The presumption of such bargaining is that reasons can be reduced to mere preferences, and that preferences can be effectively linked to strategies, as opposed to arguments, designed to win support for views that are congenial to one's own self-interests. Indeed, in this view pushing one's own private agenda is the only plausible reason anyone would ever have for discussing such matters with others. So the value of cobbling an agreement with others over what views are going to prevail in the community—of pulling off, in effect, a *quid pro quo*—is not a rational, normative one, but an emotivist, privatistic one. Insofar as the kind of deliberation specific to practice-communities is one that privileges reason giving over strategic promotion of private interests, it is apparent that its argumentative give and take has little, if anything, to do with the art of the compromise.

That practice-communities are to be construed as critical tribunals also rules out any conception of their deliberative proceedings in market terms. The beliefs and values that prevail in the marketplace are, as those that prevail in a *modus vivendi,* self-interested and self-validating ones. This time, however, the backups for these beliefs are economically shaded preferences, and whatever set of preferences carries the most financial clout usually wins the day. The difficulty here, however, is not just that the market is indifferent to preferences backed up by reasoned ideals, that it responds in the same way to unreflective desires as it does to reflective ones, but further that it provides no forum for evaluating the goods in which it trades.[52] In the market, if one doesn't like something one simply doesn't purchase it, one opts-out as it were, or in more formal parlance, one exits the situation. Hence, no provision is made for a public accounting of preferences and values, for expressing one's voice in a democratic manner about unsavory conditions that might warrant reform. This is apparent, as Anderson astutely argues, in the kind of respect accorded a chooser of commodities as opposed to that accorded a chooser of reasoned ideals. In the first instance, to respect a chooser of commodities is "to respect her privacy by not probing more deeply into her reasons for wanting a commodity than is required to effectively satisfy her want."[53] In the second instance, however, to respect a chooser of reasoned ideals is to take seriously her reasons for venturing a certain belief or view, to probe the reasons she adduces for her views, and, if those reasons are found compelling, to acknowledge the superiority of her view over other conflicting views. If the members of sporting practice-communities are properly regarded as rational choosers in this latter sense, then it is evident that the respect they deserve is at odds with that given to market players. That is why any effort to link the deliberative process proper to such communities with the ratiocination of the market must fail, and why any attempt to render social practices like sport in the idiom of a "cultural marketplace" must fail as well.

Finally, that practice-communities are best rendered as critical tribunals rules out viewing the rational consensus they seek on the Rawlsian model of an overlapping consensus.[54] Rawls's notion of an overlapping consensus is tailored to a liberal social order, one that gives its citizens wide latitude to pursue their own idiosyncratic and often incommensurable conceptions of the good. The problem such social orders confront is how to secure the social unity and cooperation required to ensure their smooth functioning. The solution, Rawls opines, is to accord justice priority over the good. Justice is to be accorded such priority because the only way in which a principle of conduct can serve as a regulative device of society is if it is publicly accepted as such by all the citizens of that society; Rawls thinks that it is possible to secure public acceptance of a system of justice in a way that it is not possible to secure public acceptance of a conception of the good. The way to achieve such public acceptance, he argues, is to seek an overlapping consensus, one which requires that individuals abstract from their own particular conceptions of the good, and from all deep interpretations and doctrines they hold about those conceptions, so that they might all settle on a fair and equitable way, that is, a just political way, to regulate their variegated pursuit of the good life.

But an overlapping consensus that requires us to, as it were, stay on the surface of things in order that we may agree to disagree about the good in the interest of fairness, is not the kind of rational consensus that practice-communities seek. They are not content to skim the surface of things because the consensus they strive for is a consensus about the good of the kinds of life embodied in sporting practices, a consensus that is itself an important part of the glue that holds these practice-communities together. In this instance, it is the good that must be accorded priority over the right, for it is that good that determines what constitutes right conduct in a practice like sport. So the kinds of questions that practice-communities wrestle with are deep ones, ones that require penetration of, rather than abstraction from, the forms of life of practices. What is at issue here is not a simple weighing of our preferences, but a strong evaluation of what shape and form we wish our sporting practices to take, and, insofar as our own identities are imprinted in those practices, who we wish to be.[55] To the extent, then, that this sort of deliberation and consensus requires that "the roles of a participant in argumentation and social actor overlap,"[56] Rawls's model of an overlapping consensus, which requires that these roles not overlap so that our wider, abstract views about justice might, is not suited to practice-communities.

The second advantage to treating the deliberative function of sporting practice-communities as a species of litigation is that it underscores the importance of locating an idiom that allows the plaintiff (in this instance our ensemble of sporting practices) to state its case in a way that adequately conveys the wrongs committed against it (in this instance the debauchery it has suffered at the hands of its institutions). Underscoring that importance reveals precisely what is wrong with our current setup of athletic practices and institutions: institutions preside over practices in the manner of a *differend* rather than a *litige.* That doesn't mean that practices have no legitimacy under this arrangement, for the aggrieved party of any *differend* has legitimacy or else there could be no dispute, or alleged resolution,[57] in the first place; it means rather that the reasons advocates of sporting practices are permitted to give to present their case are not the reasons that capture the present institutional malaise of those practices. So they are forced to couch their complaint in another language, a language native to institutions whose code words include such things as external goods, bureaucratic authority, and due process. Needless to say, this is not a language amenable to the kinds of life particular to practices; for nowhere in its rational calculus does it take into account that if one form of life is better suited to a practice like sport than another, then that is a reason, let alone a good reason, to choose it. The fate of sport then proves to be no different from that of other practices forced to adjudicate the wrongs they have suffered by submitting to the *differend:* in each case their judges become, in effect, their executioners.

If the kind of deliberation sporting communities are to engage in is, however, best treated as a litigation, then obviously the tables will have to be turned on institutions and a new idiom will have to be found to better recount the damage they have inflicted on sport. In this case, the substitution of *litige* for *differend* requires that some way be found to turn sport into a plaintiff without turning it into a victim. At the very least, that means that sporting practices will have to be allowed to speak their own language, a language whose key notions, we now know, speak to goods and virtues for which there are no adequate cognates in the language of institutions. If that is going to happen, then practice-communities will need to take their point of departure from the internal logic of sport and converse about it in terms of their own principled and shared understandings of its practice. Only in such a conversational setting will it even be acknowledged that if a form of life is found to be better suited to one particular sporting practice than another, that is a reason, in fact the best reason, to choose it over the other.

In order to make the conversational settings of sporting practice-communities litigations rather than *differends,* however, it is not necessary to turn them into "constructed" conversational pieces, into conversations, that is, that call for the idealization of the conversational setting itself and/or that of its speakers. What are required here are not the idealizing presuppositions of a Habermasian "ideal speech" situation that set out transcendental criteria of reasoned discourse, but the concrete presuppositions of practice-centered deliberations that set out contextual criteria of reasoned discourse, presuppositions that demand we enmesh ourselves in the fineries of sporting practices and produce thick ethnocentric accounts of them. These contextual presuppositions stipulate what amounts to a variation of the liberal art of separation applied to practice-communities: namely, that all nonrelevant goods, values, and judgments be bracketed from the deliberative proceedings of sporting communities. This suggests that our collective deliberations and judgments about sport will have to be framed in the same manner that Walzer argues our collective deliberations and judgments about politics will have to be framed in a well-ordered (properly demarcated) society. "Citizens [will] come into the forum," he writes, "with nothing but their arguments. All nonpolitical goods have to be deposited outside: weapons and wallets, titles and degrees."[58] Similarly, members of sporting communities will come into the athletic forum armed only with their arguments, leaving behind all titles, goods, and vantage points that derive from their standing in other spheres.

Once practice-communities are able to purge themselves of such exoteric standpoints, I contend, they can let their contextualized internal understandings of sport do all the talking, understandings that for all their distinctiveness remain "ordinary" ones. I use the notion

"ordinary" understandings here to contrast not with critically informed ones, but with "esoteric," specially contrived understandings,
as well as "common," institutionally shaped ones. In this first contrastive sense, saying that the deliberations of sporting communities
should be pitched to their ordinary understandings of sport amounts
to saying that they should appeal to those understandings of sport
that emanate from their socialization into its practice. These are the
sorts of understandings that one acquires when one is, and seeks to
be, an informed participant and commentator of its practice, literally
a devotee of its practice; as with most other crafts, the knowledge and
normative insight sport requires is quite specific to its practice, demanding little else in the way of specialized knowledge or insight.
What we are after here, then, are not the kind of recondite understandings sought by bourgeois liberals who use rights as their rulers to
draw straight and proper lines, the kind that they believed only philosophers and, ultimately, lawyers possessed. Rather, the understandings relevant to the conversational settings of practice-communities
are ones potentially available to all those who take up sport in a serious and rigorous fashion, and who make some concerted effort to
acquaint themselves with its intricacies and subtle nuances. It is in
this sense that the art of conversation that I hold to be normative to
practice-communities—normative inasmuch as if sport is not thought
about in this manner it is reasoned about wrongly—is to be regarded as a popular rather than an esoteric one.

The second contrast built into my claim that the deliberations of
sporting practice-communities should be pitched to their ordinary
understandings picks out those ordinary understandings that originate, as I argue above, with our socialization into sporting practices
from those common understandings that originate with our socialization into their institutionalized offspring. What makes this an important and useful contrast is that tapping into the former is an effective way to counter and buffer against the corrosive effects of the
latter. Lasch was one of the first to grasp the critical significance of
this contrast, as I noted in Chapter 3, when he boldly, but in my mind
correctly, argued that sports resist assimilation more effectively than
most human enterprises precisely because their socialization exacts
its "own demands and inspire[s] loyalty to the game itself, rather than
to the programs ideologues seek to impose on them."[59] What is compelling about Lasch's claim is that it is indeed these ordinary understandings of sporting practices that best militate against the baleful
effects of their institutionally sponsored socialization, a socialization
responsible for, among other things, what Walzer calls "our common

acquiescence in illegitimate conversion patterns."[60] Our common acceptance of such illicit conversions, of invasions of the logic and goods of one sphere by those of other spheres, might be effectively resisted by our ordinary, internal understandings of a sphere like sport. This is made yet more explicit by Lasch's further tantalizing, but again in my estimation correct, claim that "the anguished outcry of the true fan, who brings to sports a proper sense of awe only to find them corrupted from within by the spread of the 'entertainment ethic,' sheds more light on the degradation of sports than the strictures of left-wing critics."[61] If I am right, however, making that "proper sense of awe" the focal point of the deliberative proceedings of sporting practice-communities promises not just to shed light on the contemporary degradation of sport, but to shed that degradation itself.

While framing the deliberative setting of sporting practice-communities in the manner of a litigation does not require the idealization of that setting or its discussants, it does require, as all craft-communities do, the recognition of rational authorities of the game, and the granting of such authorities a privileged role in the conversations of practice-communities. That is because although the understandings of sport practices are ordinary ones potentially available to all members of their practice-communities, they are not shallow, uncultivated ones. It is folly to imagine that the precious fineries of sporting practices are adequately grasped by all who engage in them or reflect upon them, that they can be gleaned in one engagement or sitting all at once and once and for all. On the contrary, they demand, as I insinuate above, much cultivation, discipline, study, and diligence. That means that novices and those less accomplished in discernment and judgment will at first have to accede to the considered judgments of those who qualify as rational authorities of the game. But there is nothing particularly onerous, meaning undemocratic or uncritical, about the relation of such rational authorities to novices. The relation between them resembles more so a master-apprentice model than it does a master-slave one.[62] That is because those who reside at both the top and the bottom of athletic practice-communities are all practitioners of some sort, whether they be athletes or critics. Further, the hierarchy that separates rational authorities from novices is a linear rather than a pyramidal one. That means that novices who persevere in their craft, who pursue the practice of sport diligently and thoughtfully, will themselves eventually become rational authorities of the game. And, of course, once they achieve the requisite standards of excellence and powers of discernment that are its concomitant, they will be prepared to advance the discussion, the practical discourse, about what is the proper character and scope of sport rather than having to yield at crucial junctures to the judgment of other authorities.

The best way to think about the rational authorities of a sporting practice-community, then, is also the best way to think about the reasoning that goes on within such communities and the rationally authoritative interpretations that issue as products of that reasoning: both are meant to exemplify, and in a well-ordered society do exemplify, the highest standards of reason realized thus far regarding the character, scope, and proper context of sporting practices.[63] This is not to say that the authoritative voices, texts, and precedent-setting interpretations that come out of the deliberations of such practice-communities capture the essence of sport, which no interpretive community can lay claim to if only because the notion of an essence is, as we previously argued, a chimerical one, but that they exemplify the best interpretive rendering of sport that has yet been achieved. The best interpretation in this case means the rationally superior, most exhaustive interpretation, the one that appropriates the best insights of rival interpretations without falling prey to their manifest errors and weaknesses. The process by which we arrive at such definitive interpretations, by which we rationally adjudicate among contending interpretations of the good of the kinds of life embodied in sporting practices, is a historical process of justification and vindication. That means that the best interpretation of sport can only claim a historical superiority over its rivals, as the best we have to offer so far. That is why, as Rorty trenchantly reminds us, "we should never think that the regress of interpretations can be stopped once and for all, but rather realize that there may always be a vocabulary, a set of descriptions, around the corner which will throw everything into question once again."[64] So no matter how persuasive the interpretive decrees spun out by practice-communities concerning the proper demarcation of sport may appear to be, they are never immune from criticism, and they may be called on again and again to prove their rational mettle against yet other rival interpretations. Only those interpretations that survive this historical dialectic of vindication deserve our rational assent, and so our consideration in setting the boundaries of sporting practices and the terms of their institutional oversight.

This completes my sketch of a new, reconstructed critical theory of sport. The point of that reconstructive effort, I claimed, was to find some way to reverse the dominion institutions presently hold over sporting practices. In this regard, I argued that our best hope for reversing that dominion is to ply the liberal craft of drawing lines, and to socialize these lines by tapping the internal logic of sport and the principled and shared convictions of its practice-community. Whether boundary revisions of this sort will prove effective is, of course, a matter for history to decide. It must also be left to the verdict of history and the vagaries of social and political struggle to determine the course of radical change that might result from tampering with the boundaries of sporting practices and placing defined limits on the conduct of their institutions. It may well be that the change will be gradual and incremental. I know of no "iron" law that rules that possibility out, that mandates that radical change must come in one fell swoop or not at all. I am, however, inclined to agree with Walzer that if change comes it will probably be swift. He cites the creation of a national health service in England after the war in which "one year doctors were professionals and entrepreneurs; and the next year, they were professionals and public servants."[65] The boundary shift it would take to liberate sport from its current bondage is more difficult than this one; it is far too complex a practice to yield to such a far-flung revision. Yet at the same time it is simpler; it is far too centered and situated a practice to require this kind of broad consensus. But whatever shift would have to be made to ignite a similar precipitous change in the practice of sport, one thing is certain: absent some such radical boundary revision, the forms of life intrinsic to sport are not likely to survive. That prospect, I am persuaded, is a grim one that we should all—at least those of us who profess some affection for, if not love of, sport—try our best to prevent.

NOTES

1. This part of my argument is heavily indebted to Walzer's provocative and instructive essay, "Liberalism and the Art of Separation," *Political Theory* 12 (August 1984): 315–30.

2. Ibid., p. 323.

3. Bowles and Gintis argue that one especially pernicious consequence of this privatization of the market is that it paved the way for the treatment of the corporation as a fictive individual, which accorded ostensibly public corporations all the rights and privileges of private citizens—the most important of which was, of course, the right to conduct their businesses free of the political scrutiny of the state, and of the democratic scrutiny of their workers. See their *Democracy and Capitalism* (New York: Basic Books), pp. 171–72.

4. Walzer, "Liberalism and the Art of Separation," p. 324.

5. In arguing that liberalism should make the protection of social practices from institutions its focal point I am not arguing that it should abandon rights-talk. That would be a huge mistake, not merely because it would imperil our private lives, which it most assuredly would, but because it would

imperil our social practices as well. It would imperil our social practices because it would afford individuals no protection against arbitrary exclusion from practices on grounds of race, gender, religion, or political persuasion. It is for this reason that I think Stout is right to insist that the vocabulary of rights be conjoined to the vocabulary of virtues, and Lasch wrong to urge that they be disjoined. See Jeffrey Stout, *Ethics After Babel* (Boston: Beacon Press, 1988), p. 292; Christopher Lasch, "The Communitarian Critique of Liberalism," *Soundings* 69 (Spring 1986): 75.

6. See my previous discussion of this point, Chapter 3, pp. 151–52, 158.

7. See Chapter 3, pp. 157–59.

8. Walzer, "Liberalism and the Art of Separation," p. 318.

9. Ibid., p. 323.

10. Jürgen Habermas, "The Political Experience and the Renewal of Marxist Theory," in *Habermas: Autonomy and Solidarity*, ed. Peter Dews (London: Verso, 1986), p. 91.

11. On the distinction between, and relation of, social dominance and monopoly, see Walzer, *Spheres of Justice* (New York: Basic Books, 1983), pp. 10–13.

12. Ibid., p. 9.

13. I owe both of these statements to Walzer's *Spheres of Justice*, p. 18. It also bears mentioning here that resorting to such demarcation schemes answers at least part of Habermas's complaint against first-generation critical theorists for lacking what he calls "clearly demarcated object domains like the communicative practice of the everyday lifeworld in which rationality structures are embodied and the process of reification can be traced. The basic concepts of critical theory placed the consciousness of individuals directly vis-à-vis economic and administrative mechanisms of integration." See his *The Theory of Communicative Action, Volume 2* (Boston: Beacon Press, 1987), pp. 382–83.

14. Two points of clarification are in order here. First, my claim that all sports are games follows Suits's argument to that effect in his early seminal essay "The Elements of Sport," in *Philosophic Inquiry in Sport*, ed. William J. Morgan and Klaus V. Meier (Champaign, Ill.: Human Kinetics, 1988). In a later essay, "Tricky Triad: Games, Play, and Sport," *Journal of the Philosophy of Sport* 15 (1988): 2, Suits amended that claim and argued that certain select sports, for example, diving and gymnastics, are not games but what he now calls "judged performances." Since I do not find Suits's amended claim persuasive, I pay it no mind here. For some instructive criticisms of Suits's revised account see Meier's and Kretchmar's responses to his "Tricky Triad" essay in volumes 15 and 16 (1988–89) of the *Journal of the Philosophy of Sport*. The second point is that my accent on the rationality embodied in sportive pursuits is not meant to imply that the physical side of these pursuits is unimportant or otherwise irrelevant to their conduct. Rather, it is only meant to underscore the critical line I want to take here, one whose critical promise, I maintain, is not contingent on these physical dimensions, and one that has heretofore been ignored by critical sport theorists.

15. Bernard Suits, *The Grasshopper: Games, Life and Utopia* (Toronto: University of Toronto Press, 1978), p. 38.

16. Bernard Suits, "Sticky Wickedness," *Dialogue* 21 (1982): 757.

17. Suits, *The Grasshopper*, p. 39.

18. This point comes straight out of Rorty's essay "Solidarity or Objectivity?" in *Objectivity, Relativism, and Truth* (Cambridge: Cambridge University Press, 1991), p. 26.

19. Ibid.

20. Jacques Derrida, "Racism's Last Word," *Critical Inquiry* (Autumn 1986): 292.

21. On this point, see Rorty's essay "Cosmopolitanism without Emancipation: A Reply to Jean-François Lyotard," in *Objectivity, Relativism, and Truth* (Cambridge: Cambridge University Press, 1991), p. 217.

22. See Chapter 2, p. 86.

23. Thomas McCarthy, *Ideals and Illusions: On Reconstruction and Deconstruction in Contemporary Critical Theory* (Cambridge, Mass.: MIT Press, 1991), p. 36.

24. See Chapter 2, p. 87.

25. Hans Kamphausen, "Traditionelle, Leibesübungen bei autochthonen Völkern," as quoted and translated in Allen Guttmann's *From Ritual to Record: The Nature of Modern Sports* (New York: Columbia University Press, 1978), p. 23. The secularization of sport was already apparent, as Guttmann observes, in the sports of ancient Greek society. But it did not reach its zenith until the modern period. That is why Guttmann treats secularism as one of the seven cardinal features of modern sports.

26. As Suits argues in his refutation of "radical instrumentalism" as a theory of games, "Because of the equal but irreconcilable demands of the game and of what may be called life, although it is possible to meet the demands of the game or of life or of neither, it is not possible to meet the demands of both." *The Grasshopper*, p. 148.

27. Richard Rorty, *The Consequences of Pragmatism* (Minneapolis: University of Minnesota Press, 1982), p. 167.

28. Hilary Putnam, "Why Reason Can't Be Naturalized," in *After Philosophy: End or Transformation?* ed. Kenneth Baynes et al. (Cambridge, Mass.: MIT Press, 1987), p. 241.

29. Alaisdair MacIntyre, *Whose Justice? Which Rationality?* (Notre Dame, Ind.: University of Notre Dame Press, 1988), pp. 367–68. I should point out that my argument in this latter part of the section is entirely indebted to MacIntyre's discussion of perspectivism in *Whose Justice?*

30. Ibid., p. 368. What is pathological about this anomie, as Sandel argues, is that intolerance flourishes most where our common forms of life are uprooted and where "atomized, dislocated, frustrated selves [find themselves] at sea in a world where common meanings have lost their force." Michael Sandel, "Morality and the Liberal Ideal," *The New Republic,* May 7, 1984, p. 17. What makes this sort of dislocation and fragmentation particularly onerous, however, as Hannah Arendt argues further, is its susceptibility to totali-

tarianism, for totalitarianism takes hold in people who are uprooted and who realize they "have no place in the world recognized and guaranteed by others." Hannah Arendt, *Totalitarianism* (New York: Harcourt Brace, 1968), p. 173.

31. MacIntyre, *Whose Justice?* p. 369.

32. Hilary Putnam, *Reason, Truth and History* (Cambridge: Cambridge University Press, 1981), p. 147.

33. Bero Rigauer, *Sport and Work* (New York: Columbia University Press, 1981), p. 103; Richard Gruneau, *Class, Sports, and Social Development* (Amherst: University of Massachusetts Press, 1983), p. 58.

34. Rigauer, *Sport and Work*, p. 79.

35. For an interesting discussion of the game-trifler, see Suits, *The Grasshopper*, pp. 45–46.

36. John Searle, *Speech Acts* (Cambridge: Cambridge University Press, 1969), p. 34.

37. Fred D'Agostino, "The Ethos of Games," *Journal of the Philosophy of Sport* 8 (1981).

38. Ibid., pp. 15–16.

39. Klaus Meier, "Restless Sport," *Journal of the Philosophy of Sport* 12 (1985): 64–77.

40. D'Agostino, "The Ethos of Games," p. 16.

41. What I offer here is a gloss of Suits's formulation that one "can have no reason for accepting the rules [of a game] which is not also a reason for playing the game." *The Grasshopper*, p. 144. There is, however, an important difference between our two formulations. Whereas Suits's stakes his formulation on rule acceptance, I stake mine on the acceptance of the logic of game-playing itself. This makes my rendering more stringent than Suits's since it demands more of players than their simple adherence to the rules of games. This explains our varying treatment of instrumentally motivated players of games. My treatment questions the conventional wisdom that instrumental athletic types, most notoriously professional players, who place a premium on the external goods that can be had by participating in sport are genuine game-players, whereas Suits's less severe rendering simply endorses the conventional wisdom that such types are uncontroversially genuine players of games. Still, this difference between our accounts may be more so implied than real. One could plausibly read Suits's claim that one "can have no reason for accepting the rules that is not also a reason for playing the game" as suggesting that games have in addition to formal rules an ethos that makes its own rational demands on the conduct of its practice. This is a plausible reading of Suits's rendering because he doesn't count just any professional player of games as a genuine player, but only those professionals who make "excellence in playing the game, and in playing a game alone," (p. 146) the preeminent concern of their professional careers, which accords with my own view of such players. In order to read Suits in this manner, however, we would have to flesh in, much as I try to do in the text, what that ethos comprises and what bearing it has on the logical fabric of games.

42. For his discussion of the Smith example see, *The Grasshopper*, pp. 145–46.

43. For a trenchant critique of radical instrumentalism as a theory of games see Suits, *The Grasshopper*, pp. 147–53.

44. Milton Friedman, *Capitalism and Freedom* (Chicago: University of Chicago Press, 1962); Elizabeth Anderson, "The Ethical Limitations of the Market," *Economics and Philosophy* 6 (1990): 179–83. This part of my discussion relies heavily on Anderson's insightful analysis of the market and economic goods.

45. Anderson, "The Ethical Limitations of the Market," p. 181.

46. For a cogent analysis of the weaknesses of liberal accounts of such social groups, see Michael Walzer's essay "The Communitarian Critique of Liberalism," *Political Theory* 18 (February 1990): 15–16.

47. The right to exit practices no longer to our liking underscores once again the importance of individual rights to social practices. Enforcing the right of exit from deeply rooted practices not only protects individuals from unwarranted coercive pressures, but makes it possible for them to form new practice-communities (and perhaps even new practices) with similar-minded individuals. For an argument to this effect, see Allen Buchanan's insightful essay "Assessing the Communitarian Critique of Liberalism," *Ethics* 99 (July 1989): 858. What the emphasis on practices and their communities does require, however, is that individuals not be allowed to play their rights as trump cards to defeat the communal interests of practitioners to treat or engage in a practice in a certain way. To allow individual rights this kind of unlimited scope would undermine the joint activities of practice-communities. But denying that rights can trump joint activities in this manner does not override, *mutatis mutandis*, the rights of individuals to exit practices they no longer find compelling. To be sure, granting easy access to and exit from practices and their relevant communities may itself jeopardize the bonds of such communities—this is a constant problem of liberal democracies that give individuals this kind of license. But the best antidote for this, I argue, is not to repress the freedom of individuals to move about as they please, but to strengthen our communal attachments to social practices by sprucing them up, cultivating what it is that attracts us to them in the first place.

48. Michael Sandel, *Liberalism and the Limits of Justice* (Cambridge: Cambridge University Press, 1982), p. 150.

49. Jean-François Lyotard, *The Differend: Phrases in Dispute* (Minneapolis: University of Minnesota Press, 1988), xii.

50. Ibid., p. 9.

51. For an insightful analysis of the point and character of a *modus vivendi*, see John Rawls's essay "Justice as Fairness: Political not Metaphysical," *Philosophy and Public Affairs* 14 (Summer 1985): 247.

52. Anderson, "The Ethical Limitations of the Market," p. 183.

53. Ibid., p. 193.

54. John Rawls, "The Idea of an Overlapping Consensus," *Oxford Journal for Legal Studies* 1 (1987): 1–25.

55. As Habermas writes in this vein, "a person who questions the forms of life in which his identity has been shaped questions his very existence."

See his *Moral Consciousness and Communicative Action* (Cambridge, Mass.: MIT Press, 1990), p. 177–78.

56. Jürgen Habermas, "Individual Will-Formation in Terms of What Is Expedient, What Is Good, and What Is Just," unpublished manuscript quoted in Thomas McCarthy's *Ideals and Illusions*, p. 186.

57. As Lyotard takes pains to point out, in a *differend* "One side's legitimacy does not imply the other's lack of legitimacy." *The Differend*, p. xi.

58. Walzer, *Spheres of Justice*, p. 304.

59. Christopher Lasch, *The Culture of Narcissism* (New York: Warner Books, 1979), p. 205.

60. Walzer, *Spheres of Justice*, p. 19.

61. Lasch, *The Culture of Narcissism*, p. 215–16. By left-wing critics Lasch is thinking here primarily of American exponents of New Left sport theory such as Paul Hoch, Dave Meggyesy, and Jack Scott. If my critique of leftist theorists of sport in the first part of this book is cogent, one can throw in here French and German exponents of the New Left as well as the hegemonists.

62. I owe this point and the line of argument that immediately follows to Stephen Marglin's important essay, "What Do Bosses Do?" *Review of Radical Political Economics* (Summer 1974): 63.

63. The argument I offer here is derived from Alaisdair MacIntyre's illuminating analysis of "rational traditions" and the rational character of crafts and craft guilds. For the first analysis see his *Whose Justice? Which Rationality?*, especially chapter 18; for the second see his *Three Rival Versions of Moral Inquiry* (Notre Dame, Ind.: University of Notre Dame Press, 1990), pp. 61–66.

64. Rorty, *The Consequences of Pragmatism*, p. xlvii.

65. Walzer, *Spheres of Justice*, p. 319.

Postscript: Sport in the Larger Scheme of Things

Two guiding aims have shaped this treatise. The first was a deconstructive one that sought to dismantle two of the leading currents of critical sport theory, New Left and hegemony sport theory respectively, and to decipher what was problematic and unproblematic in each. The second was a reconstructive one that built an alternative critical theory of sport, one able to meet the objections leveled against its predecessors and a sufficiently robust one able to put the social criticism of sport on a new and surer argumentative footing. In this postscript I would like to add some final words about my reconstructed theory of sport and address a possible question about its present justification.

The justification I offered for my reconstructed critical theory of sport was an internal one. I invoked the internal logic of sport and the "inside" rational deliberations of its practice-community to justify the demarcation of the boundaries of its practice and the imposition of normative blocks on the conduct of its institutions. This mode of justification is obviously circular; it promises to provide a new ground for a critical theory of sport by petitioning its distinctive rational order and then proceeds to justify this new critical venture by petitioning this very same rational order. But it is not its circularity that is problematic. Circularity is the price that must be paid when theory eschews a God's-eye perspective on practices like sport. That is because giving up such a perspective means that one must begin with social practices themselves, and I have offered compelling reasons why beginning with the internal logic of sport is the critical place to begin our investigations of sport.

That I justify my theory of sport by appealing to rational elements that are intrinsic to it is also not objectionable because it is self-validating—because it merely endorses our existing crop of sporting practices just as they are practiced. To be sure, there is always a danger that in criticizing a practice like sport from the inside out one may unwittingly provide a status-quo justification of it. If one were to pick the wrong features of sport—say, its institutional features—to serve as the standards of one's critical analysis of it, one would have little to say about sport that is genuinely critical. In such cases, the immanent critic of sport merely replaces the "epistemological myth of the given" of her transcendent counterpart, who believes there are some privileged ahistorical ideals that can be tapped to criticize sport, with her no less pernicious "historical myth of the given," the myth that one can criticize sport by appealing to its putative features, by using, in effect, the tools and resources of the apologist. But my pointed appeal to the logic of sport and to the discursive inclinations of its practice-community was designed to guard against this very thing, to undercut any status-quo justification of sport. So it is not self-validating in this apologetic sense, at least not obviously so.

But there is one troubling sense in which my immanent justification of a new critical theory of sport is self-validating. It presupposes that sport, or at least some variation of it, warrants our support in the first place, that it is a worthwhile enterprise that deserves our full sanction. It can hardly avoid this question-begging implication, since by making the logic of its practice and the *litige* of its devoted followers the twin pillars of its critical treatment of sport, it ensures that sport in one form or another will be validated as a legitimate human undertaking. This self-validating presumption is a significant one because it imposes an unacceptable limit on the social criticism of sport: it prevents the critic from asking whether we would all be better off without sport, whether, in the larger scheme of things, sport merits a place in our hearts and in the social fabric of our culture.

In order to get around this curb on the social criticism of sport so that we might ask probing questions of the foregoing sort, I propose an additional justification of my reconstructed theory, a more open-textured and inclusive one.[1] This mode of justification takes the larger, rather than the internal, measure of sport, to see how it connects up with everything else. A good way to assess whether practices like sport are really worth the candle is to ratchet the analysis up a notch and consider how the goods specific to one practice mesh with the goods specific to other practices, to ascertain how they all fit together into some coherent pattern or whole. It is only by taking this larger measure of practices like sport, I contend, that we can adequately determine which practices deserve our assent and support and which our rebuke and censure.

The larger justificatory measure I propose to take of sport is itself an open-ended, somewhat imprecise, and underdetermined one. It does not seek to situate sport in an elaborate and detailed grid that purports to rank its comparative goodness over that of other practices in some precise fashion. Rather, it seeks to justify the inclusion of sport in societies in good working order on the liberal ideal of pluralism. The ideal of pluralism is the ideal that society should keep alive as many social practices as it can reasonably support, that a well-ordered society is a society that is able to give its members a wide range of forms of life to choose from so that each may lead an engaging and rich life. The problem, of course, is that there is no social world without loss, that no social order or culture can include within itself all forms of life, and that even those it is able to take under its wings cannot be supported in the same way and to the same degree.[2]

How are we to decide which to support, which to reject, or which simply to let wither away? The answer supplied by the liberal ideal of pluralism is a two-pronged one. First, as I mention above, society should support as many social practices as it can—the more the better. Here, the epigram "less is more," popularized by environmentalists, doesn't hold weight; it is rather the other way around: more is more and less is less. So a well-ordered society is on this first count at least an open and radically tolerant one, accepting as much diversity as it can possibly handle, and being as inclusive as it can possibly be. The second prong takes hold, however, when we begin to run out of social space to house these different forms of life. In this instance, only those practices and endeavors that make some claim on us, that contribute the most to human flourishing, that enrich, enliven, enlarge, and enhance our lives the most deserve our support. By contrast, those that no longer resonate with our social being, that are no longer found uplifting and compelling, are to be left to succumb to the process of social attrition that governs all practices in a well-ordered society. Here radical resonance rather than radical tolerance is called for.

There are obvious difficulties with each prong of this answer. With respect to the first, it might be argued that giving members of society too many choices, too many forms of life from which to choose, is more confusing and paralyzing than it is uplifting and liberating. Though there is some force to this retort, it is hardly decisive. Pluralism is best understood and defended not as an effort to present a dizzying array of choices to a populace befuddled by the choices, but as an argument against narrowing the good life to a select few forms of life. It aims to undercut the Right, which gives pride of place to religion; the Left, which wishes to privilege the workplace; the capitalist, who favors the market; and the civic republican and the communitarian, who prefer the political realm.

With respect to the second prong, it might be rejoined that it asks too much of society, that it calls for a public ranking of the intrinsic value of different forms of life that it is ill-equipped to carry out. There is some force to this argument as well, but it is misdirected. The pluralism I speak of argues that while the state is not equipped to make such qualitative rankings, civil society—what Walzer labels the "space of uncoerced human association," "the setting of settings"[3]—is so equipped, and, when left properly to its own devices and not impeded by the coercive apparatus of the state, it engages in these sorts of deep and complicated normative assessments all the time. This is the realm in which different practice-communities make their partisan pitches for support, vie for scarce resources, and are forced to adjudicate conflicts among the goods of the forms of life they embody (many of which are borne by the same practitioners who happen to be members of different practice-communities). So only those forms of life that are able to secure the democratic sanction of civil society, of the practitioners of its varied practices, will be confirmed as life-enriching ones and supported as such.

It is pluralism that justifies the inclusion of sport in well-ordered societies. This larger justification of sport is a liberal one, but only partly so. There are two parts to this justificatory scheme, and each is an admixture of liberal and socialist elements to varying degrees. The first is largely socialist and to a lesser degree liberal. It argues that the ideal of pluralism is best realized not, as some liberals hold, when individuals are left to their own devices to actuate unfettered choices, but when society is arranged in a "decentralized democratic socialist" manner that protects social practices from unwarranted encroachment.[4] What is liberal about this democratic socialist arrangement is, of course, that it is anchored in the liberal ideal of pluralism. The second part is largely liberal and to a lesser degree socialist. It argues that the ideal of pluralism is best realized in a liberally conceived state, that is, a state that is neutral regarding the different and competing conceptions of the good entertained in civil society. What is socialist about this liberal state is that it is more intrusive than most liberal theorists would allow, that it has the license to intervene in the adjudication of competing forms of the good life when such intervention is itself necessary to safeguard a pluralistic society.

Let's begin with the decentralized democratic socialist part of my justificatory scheme. A decentralized socialist arrangement is one in which the practice-communities of social practices and the local settings of instrumental activities are granted democratic control over their respective undertakings. I now want to consider this arrangement, however, not from the eye of any one particular practice-community, not from the inside out, but from the collective eyes of all such prospective communities, from the outside in. I do so by grouping these autonomous communities into two larger realms. The first realm I call, after Marx, the realm of necessity, which comprises all the instrumental and service activities of a society that contribute to its material production and reproduction.[5] The second realm I call, after Rawls, the realm of social perfectionism, which comprises all the practices of a society that contribute to the advancement of human excellence in its various forms.[6] My reason for separating the materially productive activities from the perfectionist practices of society is that each realm requires, as we shall shortly see, a different form of pluralist justification.

The realm of necessity, as Marx tells us, is so named because it is the social space in which the different instrumental activities by which we seek to satisfy our material needs are situated. What the ideal of pluralism calls for in this material sphere of life is a constrained market controlled by the workers and an autonomous service sector of medical and clinical care governed at least in part by local volunteers. Only a democratically run workplace and service sector will ensure a variety of instrumental activities to meet our material and social needs, and an open and public mechanism to evaluate the value of the services rendered. It will promote pluralism outside the realm of necessity by blocking the use of market models to direct noninstrumental practices. And it will promote pluralism within the realm of necessity by preventing the domination of the market and service spheres by capital-rich entrepreneur types. A democratically governed marketplace can avail itself of a number of different market agents to meet the needs of its members: from family businesses, to publicly owned companies, to consumer cooperatives and various nonprofit organizations.[7] Local control and democratic voice thus count here for greater diversity, not less. So at least in the material affairs of society, pluralism and democratic socialism make for a good marriage.

The realm of social perfectionism encompasses, as I suggest above, the different practices that claim excellence as their trademark. Since these practices are once removed from the material demands that occupy instrumental activities, they have nothing directly to do with the material production of society nor with the crafting of useful objects and services. Further, since these activities are not burdened with the material constraints that instrumental activities have to answer to, their pursuit of excellence is largely a gratuitous affair. This suggests a link between what Rawls calls perfectionist pursuits and what MacIntyre calls social practices. MacIntyre, it will be recalled, defines social practices as skillful, virtue-laden endeavors that seek, each in its own inimitable way, excellence. So it seems plausible to argue that the sphere of social perfectionism is co-extensive with the sphere of social practices, the paradigmatic forms of which include, according to MacIntyre, games, sports, the sciences, architecture, farming, historical research, politics (in Aristotle's sense only), painting, and music.[8]

What the ideal of pluralism requires in this sphere is also autonomously governed practice-communities, but this time in order to ensure an abundant life of excellence as opposed to an abundant material life. Turning control of social practices over to their votaries will likely have this effect since this is the only way to guarantee that every practice will get a hearing, and an informed and partisan one at that, as to its intrinsic merits. Going for local control will also promote pluralism outside of each practice within this sphere by minimizing the intrusion of practice-communities in the *litige* of other practice-communities. It will further encourage pluralism within each practice by prohibiting ruling elites from dominating the deliberative proceedings of practice-communities and by keeping at bay institutional forces of normalization. Once again, diversity and democratic socialist control seem tailored to each other's special interests and concerns rather than antipodes.

If pluralism is the right justificatory device here, then any society that fails to make some provision for excellence, for practices that make its pursuit their central aim, is a deficient society. Further, if it is plausible to count sport among those practices dedicated to excellence and its appropriate advancement, then any society that fails to make some provision for sport is a deficient society as well. Just how much support practices like sport will be able to garner in such a pluralist society is difficult to say. This is a matter to be reckoned with in civil society, in the social setting of settings in which the collective deliberations of practice-communities take place and in which the good of the forms of life they embody are evaluated and debated. Since these conversations are first conceived and propelled by the votaries of these different practices, spirited discussions will ensue. There is always the danger that things might get out of hand, that the fervor with which such discussions are engaged might get in the way of reasoned discourse. This is a danger precisely because it constitutes a genuine threat to pluralism. Although such fervor is in one sense encouraged by the democratic socialist arrangement I am arguing for, insofar as it promotes partisan championing of the goods of particular practices, it is also stemmed by that arrangement, insofar as socialized communities secure within their own demarcated spheres are less likely to be intimidated by such partisan clashes, and more apt to understand, if not appreciate, what accounts for their fervor.[9] So while it can't be reasonably claimed that sport will play a large role in a democratically ordered society that takes the claims of pluralism seriously, it can be reasonably claimed, I contend, that it will play some determinate role in such a society. It can be further reasonably claimed that that role will be greater in a society that gives scope to partisan advocacy of practices and that disempowers practice-communities from using the coercive power of the state to ensure themselves a piece of the action, than a society that denies such partisan advocacy and that allows the state to interject itself in the reflective process of evaluating the worth of social practices.

It is apparent from what I have said thus far that a pluralist society is synonymous with a well-ordered one, and that a well-ordered society is synonymous with a carefully demarcated one that is subject to the local control of socialized communities. We know that we live in such a society when the instrumental undertakings vital to its well being and the perfectionist pursuits vital to its excellence fall into the hands of their proper constituencies, that is, when workers preside over our workplaces, believers over our churches and synagogues, scholars over our universities, artists over our galleries, and athletes and their devotees over our sports.[10] This is the way a truly pluralist society—and on my account the way a justified society that accords a place for sport within it—is supposed to look and function. But the picture is not quite complete. A pluralist society also needs a state to protect and nurture its diverse and democratically controlled practices. However, not just any sort of state will do; it must be one that looks and functions like a liberal state. It is to a consideration of such a state then, and to the role it plays in the justification of practices like sport, that I now turn.

Why a pluralist society requires a liberal state rather than some other version of this political body has to do with the two central features that such a state must possess if it is to encourage, rather than discourage, true diversity. First, the state must be a chastened one; it must conduct itself in a manner that befits the delimited role it is to play in presiding over the affairs of civil society. Specifically, it is to conduct itself as a regulatory agency, correcting unforeseen and unseemly outcomes or patching up structural defects that plague the social networks of civil society, not a normative one. It is to stay out of the business of ranking the intrinsic value of forms of life because its intrusion is likely to impede rather than foster pluralism. The second feature that a state congenial to pluralism must possess is a capacity to exert some real influence on social forces that stifle diversity; it must be able to intercede effectively on behalf of practices and their votaries when their forms of life are unduly threatened by systemic imperatives. If it is unable to mobilize itself in this manner, the interests of pluralism will be seriously jeopardized.

So it seems that the state most conducive to a pluralist society is a neutral rather than a perfectionist one. And if that is so, then a liberal state is what we want. A liberal state is defined by its principled neutrality, its studied indifference to the different goods that circulate in civil society. It is this cultivated indifference that ensures that whatever action the state takes in managing the daily detail of social life will be of a regulative rather than a normative sort.

It might be quickly rejoined that while a liberal state so conceived meets the nonperfectionist requirement of a pluralist-friendly state, it fails the regulative-activist requirement of such a state. The problem here is the neutrality of the state itself, which nullifies its regulative role by forbidding it to act on any conception of the good. This is so, it is argued, on two grounds. First, a neutral state is one whose justification excludes reference to any conception of the good. Second, a neutral state is one in which all particular conceptions of the good must fare equally well. Taken together, these suggest that if the state is to maintain its vaunted neutrality toward the good, it must refrain from doing anything. If it takes some action then it must either appeal to some good to justify its intervention, lest it be subject to the charge of arbitrary intercession, or face the ineluctable fact that the action it took could not avoid advancing some conceptions of the good over others. A neutral state is for all intents and purposes, therefore, a paralyzed, dormant state.

This rejoinder fails on both counts because it misconstrues what the neutrality of the state entails. To begin with, to say that the state must remain neutral is not to say that it is disallowed from making reference to *any* conception of the good, but only reference to any *particular* conception of the good. So it can perfectly well justify its intervention in the social world by appealing to a general, common conception of the good. With regard to the second point, to say that the state must remain neutral is not to say that all particular conceptions of the good must fare equally well under its jurisdiction, but only that the state is to refrain from doing anything whose stated aim is to promote or assist one form of the good over, and at the expense of, other forms of the good. The state, in other words, is required to maintain ideological neutrality in its dealings with particular conceptions of the good (what some theorists call "justificatory neutrality" or "neutrality of grounds"), but it is not required, per impossible, to advance all conceptions of the good equally (what some theorists call "consequential neutrality" or "neutrality of effects").[11] No social agency, least of all the state, can intervene in the course of social life without influencing, positively or negatively, particular conceptions of the good, but the state can so intervene, and be expected to so intervene, so as to effect only the common good—bracketing whatever the particular results of that intervention may turn out to be.

If a state can prevail upon the social world without violating its neutrality, then a liberal state that prides itself on its neutrality can surely do the same without pain of contradiction. If that is so, then, as I suggest above, a liberal state is congenial to the interests of a pluralist society. It can intervene in civil society by endorsing and sponsoring certain instrumental undertakings and social practices as long as its justification for doing so is not to advance the particular forms of the good they embody—though, to be sure, this is likely to be the effect of its intervention—but to advance the good of pluralism itself. Yet it cannot so intervene willy-nilly; it can endorse and sponsor, but not evaluate, activities of this sort only under certain specified conditions, and these conditions vary somewhat depending on whether one's reference is the realm of necessity or the realm of perfectionism.

In the material sphere of life, the state may not intercede to bolster market and service arrangements that no longer curry favor with the relevant communities. Nor may it intercede to remedy mere disparities of income or life style that may justifiably be taken to be rewards of success in the market. But it may intervene, I argue, when such market disparities—the fact that some people have more money and fancier cars than others—translate into social domination, when, that is, the monied are able to exert undue influence over the lives of the unmonied. If families, churches, unions, worker communes, and the like are unable to offset the pernicious effects of such market-induced social domination, then the state is permitted to use its offices to neutralize or overturn these effects, and its justification for doing so is pluralism. Dominated social groups who lack the material wherewithal to make and enact meaningful choices severely limit their own, and their society's, diversity. At the very least, this requires a strong welfare state administered by both state officials and local volunteers. A privately run welfare system would be woefully inadequate, and a nationalistically run welfare system would discount the voice of local groups and communities.[12]

In the sphere of perfectionist practices, the state is similarly debarred from propping up practices that have lost favor with their relevant practice-communities, that no longer resonate with those communities. Nor is it permitted to meddle in the social accretion and attrition process that goes on as a matter of course in civil society in which practices are variously added to and deleted from our repertoire of perfectionist pursuits. But it does have license to intercede on behalf of particular practices and their communities that are imperiled by social domination, and its license derives once again from the ideal of pluralism. In this case, social domination springs either from monopolies that control resources necessary to put on and conduct perfectionist endeavors (the problem of scarce resources) or from structural defects in society that allow for illicit conversion of goods, for the invasion of one sphere by another sphere; the net effect of both is to limit the diversity of social practices and that of their social settings. In the case of scarce resources, the state may offer, for example, tax credits to individuals who invest in such practices, or undertake modest shifts in distribution of income to support a wider range of social practices. In the case of structural defects, the state's principal role is to enforce existing partitions and to encourage and empower practice-communities to fortify old ones and, if necessary, to build new ones. We can hardly afford for the state to do less, if, that is, we expect to keep endangered ways of living that still resonate with people in meaningful ways from becoming extinct.

This is how a pluralist society would look and function from the standpoint of the state. When conjoined with my above account of a pluralistically ordered civil society, we get a glimpse of the total picture and an idea of the way a fully justified society that reserves an important social space for sport would look and function. It is just such a well-ordered society, in which a perfectionist civil society works in tandem with a neutral state to promote pluralism, that provides the most compelling justification, in the larger sense intended, of perfectionist practices like sport.

The choice we face here, as before, is a rather stark one. We can either, as Stout tells us, "transform our social practices and institutions in quite particular ways, exerting humane control over [them] . . . or . . . find ourselves out of the action."[13] I have offered one scheme for inserting ourselves back in the action. The immanent and synoptic backing I provide is meant to disarm the right-wing skeptic who is inclined to reject all such proposals for social change as pie-in-the-sky nonsense and the left-wing skeptic who is inclined to reject all liberally tinged proposals for social change. It is also meant, of course, to persuade less ideologically disposed skeptics and doubters that this is one promising way to address some of the serious social problems that currently confront sport and the like. It is in this critical and practical spirit that I invite the reader to ponder its merits, criticize its shortcomings, and join in the dialogue and effort to undo the degradation that practices like sport have had to suffer for too long.

NOTES

1. I also offer this latter justificatory effort to correct a possible misapprehension that might arise from my use of the liberal art of separation to this point. In arguing for a separation of sport from unwholesome outside influences I am *not* implying that efforts to locate connections between practices like sport are dismal, meaningless, and ideological exercises. I do hold that the present institutionally driven constellation of social forces makes it imperative to wall off practices like sport from their pervasive influence. The implication to be drawn from this is not that looking for linkages between practices is an ideologically suspect thing to do, but only that denying distinctions between them is. My full view is that the assimilationist tendencies and biases of the current social system require that we first understand what marks social undertakings off from one another before we can tackle the question of what it is that binds them together.

2. On the notion of social loss, see John Rawls, "The Priority of Right and Ideas of the Good," *Philosophy and Public Affairs* 17 (Fall 1988): 265.

3. Michael Walzer, "The Idea of a Civil Society," *Dissent* (Spring 1991): 293, 298.

4. On the notion of a "decentralized democratic socialism" see Michael Walzer, *Spheres of Justice* (New York: Basic Books, 1983), p. 318.

5. Karl Marx, *Capital, Volume 3* (New York: International Publishers, 1977), p. 820.

6. John Rawls, *A Theory of Justice* (Cambridge, Mass.: Harvard University Press, 1971), pp. 25, 325–32.

7. I owe these examples to Walzer, "The Idea of a Civil Society," p. 300.

8. Alaisdair MacIntyre, *After Virtue* (Notre Dame, Ind.: University of Notre Dame Press, 1984), p. 187. Farming is the one entry on this list that strains the apparent connection between perfectionist pursuits and social practices. This is not because farming is a stranger to excellence, but because its instrumental demeanor suggests a closer link to material pursuits than perfectionist ones.

9. Walzer makes a similar argument in his essay "Liberalism and the Art

of Separation," *Political Theory* 12 (August 1984): 329. Even this socialist part of my argument is laced with liberal influences. The notion that practice-communities that are secure within their own settings are less likely to be disturbed by, or interfere with, the affairs of other practice-communities is merely, as Walzer tells us, "the socialist form of the old liberal hope that individuals secure in their own circles won't invade the circles of others." Ibid., p. 329.

10. Ibid., p. 327.

11. For various renditions of this distinction see Will Kymlicka, "Liberal Individualism and Liberal Neutrality," *Ethics* 99 (July 1989): 883–905; John Rawls, "The Priority of the Right and Ideas of the Good," *Philosophy and Public Affairs* 17 (Fall 1988): 251–76; Peter De Marneffe, "Liberalism, Liberty, and Neutrality," *Philosophy and Public Affairs* 19 (Summer 1990): 253–74.

12. I owe this point to Michael Walzer, "The Communitarian Critique of Liberalism," *Political Theory* 18 (February 1990): 18.

13. Jeffrey Stout, *Ethics After Babel* (Boston: Beacon Press, 1988), p. 277.

Index

WILLIAM J. MORGAN is a professor in the cultural studies unit and an adjunct professor of philosophy at the University of Tennessee, Knoxville. He is the editor of *Sport and the Humanities: A Collection of Original Essays* and coeditor, with Klaus V. Meier, of *Philosophic Inquiry in Sport*. Professor Morgan is the author of numerous articles on the philosophy and social theory of sport.

Books in the Series Sport and Society

A Sporting Time: New York City and the Rise of Modern Athletics, 1820–70
Melvin L. Adelman

Sandlot Seasons: Sport in Black Pittsburgh
Rob Ruck

West Ham United: The Making of a Football Club
Charles Korr

Beyond the Ring: The Role of Boxing in American Society
Jeffrey T. Sammons

John L. Sullivan and His America
Michael T. Isenberg

Television and National Sport: The United States and Britain
Joan M. Chandler

The Creation of American Team Sports: Baseball and Cricket, 1838–72
George B. Kirsch

City Games: The Evolution of American Urban Society and the Rise of Sports
Steven A. Riess

The Brawn Drain: Foreign Student-Athletes in American Universities
John Bale

The Business of Professional Sports
Edited by Paul D. Staudohar and James A. Mangan

Fritz Pollard: Pioneer in Racial Advancement
John M. Carroll

Go Big Red! The Story of a Nebraska Football Player
George Mills

Sport and Exercise Science: Essays in the History of Sports Medicine
Edited by Jack W. Berryman and Roberta J. Park

Minor League Baseball and Local Economic Development
Arthur T. Johnson

Harry Hooper: An American Baseball Life
Paul J. Zingg

Cowgirls of the Rodeo: Pioneer Professional Athletes
Mary Lou LeCompte

Sandow the Magnificent: Eugen Sandow and the Beginnings of Bodybuilding
David Chapman

Big-Time Football at Harvard, 1905: The Diary of Coach Bill Reid
Ronald A. Smith

Leftist Theories of Sport: A Critique and Reconstruction
William J. Morgan

REPRINT EDITIONS

The Nazi Olympics
Richard D. Mandell

Sports in the Western World
Second Edition
William J. Baker